DISEQUILIBRIA, ECONOMIC REFORMS AND ECONOMIC POLICIES

To my wife Hui Ye

Disequilibria, Economic Reforms and Economic Policies

A theoretical and empirical investigation for China

XIAOMING LI
School of East Asian Studies
University of Sheffield
England

Avebury
Aldershot • Brookfield USA • Hong Kong • Singapore • Sydney

© X. Li 1995

All rights reserved. No part of this publication may be reproduced, stored in a retrieval system, or transmitted in any form or by any means, electronic, mechanical, photocopying, recording or otherwise without the prior permission of the publisher.

Published by
Avebury
Ashgate Publishing Limited
Gower House
Croft Road
Aldershot
Hants GU11 3HR
England

Ashgate Publishing Company
Old Post Road
Brookfield
Vermont 05036
USA

A CIP catalogue record for this book is available from the British Library

Library of Congress Catalog Card Number: 95-76853

ISBN 1 85972 081 1

Printed and bound by Athenæum Press Ltd., Gateshead, Tyne & Wear.

Contents

List of figures	viii
List of tables	xi
Acknowledgements	xii
List of abbreviations	xiv

1 Introduction   1

    1.1 Brief retrospect of China's economic reforms   1
    1.2 The purpose of the study   3
    1.3 Outline of the book   5

2 Disequilibrium approaches to modelling socialist economies   9

    2.1 Introduction   9
    2.2 Disequilibrium economics and econometrics   9
    2.3 Basic approaches to modelling CPEs   22
    2.4 Some studies of the Chinese economy   29
    2.5 The plan for this study   33

3 Investment demand in the public-ownership economy: a game theory approach   36

    3.1 Introduction   36
    3.2 Investment demand's determinant 1: contradiction between

		consumption and accumulation	37
	3.3	Investment demand's determinant 2: conflicts between sectors for investment resources	62
	3.4	The investment behaviour of local governments	70
	3.5	Investment demand and interest rates	78
4	**Econometric model of investment-production block and its estimation**		**89**
	4.1	Introduction	89
	4.2	Structure of the model	90
	4.3	Specification of the behavioral equations in the model	94
	4.4	Disequilibrium indicators	99
	4.5	Estimation results	103
	4.6	Conclusions	113
		Appendix 4A - Sources of data	116
5	**Consumption and savings**		**117**
	5.1	Introduction	117
	5.2	Analytical framework	120
	5.3	Econometric model and estimation results	130
	5.4	Extension of the model	141
	5.5	Conclusions	144
6	**Ex-post policy experiments**		**149**
	6.1	Introduction	149
	6.2	Simulation results	153
	6.3	Summary and conclusions	161
		Appendix 6A - Simulation results	166
7	**Searching for a policy package of further Market-Oriented Reforms**		**175**
	7.1	Introduction	175
	7.2	The amended model structure corresponding to the policy package of further reforms	177
	7.3	The simulation results	188
	7.4	Model calibration and robustness of simulation results	193
	7.5	Conclusions	199
		Appendix 7A - Policy simulations of Model 2 and Model 1	203

	Appendix 7B - Simulations of Model 2 with parameter perturbations	220
	Appendix 7C - Sensitivity elasticities	228
8	**Concluding remarks**	**230**
	8.1 Summary and conclusions	230
	8.2 Tasks for the future	232
Bibliography		**235**

List of figures

Figure 2.1	Disequilibrium regimes	16
Figure 2.2	Disequilibrium regimes including an under-consumption regime	16
Figure 3.1	Income distribution and aggregate demand structure	40
Figure 3.2	Effect of excess money supply on aggregate demand	40
Figure 3.3	The state sovereignty mechanism	51
Figure 3.4	An increase of the central government's desire to accumulate	52
Figure 3.5	The multi-sovereignty mechanism	53
Figure 3.6	The central government's and individuals' reaction functions	55
Figure 3.7	The Nash solution line	58
Figure 3.8	Conflicts between the central government and individuals in national income distribution under MSM	62
Figure 3.9	Conflicts between the central government and subunits for investment resources under MSM	68
Figure 3.10	A box diagram of two localities' investments	73
Figure 3.11	The planned allocative ratio of investment resources between regions	74
Figure 3.12	Conflicts between localities for investment	77
Figure 3.13	Definiteness of the whole POE's income sources	80
Figure 3.14	Indefiniteness of subunits' income sources (1)	81
Figure 3.15	Indefiniteness of subunits' income sources (2)	81
Figure 3.16	Interest-rate rigidity of the POE's investment demand	83
Figure 5.1	Macroeconomic indicators of China 1968-1989	119
Figure 5.2	Index of retail prices	119
Figure 6.1	A permanent 5% increase in domestic credit	166-167

Figure 6.2	A temporary increase in domestic credit of 214 billion yuan; and a temporary increase in government construction spending of 214 billion yuan	168
Figure 6.3	A permanent 10% increase in government construction spending	169-170
Figure 6.4	A permanent increase in nominal interest rates by 1.1 times	171-172
Figure 6.5	A permanent 10% cut in government non-construction spending	173-174
Figure 7.1	A permanent 5% increase in domestic credit	203-205
Figure 7.2	A permanent 10% increase in government construction spending	206-208
Figure 7.3	A permanent increase in nominal interest rates by 1.1 times	209-211
Figure 7.4	A permanent 10% cut in government non-construction spending	212-214
Figure 7.5	A temporary increase in domestic credit of 219 billion yuan	215-216
Figure 7.6	A temporary increase in government construction spending of 219 billion yuan	217-218
Figure 7.7	Monetary and fiscal policy multipliers	219
Figure 7.8	Altering the consumption demand-expected inflation rate parameter	220
Figure 7.9	Altering the consumption demand-price parameter	220
Figure 7.10	Altering the consumption supply-price parameter	221
Figure 7.11	Altering the current savings-disposable income parameter	221
Figure 7.12	Altering the current savings-interest rate parameter	222
Figure 7.13	Altering the current savings-its lagged stocks parameter	222
Figure 7.14	Altering the upstream investment demand-inflation rate parameter	223
Figure 7.15	Altering the upstream-downstream investment demand parameter	223
Figure 7.16	Altering the upstream investment demand-national income parameter	224
Figure 7.17	Altering the aggregate investment supply-price parameter	224
Figure 7.18	Altering the downstream investment demand-price parameter	225
Figure 7.19	Altering the downstream investment demand-interest rate parameter	225

Figure 7.20	Altering the import-inflation rate parameter	226
Figure 7.21	Altering the consumption price adjustment parameter	226
Figure 7.22	Altering the investment price adjustment parameter	227

List of tables

Table 4.1	Price indices of retail sales	102
Table 4.2	Estimates of excess investment demand/supply	112
Table 5.1	Prices and excess demand	140
Table 5.2	Changes in MPS and components in gross savings	146
Table 6.1	Policy multipliers for excess demands	157
Table 7.1	The sensitivity of DCE and DIE to variations in individual parameters in the consumption block	228
Table 7.2	The sensitivity of DCE and DIE to variations in individual parameters in the investment block	229

Acknowledgements

This book grew out of my PhD thesis at the University of Strathclyde, Department of Economics. I would like to take this opportunity to thank several individuals for their assistance and co-operation during the research work leading to this book.

First of all, I want to express my heartfelt gratitude to Professor Andrew Hughes Hallett, who served as my thesis supervisor. Besides helping me to resolve some of the problems encountered, he provided expert guidance, encouragement, so many stimulating comments and careful review of the manuscript. Sincere thanks are also due to Rod Cross, my thesis co-supervisor, whose valuable suggestions, advice and comments are greatly appreciated.

Discussion with a number of people also proved invaluable. In particular, I would like to mention Darryl Holden, who assisted me in the testing of the econometric model and TSP programming; Peter McGregor, who introduced me to the arts of model calibration and sensitivity analysis and provided constructive comments on my work; Yue Ma, who was the source of my knowledge of game theory and econometric methods. To them, I acknowledge my deep indebtedness.

I also owe my special thanks to Professor Cheng Enfu and Professor Li Hongfeng (in China). They made available to me some statistical data, research papers and information concerning the Chinese economy, which were unavailable in Britain but were so important at the stage of my empirical study. Without this material, the conclusions of the research could have been biased, and some of the empirical analysis could not have been conducted.

Over the past several years, I enjoyed and benefited from a highly academic and hospitable environment in the Department's postgraduate study rooms. Among those fellow students, I should particularly thank Ruifang Wang, Harminder Battu, Trevor Sikorski, Mark McFarland, Maria Demertzis and Aklilu Tefera for informal discussions on many issues and for their friendship. However, none of the above individuals hold responsibility for the opinions expressed, or for any remaining errors and omissions, which lies solely with the author.

Last but not least, my thanks go to the Chinese State Education Committee and the British Council for providing me the opportunity and financial support to study in the United Kingdom.

List of abbreviations

ACFB	Almanac of China's Finance and Banking
ACFT	Almanac of China's Foreign Trade
CESRRI	Chinese Economic System Reform Research Institute
CGS	Consumption goods sector
CPE	Centrally planned economy
EVM	Errors-in-variables method
IGS	Investment goods sector
IV	Instrument variables
MSM	Multi-sovereignty mechanism
OLS	Ordinary least squares
POE	Public-ownership economy
RE	Rational expectation
SM	Substitution method
SSM	State sovereignty mechanism
SYBC	Statistical Year Book of China
2SLS	Two stage least squares

1 Introduction

1.1 Brief retrospect of China's economic reforms

Recognizing that the rigidities inherent in central planning seriously inhibited the efficient allocation and uses of resources, and did not provide adequate incentives for productivity gains, China has moved to enhance freedom of choice for economic agents in the decision-making process, and strengthen the role of market forces through the gradual removal of administrative controls and fostering of competition. The process of China's economic reforms has so far experienced two phases: 1979-1989 and 1992 to date. There are indeed lessons that can be generalized from the previous reform experience and that are relevant for the further reform program. Briefly the achievements of the 'first-phase' reform can be summarized as follows:

1. As far as income (output) is concerned, the basic structure of ownership had moved from the mono-public ownership to one where multi-ownerships coexist. In gross industrial output, for example, the share of state ownership economy had declined from 80.8% in 1978 to 64% in 1989.[1]

2. There have been great changes in the management environment of enterprises. By 1989, 90% of state-owned enterprises had adopted the contract responsibility system, and the retained profits rate of enterprises reached 45% in 1987, in contrast with less than 5% before reform. This has given rise to a certain degree of autonomy enjoyed by enterprises regarding their pricing, marketing of products, financial affairs, investment and income distribution.

3   Under strict central planning, the scope of the market was limited, applying only to certain consumer goods. As the role of central planning gradually diminished, the market for production materials and factors has developed. In 1988, market prices covered 65% of agricultural products and non-staple foods, 55% of industrial consumption goods, and 40% of industrial production materials.

4   Regarding macroeconomic management, direct administrative interference has been progressively replaced by the use of indirect levers. The categories of products and materials subject to mandatory plans and unitary distribution have been considerably reduced. In the allocation of production funds, the proportion of budgetary appropriations decreased from 75% to less than 33%, while the proportion of bank loans rose from 25% to less than 70%, over the last decade. Also the decision-making power has been decentralized. From 1979 to 1984, local governments (at the provincial level) had authorities to determine each investment project of up to 10 million yuan. After 1984, this figure rose to 30 million yuan, and in terms of non-productive investment projects, local governments could enjoy full autonomy.

5   The closed or semi-closed Chinese economy has now become a more open economy. In the last decade, total foreign capital introduced amounted to $477 billion. Total imports and exports in 1989 reached $826 billion, about four times the $206 billion figure for 1978.

Today it can hardly be doubted that the reform in the 1980s had brought about significantly historical changes to China, and had carried the potential to increase dramatically the efficiency of the Chinese economy and the welfare level of Chinese households: the average growth rate of national income in the pre-reform period (1953-1978) was 6%, rising to 9.3% in the post-reform period (1978-1989); during the 1980s per capita household income grew at an average rate of 6.5%, much higher than the pre-reform level of 1.5%.

At the same time, however, the Chinese economy and China's economic reform programme suffered many difficult problems. These problems posed grave challenge to the reform programme, and led to a three-year 'economic rectification' (1989-1991). One of the most critical economic problems is that of significant macroeconomic imbalances. When the central government loosened the constraints on the economy — allowing greater leeway to local governments and enterprises to set prices, initiate investment projects, determine income distribution and engage in foreign trade — it was as if it had slipped the tether on a frisky colt without first constructing the corral. The results had been a very large rise in investment flows (principally outside the government budget) and a rapid expansion of consumption funds. These waves of purchasing power generated an alarming burst of inflation in retail prices: 8.8% in 1985, 18.5% in 1988, and 27% in the first quarter of 1989 compared to that of 1988.[2] For a society that still remembers vividly the hyper-inflation that accompanied the collapse of the Nationalist government in 1948-1949, and the meticulous price stability of the subsequent thirty years, such a level of inflation is extremely unsettling. This led to nation-wide 'panic-buying' in 1988, and was one of the main reasons why the student demonstrations in the spring of 1989 acquired sympathy and support from the majority of the people.

Subsequent to the three-year economic rectification (1989-1991), the second phase of economic reform started in 1992. Accompanying this further liberalization have been a new-round of Chinese booming economy which reached overheating even faster than ever before. The growth rate of total fixed-assets investment (in nominal terms), for instance, jumped from 18.6% (in 1991) to 42.6% (in 1992) and 50.6% (in 1993), which resulted in 'Four Tensions' (see Li J. and Liu S., 1994): tension of communications and transportation, tension of energy resources, tension of raw materials and tension of funds. Triggered by this 'investment fever', inflation rate of retail prices continued to rise over the last several years: 5.4% (in 1992) and 13.0% (in 1993); and in January and February 1994, prices in the country's 35 major cities soared 23.3% and 26% year-on-year respectively. Widespread concern has been caused over the current situation in the Chinese economy. For example, the chief of IMF Managing Director Camdessus M. told Reuters in an interview (*China News Digest*, 4 May 1994) that China must take strong macro-economic steps in order to reduce internal demand and get rid of overheating; otherwise this will threaten to derail Beijing's plans for deep-seated economic reform.

Thus it can be seen that the problem of macroeconomic imbalances inhibits the smooth economic reform and development, and the studies of, and solutions to, this problem are required urgently.

1.2 The purpose of the study

Responding to the needs of economic reform and development, many Chinese economists have made considerable efforts to analyze and understand the problems in question. Systematic and comprehensive analyses have appeared in Zhong P.(1990), Shi J. (1989) and Li L. (1991), to name only a few important works. These contributions provide many interesting insights into the relationships between the structure of the economic system, economic policy and inflation. They are, however, non-technical works which do not, or only rarely, apply formalization or quantification, let alone construct econometric models and propose policy recommendations based on simulation experiments. Without the latter work, the hypotheses propounded in the non-technical accounts could not be tested, and the theories suggested would lack operability and practicability.

In view of this, the primary objective of the research described in this book is to establish theoretical-mathematical models which investigate the functioning and behavioral rules of different economic agents in the context of China's economic reforms. Particular attention is paid to the investment behaviour of the central government and local governments, and the consumption behaviour of households.

Based on theoretical-mathematical models, we formulate and estimate a systematic macro-econometric model. This work has two aims. The first is to test the hypotheses embodied in the theoretical analysis using time series data. The second is to calibrate the interrelationship between economic policies and macroeconomic imbalances under the existing institutional arrangement. Among the controversial questions we intend to answer are: Is shortage (or inflation) demand-determined or supply-determined? Can interest rates be used as an efficient lever in reducing disequilibrium? Given the very limited financial markets that exist in China, what is the role of money supply and government expenditure in the determination of excess demand? Which one, monetary or fiscal policy, is more effective in controlling inflation, and which is the more effective in maintaining output? How limited is the efficacy of macroeconomic policies in equilibrating markets (going sufficiently close to equilibrium) in the existing institutional setting?

Perhaps the most important question is: Would further market-oriented reforms considerably improve the behaviour of the Chinese economy with respect to equilibrium and if so, how do we push forward the reform? To answer this question is the final objective. Our intention is to build a new econometric model which represents a counterfactual economy generated by a policy package of further reforms. This 'new' model is then simulated as the 'historical' one is to see what the impacts of the same policy shocks would have been on a more market-oriented economy.

Throughout the research presented here, the basic approach to modelling the Chinese economy is of *disequilibrium* type. It is, to our knowledge, the first attempt to construct, estimate and simulate a systematic disequilibrium macro-model for the Chinese economy; and also the first attempt to base policy proposals concerning economic reforms in China on model calibration and simulation results rather than on non-technical analysis and reasoning.

1.3 Outline of the book

The rest of this book consists of seven chapters which mainly contain theoretical and empirical investigation of investment and consumption markets in disequilibrium, and estimation and simulation of macro models for China.

Chapter 2 presents a wide-ranging literature survey covering the area of disequilibrium modelling. The basic disequilibrium theory and estimation techniques for a disequilibrium model are reviewed, as are the foundations of the theoretical and econometric approaches adopted in this study. Then our attention is paid to the development of, and the difference between, three major ways of modelling markets in disequilibrium: disequilibrium indicator models; testable excess demand models; and the virtual price approach. Having looked at some empirical studies of the Chinese economy, we decide to employ the disequilibrium indicator modelling, which has not yet been applied before to the case of China. We also find that only a few of the major economic issues facing China have been resolved in the existing literature; some problems, such as disequilibrium in the investment goods market, and its interrelation with the consumption goods market, do not appear to have been dealt with at all in previous model building exercises; and the controversy concerning the households' saving behaviour in the Chinese economy still remains unsettled.[3]

The original research is reported in chapters 3 through to 7. Chapter 3 considers the problem of investment behaviour and its role in the expansion of aggregate demand. Since the public-ownership economy is still a dominant sector,[4] and is a major source of macroeconomic imbalances, it is the focus for our discussion. Since strategic analysis can provide insight into one agent's interaction with another, the game theory approach is adopted to develop theoretical investment models of the central and local governments which capture the new economic mechanisms generated by economic reforms. These models are built leaning on some results suggested elsewhere in the literature. The relationship between interest rates and investment demand is also discussed, and we consider the problem of investment swelling institutionally caused by the fundamental contradictions inherent in the public ownership. The study in this chapter thus yields some theoretical foundations for the econometric modelling of investment demand in the state-owned sector.

In chapter 4, we proceed with the specification and estimation of an econometric model of the investment-production block. The investment block contains supply equations; demand equations for the central government, local governments and non-state sector; and a few auxiliary equations linking endogenous variables to policy variables, and one block to the other. The production block encompasses aggregate production and capital formation functions. In addition, disequilibrium indicators are specified to facilitate the respecification in the estimation process. The model is then estimated using yearly data over 1979-1989, except for the production function, which is estimated over 1967-1989. This is done partly because of the lack of data in the pre-reform period, and more importantly, because the investment model is derived in the context of the economic reform programme, which has resulted in great changes in the investment system. Consequently there is a clear break in investment behaviour in the pre-1979 part of the time series.

We devote chapter 5 to the issues of consumption and savings. The classical budget constraint is discussed at length and modified before theoretical models of consumption demand and savings are derived. A distinction is drawn between forced and voluntary savings, and a gradual rise in households' marginal propensity to save is assumed, in an attempt to resolve the continuing controversy regarding savings behaviour in China. The effects of households' expectations about the market situation on their consumption decisions are also considered. In specifying the consumption supply equation, we try to reflect the gradual process by which the role of central planning declines, and the role of the market mechanism increases. Some effort is then devoted to the issue of disequilibrium indicators, which is of crucial importance to the respecification of the econometric model to be estimated. The model is estimated over 1968-1989. The model is then extended to introduce some auxiliary equations.

Chapter 6 reports simulation results for various policy shocks. First, to obtain a complete macro-model for policy simulation, the sub-models of the consumption and investment-production blocks are combined. Next, several *ex post* policy scenarios are designed for simulation experiments, which mainly involve fiscal and monetary policy shocks. The results of these exercises are examined, discussed and compared. We conclude that the efficacy of macroeconomic devices is fairly limited in moving the economy towards equilibrium under the existing regime.

Therefore in chapter 7 we undertake reform experiments, searching for a policy package which could remove the institutional drawbacks, and increase the proportion of activity subject to market-clearing. The historical model in chapter 6 is replaced by the counterfactual one corresponding to a policy reform package. In doing this, however, we are faced with the problem of how to obtain a fully specified numerical model. Since the counterfactual economic relations are not fitted to the historical time series data, the formal procedure of econometric estimation is inapplicable. We thus have to resort to a calibration procedure used in applied general equilibrium analysis. After that the counterfactual model is simulated with the same policy scenarios as considered in chapter 6. This serves to provide a basis for comparison, and we find that further market-oriented reforms would generate an economy which had self-stabilized mechanisms in response to policy shocks so that the degree of disequilibrium could be quickly reduced, and the growth of output would be maintained at much lower cost in terms of inflation. The experiments with different reform packages are followed by sensitivity analysis, which shows a degree of robustness in the results obtained.

Finally, chapter 8 contains a summary of the conclusions reached, and the directions suggested for further research.

Notes

1. This figure further declined to less than 50% in 1993 (see Fan G. et al, 1993).
2. These figures only reflect the official inflation rate. As we will see later, the 'true' inflation rate would be much higher, if the repressed one was also taken into account.
3. Recently there has been a paper (Ma G., 1993) attempting to address this controversial issue.
4. From the perspective of expenditure and particularly regarding investment expenditure, the public-ownership economy is still in a dominant position (Fan G. et al, 1993).

2 Disequilibrium approaches to modelling socialist economies

2.1 Introduction

The Socialist economies, including the centrally planned economies of the type of the ex-Soviet Union and the dual-system economies of the type of the post-reform China, have all experienced severe imbalances in domestic markets over the past several decades. Economists and econometrician realized quite early that the traditional equilibrium theories and modelling were not of great use in analysing phenomena such as formal or informal rationing, forced substitution and savings, waiting lists, repressed inflation or monetary overhang etc.. Accordingly they have constructed and developed analytical frameworks and empirical models designed to explain these phenomena. Among these studies, disequilibrium and shortage economy models form the two main schools of thought. This literature has mushroomed during the last couple of decades. A full review of this literature is beyond the scope of this book. Since the approach adopted in this book falls into the first school, the emphasis in this review is placed on the prominent contributions to the disequilibrium approach.

2.2 Disequilibrium economics and econometrics

Some economic theories

(i) The effective demand (supply) concept Traditional general equilibrium theory goes to great lengths to make sure that prices clear markets. The most famous example of this is the Walrasian auctioneer who calls out various price vectors until he/she shouts out the price vector at which *ex ante* supply

is equal to *ex ante* demand in all markets. Moreover, an important assumption in this story is that no trade at all takes place until market-clearing price vector is called out. This suggests that if prices are exogenous, then demand for the ith good in a market-clearing general equilibrium will be a function of the price vector:

$$c_i^d = c_i^d(p) \qquad (2.1)$$

where $p=(p_1, p_2, ..., p_n)'$ is the market-clearing price vector shouted out by the auctioneer. Now if the price vector is at other than p, say p^1, then (assuming uniqueness of equilibrium) there must be excess supply/demand in some markets, and agents on the 'long' side of these markets will face quantity constraints. In such circumstances, it seems unlikely that consumers rationed in the labour market will continue to demand the same value of goods as if they were fully employed. Firms finding that they are unable to sell all their output are quite likely to reduce their demand for factors of production, including labour. From this arises the concept of effective trade offers as against Walrasian (or notional) trade offers.

Patinkin (1956) is generally credited with the first model which distinguishes between Walrasian and effective trade offers. Specifically, the demand for labour by firms is shown to depend on their expectation of how much output they can sell and not only on the level of real wages. Clower (1965), with more general insight, conducted a similar analysis on household behaviour. He described this process as the 'dual decision hypothesis'. If a consumer can not sell all the labour he/she wishes, the dual decision hypothesis implies that the consumer will recompute his/her demand for the ith commodity to take account of this fact. Clower proposed a construction of the effective demand for commodity i that is based on satisfying the budget constraint and the quantity constraints for all other commodities but on neglecting the quantity constraint on commodity i itself. In this case the consumer is supposed to solve n separate optimization problems that differ from one another by which quantity constraint is omitted. The Clower effective demand concept has been further developed by Barro and Grossman (1971 and 1976), and in most detail by Benassy (1975). Another definition of effective demand is provided by Dreze (1975). Here each agent chooses the most preferred trade vector, subject to the budget constraints as well as *all* perceived constraints including the market in question. The Dreze demand concept has been further used by Younes (1975), Grandmont and Laroque (1976), Hahn (1978) and others.

By further investigation Svensson (1980) has found the behavioral theory underlying the Clower and Dreze demand concepts unsatisfactory. He finds that, under the Clower's proposal, the budget constraint may be violated. For example, consider a case where there are three goods: a consumption good x_1, hours of labour offered for sale x_2, and the real money balance x_3. Suppose that a consumer is rationed in both consumption and labour markets, and the amount rationed for x_1 and x_2 are $\bar{x}_1$ and $\bar{x}_2$. When calculating the effective demand for consumption goods, he/she respects the quantity constraint on labour market but neglects that on consumption market, and thus the budget constraint becomes:

$$p_1 x_1 - p_2 \bar{x}_2 + p_1 x_3 = m_0 \qquad (2.2)$$

When calculating the effective labour supply, he/she considers only the quantity restriction on consumption market, and the budget constraint is

$$p_1 \bar{x}_1 - p_2 x_2 + p_1 x_3 = m_0 \qquad (2.3)$$

The effective demand for consumption goods obtained under the budget constraint (2.2) is certainly larger than the rationed amount, i.e. $x_1^e > \bar{x}_1$. If one substitutes x_1^e for $\bar{x}_1$ in (2.3), then the left hand side will be larger than m_0. At the same time, if one maximizes the utility function subject to the budget constraint and *all* quantity constraints that are known to exit as suggested by Dreze, then the effective demand/supply will equal to the rationed amounts, namely, $x_1^e = \bar{x}_1$ and $x_2^e = \bar{x}_2$. This seems to be inexplicable in empirical disequilibrium analysis since effective demand/supply always satisfies restrictions and consequently the estimation of a disequilibrium gap is not feasible.

Ito (1980) discusses in greater details how to specify spill-over effects in the formation of effective demand/supply. The spill-over effect is stressed by Ito as an essential feature of a disequilibrium model, and illustrated as follows. A consumer maximizes his/her utility function of the Cobb-Douglas form

$$U = x_1^\alpha (T-x_2)^\beta x_3^\gamma \qquad (2.4)$$

subject to the budget constraint

$$p_1 x_1 - p_2 x_2 + p_1 x_3 = m_0 \qquad (2.5)$$

where T is the endowment of time. Solving the first-order conditions, one may obtain the Walrasian functions below:

$$\tilde{x}_1 = \frac{\alpha}{\alpha+\beta+\gamma} \frac{m_0 + p_2 T}{p_1}$$

$$\tilde{x}_2 = \frac{\alpha+\gamma}{\alpha+\beta+\gamma}T - \frac{\beta}{\alpha+\beta+\gamma}\frac{m_0}{p_2}$$

$$\tilde{x}_3 = \frac{\gamma}{\alpha+\beta+\gamma}\frac{m_0+p_2T}{p_1}$$

In order to calculate the effective demand for consumption goods, the consumer takes into account the amount $\bar{x}_2$ ($<\tilde{x}_2$) to which his/her labour offer is rationed, and the budget constraint (2.5). Then his/her effective demand for consumption goods is

$$x_1^e = \frac{\alpha}{\alpha+\gamma}\frac{m_0+p_2\bar{x}_2}{p_1} = \tilde{x}_1 + \frac{\alpha}{\alpha+\gamma}\frac{p_2}{p_1}(\bar{x}_2-\tilde{x}_2) \qquad (2.6)$$

The term containing $(\bar{x}_2-\tilde{x}_2)$ in (2.6) is the spill-over effect of unemployment onto the consumption goods market.

When coming to the effective labour supply, he/she then respects the quantity restriction $\bar{x}_1$ ($<\tilde{x}_1$) on consumption markets as well as the budget constraint. Maximizing (2.4) subject to $x_1=\bar{x}_1$ and (2.5) gives

$$x_2^e = \frac{\gamma}{\beta+\gamma}T - \frac{\beta}{\beta+\gamma}\frac{m_0}{p_2} + \frac{\beta}{\beta+\gamma}\frac{p_1}{p_2}\bar{x}_1 = \tilde{x}_2 + \frac{\beta}{\beta+\gamma}\frac{p_1}{p_2}(\bar{x}_1-\tilde{x}_1) \qquad (2.7)$$

The term containing $\bar{x}_1-\tilde{x}_1$ in (2.7) is the spill-over effect of consumption good shortage on the labour market.

More clearly than his preceding researchers, Ito stated that the effective demand for commodities can be expressed as a sum of the Walrasian demand and the spill-over effect. In addition, he made a proposition that for a consumer with the Cobb-Douglas utility function, the nominal value of the spill-over effect is proportional to the nominal value of dissatisfaction, or the difference between the actual transaction and the Walrasian demand (supply). The spill-over coefficient is then less than one and determined by the coefficient of the utility function.

(ii) Disequilibrium regimes Numerous theoretical studies have analyzed a stylized economy in which there are two markets, namely a market for consumption goods and a market for labour, and the combinations of different disequilibrium situations in these two markets. Barro and Grossman (1971) analyzed two fundamentally different disequilibrium situations. The first one is a general excess supply, i.e., at the initial price vector there are excess supplies of both consumption goods and labour. This situation is appropriately labelled *Keynesian unemployment* ($C^d<C^s$, $L^d<L^s$). The second disequilibrium situation is characterized by general excess demand, i.e.,

excess demand in both labour market and consumption market. As prices and wages are fixed and can not rise to alleviate these excess demand in the short run, this situation has been called *repressed inflation* ($C^d > C^s$, $L^d > L^s$). Later in Barro and Grossman (1976) and Malinvaud (1977), they treated the disequilibrium combination called *classical unemployment* ($C^d > C^s$, $L^d < L^s$), the case of excess demand for consumption goods and excess supply of labour. In an inter-temporal frame work with nonperishable goods, however, the *under-consumption* case ($C^d < C^s$, $L^d > L^s$), characterized by an excess supply of goods and an excess demand for labour, may arise. It was initially discussed by Malinvaud (1977) and, in a more explicit intertemporal framework, by Muellbauer and Portes (1978).

Consider an economy with three representative agents: household, firm and government. The government enters the economy through fixing the volume of real government expenditure, which is a prior claim on output (the government is never rationed). Now under the dual decision hypothesis, household and firm have the following decision-making functions concerning consumption demand and supply:

$$C^d = \begin{cases} \tilde{C}^d \left[\underset{(+)}{\frac{W}{p}}, \underset{(+)}{\frac{\pi}{p}}, \underset{(+)}{\frac{M}{p}} \right], & \text{if } \bar{L} = L^s \leq L^d ; \\ \bar{C}^d \left[\underset{(+)}{\frac{W}{p}}, \underset{(+)}{\frac{\pi}{p}}, \underset{(+)}{\frac{M}{p}}; \underset{(+)}{\bar{L}} \right], & \text{if } \bar{L} = L^d < L^s . \end{cases} \quad (2.8)$$

$$C^s = \begin{cases} \tilde{Y}^s \left[\underset{(-)}{\frac{W}{p}} \right] - G, & \text{if } \bar{L} = L^d \leq L^s ; \\ \bar{Y}^s \left[\underset{(-)}{\frac{W}{p}}; \underset{(+)}{\bar{L}} \right] - G, & \text{if } \bar{L} = L^s < L^d . \end{cases} \quad (2.9)$$

$$C = \min \{ C^d, C^s \} \quad (2.10)$$

where C, C^d, C^s, $\tilde{C}^d$ and $\bar{C}^d$ are actual consumption, consumption demand, consumption supply, notional consumption demand and effective (or labour-rationed) consumption demand respectively; L^d, L^s and $\bar{L}$ denote labour demand, labour supply and labour ration faced by the household (or the firm) respectively; $\tilde{Y}^s$ and $\bar{Y}^s$ represent total notional consumption supply and total effective (or labour-rationed) consumption supply respectively; W/p, π/p, M/p are real wage, real profits, and real money balances.

Precisely analogously, for the labour markets the household and firm's dual decision-making function can be written as

$$L^d = \begin{cases} \tilde{L}^d\left[\underset{(-)}{\dfrac{W}{p}}\right], & \text{if } \overline{C}=C^s \leq C^d ; \\[2ex] \overline{L}^d\left[\underset{(-)}{\dfrac{W}{p}}; \underset{(+)}{\overline{C}}\right], & \text{if } \overline{C}=C^d<C^s . \end{cases} \qquad (2.11)$$

$$L^s = \begin{cases} \tilde{L}^s\left[\underset{(+)}{\dfrac{W}{p}}, \underset{(-)}{\dfrac{\pi}{p}}, \underset{(-)}{\dfrac{M}{p}}\right], & \text{if } \overline{C}=C^d \leq C^s ; \\[2ex] \overline{L}^s\left[\underset{(+)}{\dfrac{W}{p}}, \underset{(-)}{\dfrac{\pi}{p}}, \underset{(-)}{\dfrac{M}{p}}; \underset{(+)}{\overline{C}}\right], & \text{if } \overline{C}=C^s<C^d . \end{cases} \qquad (2.12)$$

$$L = \min\{L^d, L^s\} \qquad (2.13)$$

where L, $\tilde{L}^d$, $\overline{L}^d$, $\tilde{L}^s$, $\overline{L}^s$ and $\overline{C}$ stand for actual labour amount, notional labour demand, effective (or consumption-rationed) labour demand, notional labour supply, effective (or consumption-rationed) labour supply, and consumption ration respectively.

Examining (2.8)-(2.10) and (2.11)-(2.13) together, we can begin to see the two markets interact. For example, when actual trading is taking place with excess supply in consumption goods market, the notional labour demand function of the firm becomes irrelevant and is replaced by the effective demand function which, through the minimum condition, may then determine the amount of labour actually transacted. At the same time when actual trading is taking place with excess supply in the labour market, the notional consumption demand function of household becomes irrelevant and is replaced by the effective demand schedule. This, via the minimum condition, may again has an impact on firms if consumption demand is even less than firms initially anticipated.

We start with Figure 2.1 (a) showing how the different regimes depend on the real wage W/p and real money balances M/p. The broken curves are drawn by equilibrating *notional* demands and supplies in the labour and consumption markets, that is,

$$\begin{cases} \tilde{C}^d(x_h) = \tilde{C}^s \equiv \tilde{Y}^s(x_f) - G ; \\ \tilde{L}^d(x_f) = \tilde{L}^s(x_h) . \end{cases} \qquad (2.14)$$

14

where $x_h = (W/p, M/p, \cdots)$ is the vector of exogenous arguments in the households' utility function, and $x_f = (W/p, \cdots)$ is the vector of exogenous arguments in the firms' objective function. The solid curves denote equity between *effective* demands and supplies in the corresponding markets, namely

$$\begin{cases} \overline{C}^d(x_h;\overline{L}) = \tilde{C}^s \equiv \tilde{Y}(x_f) - G, & \overline{L} = \tilde{L}^d(x_f); \\ \overline{L}^d(\overline{C}) = \tilde{L}^s(x_h), & \overline{C} = \tilde{C}^d(x_h); \\ \tilde{C}^d(x_h) = \overline{C}^s \equiv \overline{Y}^s(\overline{L}) - G, & \overline{L} = \tilde{L}^s(x_h); \\ \tilde{L}^d(x_f) = \overline{L}^s(x_h;\overline{C}), & \overline{C} = \tilde{C}^s \equiv \tilde{Y}^s(x_f) - G. \end{cases} \quad (2.15)$$

In equation group (2.15) it is assumed, as Lee does (1986), that households and firms will not both be rationed simultaneously in the same market. Thus, for example, when households express effective demand for goods because of labour rations they face, firms' effective supply coincides with notional one as they are not rationed in labour market. Equations in (2.15) are the effective market-clearing conditions in the Barro-Grossman sense. They state that when the firm is rationed in the labour market, 'the effective supply of commodities can vary even with the real wage fixed. Changes in the level of the constraint $\overline{L}$ determine effective commodity supply independently of changes in W/p' (Barro and Grossman 1976, p. 69). Similarly in the case of the firm being constrained in consumption market, 'the effective demand for labour can vary even with the real wage rate fixed. Changes in the level of the constraint $\overline{C}$ influence effective labour demand independently of changes in W/p' (Barro and Grossman 1976, p. 43). In Barro-Grossman's study, x_f only contains W/p, and thus it disappears from firms' effective decision demand/supply functions. As such, differentiating both sides of (2.15) yields identical slopes $\partial(W/p)/\partial(M/p)$ for curves $\tilde{C}^d = \overline{C}^s$ and $\overline{L}^d = \tilde{L}^s$ (given $(\partial \tilde{C}^s/\partial \tilde{L}^s) = (\partial L^d/\partial \tilde{C}^d)^{-1}$), although the signs of the slopes are ambiguous. But the slopes for loci $\tilde{C}^d = \tilde{C}^s$ and $\overline{C}^d = \tilde{C}^s$ are negative $((W/p)/\partial(M/p)<0)$, and $\partial(W/p)/\partial(M/p)>0$ for curves $\tilde{L}^d = \tilde{L}^s$ and $\tilde{L}^d = \overline{L}^s$. Since $\tilde{C}^d = \overline{C}^s$ and $\overline{L}^d = \tilde{L}^s$ are coincident with each other, the effective market-clearing conditions divide wage-money space into three regions in Figure 2.1 where we depict the loci of $\tilde{C}^d = \tilde{C}^s$ ($\tilde{L}^d = \tilde{L}^s$) somewhere to the right of $\tilde{L}^d = \tilde{L}^s$. Suppose that there happen to be a pair of values $(W/p)^*$ and $(M/p)^*$ which simultaneously clear both consumption and labour markets. Thus point E $[(W/p)^*, (M/p)^*]$ locates on both loci labelled $\tilde{C}^d = \tilde{C}^s$ and $\tilde{L}^d = \tilde{L}^s$. Since neither households nor firms face quantity constraints, the consumption demand/supply and labour demand/supply corresponding to point E are all notional as well, and hence point E generates the unique Walrasian equilibrium, i.e., $\tilde{C}^d = \tilde{C}^s$ and $\tilde{L}^d = \tilde{L}^s$.

Starting from E an economy could reach one of three alternative states.

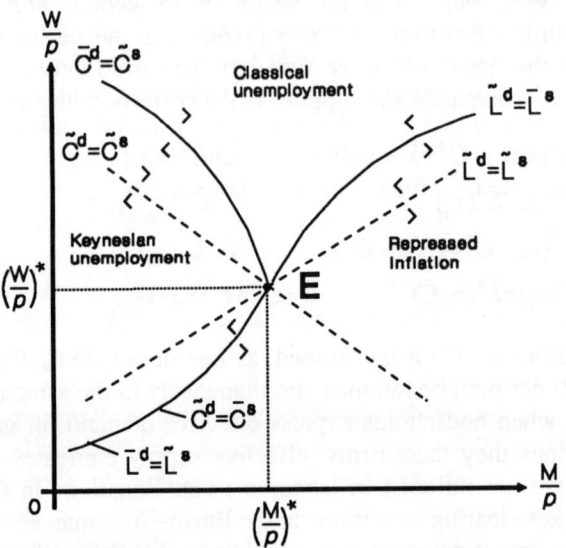

Figure 2.1 Disequilibrium regimes

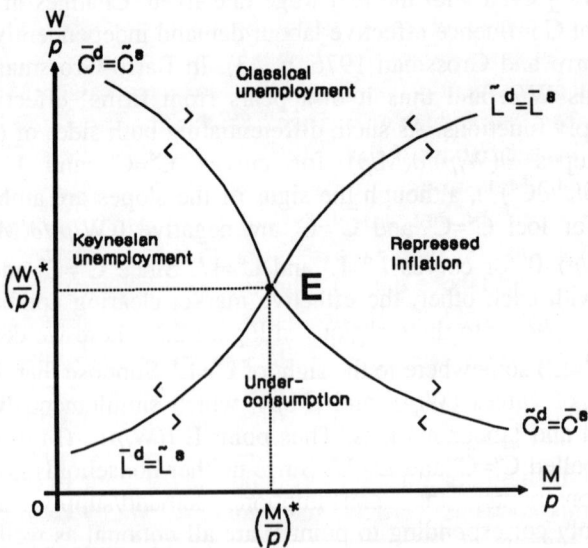

Figure 2.2 Disequilibrium regimes including an under-consumption regime

If the real wage rate is kept at $(W/p)^*$ while real money balances are decreased, firms' demand for labour and supply of consumption goods will be unchanged (see equations (2.9) and (2.11)), while households' demand for consumption goods will fall but their supply of labour will rise (see equations (2.8) and (2.12)). Hence a general excess supply in both markets is generated, and the economy moves into the disequilibrium regime of Keynesian unemployment. Being labour-rationed, households' consumption decision schedule shifts to the effective consumption demand function which is less than notional demand function. As such the equating of $\bar{C}^d$ to $\tilde{C}^s$ requires for any given real wage a level of real money balances above the level which would equate $\tilde{C}^d$ to $\tilde{C}^s$. Consequently, the locus $\bar{C}^d=\tilde{C}^s$ originates at point E and lies everywhere to the right of locus $\tilde{C}^d=\tilde{C}^s$. Thus the existence of excess supply in the labour market enlarges the region of excess supply in the consumption market. If on the other hand the real money balances are increased holding (W/p) at $(W/p)^*$, general excess demand in both markets will be generated as a higher demand for consumption goods and a smaller supply of labour emerges. In this circumstance the economy is in the disequilibrium regime known as repressed inflation. Similarly we observe that the presence of excess demand for consumption goods enlarges the region of excess demand in labour market. Now suppose real money balances are kept constant at Walrasian equilibrium level $(M/p)^*$ while real wage is increased. Firms demand less labour and supply less output. The household will demand more goods and supply more labour as the increase of the real wage makes leisure more expensive relative to goods. So a situation where there is excess consumption demand and excess labour supply appears, which is called 'classical unemployment'. Finally assume constant value $(M/p)^*$ for real money balances, but reduce real wage. This is the most ambiguous case, since we know least about the probable outcomes: for the household, both labour supply and consumption demand will fall; for the firm, which should increase labour demand and hence the output only with respect to real wage, perceive restrictions on both markets, and with the effective consumption supply function and labour demand function at work (see equation (2.15)), both labour demand and consumption supply also decrease as a result of falls in $\bar{C}$ ($=\tilde{C}^d$) and $\bar{L}$ ($=\tilde{L}^s$). But which region, the Keynesian unemployment or the represses inflation regime, the economy will eventually go to depends on the comparative speed of decreases in households' consumption demand and firms' consumption supply, and in households' labour supply and firms' labour demand. Diagrammatically, it depends on the slope of the locus $\tilde{C}^d=\bar{C}^s$ ($\bar{L}^d=\tilde{L}^s$). If this locus is vertical, the economy would be on the border between the regions of Keynesian unemployment and repressed inflation. This implies that households' demand for goods and supply of labour would decline at the same speed as firms' supply of goods and demand for labour do. If the slope of this locus is negative, the economy would be in the Keynesian unemployment regime. If the slope of this locus is positive as shown in Figure 2.1, the economy would then be in the regime of repressed inflation.

There is no region of excess supply of goods and excess demand of labour in Figure 2.1. In the intertemporal approach used in Muellbauer and Portes (1978), however, an under-consumption regime is a distinct possibility. Muellbauer-Portes's study has extended the analysis of Barro and Grossman by allowing firms to carry over inventories from one period to the next, just as households may hold money balances. This approach has led to the effective market-clearing conditions given below:

$$\begin{cases} \bar{C}^d\left(\frac{W}{p},\frac{\pi}{p},\frac{M}{p};\bar{L}\right)=\tilde{C}^s\left(\frac{W}{p},G\right), & \bar{L}=\bar{L}^d\left(\frac{W}{p}\right); \\ \bar{L}^d\left(\frac{W}{p},\bar{C}\right)=\tilde{L}^s\left(\frac{W}{p},\frac{\pi}{p},\frac{M}{p}\right), & \bar{C}=\tilde{C}^d\left(\frac{W}{p},\frac{\pi}{p},\frac{M}{p}\right); \\ \tilde{C}^d\left(\frac{W}{p},\frac{\pi}{p},\frac{M}{p}\right)=\bar{C}^s\left(\frac{W}{p},G;\bar{L}\right), & \bar{L}=\tilde{L}^s\left(\frac{W}{p},\frac{\pi}{p},\frac{M}{p}\right); \\ \tilde{L}^d\left(\frac{W}{p}\right)=\bar{L}^s\left(\frac{W}{p},\frac{\pi}{p},\frac{M}{p};\bar{C}\right), & \bar{C}=\tilde{C}^s\left(\frac{W}{p},G\right). \end{cases}$$ (2.16)

Thus the resulting effective demand for labour and the effective supply of goods, unlike the ones in Barro-Grossman sense, are determined by perceived quantity constraints as well as initial endowments and prices. This is reflected by the vector x_f also being an argument of the effective demand/supply functions of firms. Now differentiating both side of (2.16) with respect to W/p no longer gives identical slopes for loci $\tilde{C}^d=\bar{C}^s$ and $\bar{L}^d=\tilde{L}^s$, and the divergence between these two curves makes one more constraint regime (i.e., under-consumption regime) possible. The diagram describing the different disequilibrium regimes under such circumstances would look like Figure 2.2, with the under-consumption regime situated between the Keynesian unemployment and repressed inflation regions.

Estimation techniques

During the last a few decades, major advances were made as well in all components of quantitative economics of disequilibrium: computational capabilities, data collection, mathematical modelling, and econometric estimation and hypothesis testing. Due to the focus of this analysis, we limit our survey here to some developments of estimation technique for disequilibrium models.

Fair and Jaffee (1972) developed the first disequilibrium econometric model with minimum conditions, and proposed alternative methods of estimation. The simplest form of the Fair-Jaffee model is as follows:

$$D_t = \alpha_0 X_t^D + \alpha_1 p_t + \mu_t^D, \quad \alpha_1 < 0. \tag{2.17}$$

$$S_t = \beta_0 X_t^S + \beta_1 p_t + \mu_t^S, \quad \beta_1 > 0. \tag{2.18}$$

$$Q_t = \min\{D_t, S_t\} \tag{2.19}$$

D_t denotes the quantity demanded during period t, S_t the quantity supplied during period t, and p_t the price of the goods during period t. X_t^D and X_t^S denote the variables, aside from p_t, and the error terms are μ_t^D and μ_t^S, that influence D_t and S_t respectively. The distinguishing feature of the model is that p_t is not assumed to adjust each period so as to equate D_t and S_t. Fair and Jaffee suggested that the maximum likelihood method can be used to estimate the values of the parameters α_0, α_1, β_0 and β_1, given observations on X_t^D, X_t^S, p_t and Q_t. The log of likelihood function of the entire sample is:

$$\log L = -\frac{m}{2}\log(2\pi\sigma_D^2) - \frac{n}{2}\log(2\pi\sigma_S^2) - \frac{1}{2\sigma_D^2}\sum_t^m (D_t - \alpha_0 X_t^D - \alpha_1 p_t)^2$$

$$- \frac{1}{2\sigma_S^2}\sum_t^n (S_t - \beta_0 X_t^S - \beta_1 p_t)^2 \tag{2.20}$$

where m is the number of observations for which $Q_t = D_t$ so that D_t is replaced by Q_t and the fourth term is equal to zero; n is the number of observations for which $Q_t = S_t$ so that S_t is replaced by Q_t and the third term is equal to zero. The sums $\sum_t^m$ and $\sum_t^n$ denote summation over those observations (not necessarily sequential) for which $Q_t = D_t$ and $Q_t = S_t$ respectively. The terms σ_D and σ_S are the standard errors of μ_t^D and μ_t^S respectively. Substituting the estimates for the six parameters ($\hat{\alpha}_0$, $\hat{\alpha}_1$, $\hat{\beta}_0$, $\hat{\beta}_1$, $\hat{\sigma}_D^2$ and $\hat{\sigma}_S^2$) into (2.20) yields:

$$\log L = -(m+n)\log(\sqrt{2\pi}) - m\log(\hat{\sigma}_D) - n\log(\hat{\sigma}_S) - \frac{m+n}{2} \tag{2.21}$$

The solution to the problem is then to choose the sample separation m or n and the corresponding values of $\hat{\alpha}_0$, $\hat{\alpha}_1$, $\hat{\beta}_0$ and $\hat{\beta}_1$ that maximize (2.21). In this way, the sample is effectively reduced to m and n, which leads to loss of precision, because of small degree of freedom.

A slightly more complicated model arises if p_t is made endogenous by the addition to (2.17), (2.18) and (2.19) of, say, a dynamic adjustment equation:

$$\Delta p_t = \gamma(D_t - S_t) \qquad (2.22)$$

where γ is an unknown positive scalar parameter. Equation (2.22) actually provides investigators with more information about price-setting behaviour to help in the estimation problem. Fair and Jaffee discussed three estimation methods for this model. The first one (Directional Method I) is implemented by separating the sample into periods of excess demand and excess supply on the basis of the observed direction of price changes. The supply function can be estimated over periods of excess demand (using Q as the dependent variable), and the demand function can be estimated over periods of excess supply (also using Q as the dependent variable). Period of temporary equilibrium ($\Delta p_t = 0$) are included in both samples since both demand and supply schedules are observed at such times. The second one (Directional Method II) operates by postulating a number of different sample separations corresponding to alternative assumptions about the excess demand status of the market during the periods in which the change in price is either so small or so variable as to leave that status in doubt. This method is less dependent on the price change as an indicator of disequilibrium in the market, and *a priori* information on price changes is merely used to reduce the number of sample separations. Then the supply and demand equations are fitted to each set of sample separations and the log of likelihood function (2.20) is evaluated for each case. The sample separation which maximizes (2.20) is the preferred one. The most interesting method is the fourth one so called 'The Quantitative Method'. For this method the system of equations (2.17)-(2.19) and (2.22) can be reduced to a single demand equation and a single supply equation:

$$Q_t = D_t - \frac{k_1}{\gamma}\Delta p_t = \alpha_0 X_t^D + \alpha_1 p_t - \frac{k_1}{\gamma}\Delta p_t + \mu_t^D \qquad (2.23)$$

$$k_1 = \begin{cases} 1, & \text{if } \Delta p_t > 0 \text{ ;} \\ 0, & \text{otherwise .} \end{cases}$$

$$Q_t = S_t + \frac{k_2}{\gamma}\Delta p_t = \beta_0 X_t^S + \beta_1 p_t + \frac{k_2}{\gamma}\Delta p_t + \mu_t^S \qquad (2.24)$$

$$k_2 = \begin{cases} 1, & \text{if } \Delta p_t < 0 \text{ ;} \\ 0, & \text{otherwise .} \end{cases}$$

For the problem that the same coefficient γ appears in both equations, it can be solved using the estimation technique developed in Fair ('The Estimation of Equation System with Restrictions Across Equations and Serial Correlated Errors', mimeographed). For the problem of simultaneity, Fair and Jaffee suggested applying the standard two-stage least squares technique. Consider the estimation of equation (2.23) for example. In the first stage, the fitted values $\Delta \hat{p}_t$ are obtained by regressing Δp_t against appropriate instruments over that part of sample for which Δp_t is non-negative ($k_1=1$). In the second stage, use $\Delta \hat{p}_t$ and the inserted zeros ($k_1=0$) for the periods of negative Δp_t to construct series $k_1*\Delta \hat{p}_t$ which replaces $k_1*\Delta p_t$ in the equation (2.23). The same idea can be applied to the treatment of endogeneity of Δp_t in (2.24) and p_t in both equations.

However, Amemiya (1974, p. 760) points out that 'a variant of the two-stage least squares method which Fair and Jaffee propose and claim to be consistent is inconsistent'. The problem is that the quantitative method discussed by Fair and Jaffee uses only the part of the sample where $\Delta p_t>0$ for estimating demand equation (or $\Delta p_t<0$ for estimating supply equation). This would lead to $E\mu_t^D \neq 0$, which then would give rise to the bias of the Fair and Jaffee estimators. On the other hand, Amemiya argued, the fact that g_t (= $k_1*\Delta p_t$) contains zero values does not in any way violate the conditions for the consistency of two-stage least squares estimator. Thus the parameters of (2.23), for example, can be consistently estimated by first regressing g_t on all the exogenous variables (X_t^D and X_t^S) thereby defining its predictor $\hat{g}_t$, and second regressing Q_t on X_t^D, $\hat{p}_t$ (obtained in a similar way as $\hat{g}_t$) and $\hat{g}_t$. Next Amemiya discussed the efficiency of an estimator resulting from the constraint that γ appears in both demand and supply equations. Fair and Jaffee noticed that two-stage least squares technique would obtain consistency at the cost of efficiency, but they failed to find a solution to the problem of contradiction between consistency and efficiency. Amemiya proposes the maximum likelihood estimator, which he expects to be consistent and asymptotically efficient, and which he thinks can be obtained by an iterative scheme. In addition, Amemiya also considered two cases where μ_t^D and μ_t^S are serially correlated, and where μ_t^D and μ_t^S are contemporaneously correlated but serially uncorrelated. For the first one the maximum likelihood method becomes computationally intractable, but the two-stage least squares method can be easily modified to take account of the serial correlation. For the second one, a somewhat different and complicated likelihood function is proposed.

In the subsequent years further progress in estimation techniques for disequilibrium models was made, among others, by Fair and Kelejian (1974), Maddala and Nelson (1974), Goldfeld and Quandt (1975). These studies of methods of estimation for markets in disequilibrium have been limited to the single market case. Ito (1980) develops the first two-market disequilibrium model, and makes several possible assumptions on the price and wage adjustment mechanism in the consumption goods and labour markets respectively. These different assumptions lead to four types of model, among which two types are characterized by allowing asymmetric price adjustment mechanism. The maximum likelihood method is provided to estimate three of his models, while the two-stage least squares method is proposed for estimating one of them. But finally one of his models, which does not allow price and wage to be included as exogenous variables, has to be dropped from consideration.

2.3 Basic approaches to modelling CPEs

The centrally planned economies, as is generally recognized, possess unique features. They persistently operate in a state of general excess demand and pervasive shortage outside the conventional equilibrium state. This has stimulated extensive theoretical and empirical research in the behaviour of CPEs. A selective review of that research is presented in this section, covering disequilibrium indicator models, testable excess demand models, and the virtual price approach to disequilibrium analysis.

Disequilibrium indicator models of CPEs

Disequilibrium econometric models were based on the Western theoretical and econometric approaches discussed above, but adapted to take into account the institutional characteristics and data constraints of socialist countries. The disequilibrium econometric models of CPEs were diverse in nature and can be subdivided into two groups according to their approach: (1) chronic (i.e., known) excess demand (or disequilibrium indicator) models; (2) testable excess demand models. The disequilibrium indicator modelling approach assumes the existence of excess demand and seeks to represent it by an observable synthetic indicator. The testable excess demand models, on the other hand, generally make no *a priori* assumption concerning the existence of disequilibrium, but rather use demand and supply equations plus the minimum condition to detect and measure it if found.

The disequilibrium indicator models originated with the Fair and Jaffee (1972) model, although they did not explicitly use the terminology. It was claimed in Welfe (1978) that it is usually possible to define a set of variables which directly determine (or are directly determined by) excess demand. These variables are called 'disequilibrium indicators' and can be used to solve out the unobservable demand (and/or possibly supply) variable. In this sense, the difference of price in the original Fair-Jaffee model (see equation (2.22)) would be the first disequilibrium indicator appearing in the literature. Nevertheless, the model of the Fair-Jaffee types with endogenous, freely negotiated prices and perfect information cannot be explicitly employed for the most of CPEs. The solution usually adopted for this problem was given in the first quantitative disequilibrium consumption model developed by Charemza and Gierusz (1978) which was written as:

$$Q_t^d = Q^d(\cdot) + \mu_t \qquad (2.25)$$

$$Q_t^s = Q^s(\cdot) + v_t \qquad (2.26)$$

$$Q_t^d - Q_t^s = \gamma \frac{\Delta S_t}{\overline{Y}_t}, \quad \gamma > 0 \qquad (2.27)$$

where Q_t, Q_t^d and Q_t^s are the quantity transacted, demanded and supplied respectively, ΔS_t the increase in personal savings between current and last periods, $\overline{Y}_t$ the average money income of households over the current and last periods. An additional assumption is imposed that $Q_t^d - Q_t^s \geq 0$, and $Q_t = Q_t^s$ over entire sample period. Substituting (2.25) into the demand function leads to:

$$Q_t = Q^d(\cdot) - \gamma \frac{\Delta S_t}{\overline{Y}_t} + \mu_t \qquad (2.28)$$

which was estimated by OLS. Charemza (1989) pointed out that this procedure has some flaws. First it makes ΔS_t and/or $\overline{Y}_t$ endogenous and hence the OLS estimator inconsistent. Second the assumption of a deterministic excess demand equation would reduce the problem to estimating the parameter γ. Another major problem with disequilibrium indicator approach is that the exogenous and endogenous nature of the disequilibrium indicators remains undecided.

While insufficient attention was paid to difficulties associated with that approach, the number of empirical studies adopting deterministic disequilibrium indicators to model consumption market imbalances have grown significantly. In those studies, for example, Michalak and Starzynska (1979) assumed excess demand to be proportional to the difference between the free market prices and official state prices for food; Gronicki and Szreder (1981 and 1986) constructed a model for the TV market which expressed the excess demand as a function of changes in TV inventories; Hulyak (1985) used a disequilibrium indicator of the first difference of total personal savings. Although the above listed models possess relatively good *ex post* statistical diagnostics, non of them has been used for *ex ante* forecasting or simulation exercises. The main reason is that models with deterministic, extraneously driven, disequilibrium indicators do not permit well-defined *ex ante* computation of excess demand. Their utility in the *ex post* simulation of excess demand is also questionable: What is the point of building and estimating a complicated disequilibrium model if it is recognized in advance that excess consumption demand is entirely determined by one known variable? Charemza and Gronicki (1988) proposed a deterministic disequilibrium indicator of an endogenous nature: a wage illusion mechanism. They assumed that workers are additionally paid for disutilities connected mainly with consumption market shortages. This eventually leads to the wage relation used as disequilibrium indicator equation:

$$w_t = w_{t-2} + \alpha (C_t^d - C_t^s) \qquad (2.29)$$

With the disequilibrium indicator of this type, the *ex ante* computation of excess consumption demand is well-defined, and it makes the disputable point of *ex post* simulation unnecessary, since the excess consumption demand is here determined by $C_t^d(\cdot) - C_t^s(\cdot)$, but not entirely determined by one known variable as a disequilibrium indicator. Their model was indeed used for simulation and optimal control experiments to reveal a feasible *ex post* macroeconomic policy with an objective to reduce the level of consumption disequilibria in Poland. Despite this development, the equation (2.29) has also received a substantial critique, mainly stressing an absence in the equation of some relevant explanatory variables, especially labour productivity and a cost of living index. Charemza responded to these criticism, and the details can be found in Charemza (1989).

Substantial recent progress were achieved in disequilibrium indicator modelling (see book edited by Davis and Charemza, 1989). Some researchers express scepticism about the value of traditional deterministic univariate disequilibrium indicators and introduce multivariate forms. Welfe (1989), for example, uses a multivariate deterministic disequilibrium indicator model in his investigation of consumption and savings in Poland. Disequilibrium was defined there as the result of functioning factors included in the indicator. To construct this kind of indicator, Welfe first transforms the identity defining excess demand, $DE_t = D_t - S_t$, as follows:

$$DE_t = S_t \left(\frac{D_t}{S_t} - \frac{D_{t-n-1}}{S_{t-n-1}} \right) + S_t \frac{DE_{t-n-1}}{S_{t-n-1}} = \alpha_E S_t \left(\frac{D_t}{S_t} - \frac{D_{t-n-1}}{S_{t-n-1}} \right) \qquad (2.30)$$

The general assumption is that excess demand in the initial period DE_{t-n-1} has a normal value, and hence D_{t-n-1}/S_{t-n-1} and DE_{t-n-1}/S_{t-n-1}. To replace the unobservable variables demand D_t and supply S_t, The potential limit for demand $\tilde{D}_t$ and for supply $\tilde{S}_t$ has to be employed. In the former case $\tilde{D}_t$ is the volume of current income or the income increased by forced savings; for the latter, $\tilde{S}_t$ is sales in socialized trade. They can be treated as instrumental variables. It was also suggested that the solution to the problem of finding

D_{t-n-1}/S_{t-n-1} is to use the minimum ratio of $\tilde{D}_t$ to $\tilde{S}_t$. The above considerations give rise to:

$$DE_t = \tilde{\alpha}_E I_t$$

where

$$I_t = \tilde{S}_t\left(\frac{\tilde{D}_t}{\tilde{S}_t} - \min\left\{\frac{\tilde{D}_1}{\tilde{S}_1},...,\frac{\tilde{D}_T}{\tilde{S}_T}\right\}\right)$$

is a disequilibrium indicator. This disequilibrium indicator is then used to determine the forced savings. In his study, Welfe made a distinction between forced and voluntary savings, assumed the neutralization and activation of forced savings, and modified classical budget constraint for consumers. By doing so, he finds that consumers add partly the unspent money (forces savings) to current income to spend in the next period, and hence increase demand even more. Without adopting the novel disequilibrium indicator approach, Welfe's findings would have been impossible.

Testable excess demand models

Parallel with disequilibrium indicator models have been testable excess demand models which stemmed mainly from Maddala and Nelson (1974) and Goldfeld and Quandt (1975). As the name suggests, such a model consists of demand and supply equations together with minimum condition, without any additional information about excess demand. For estimation, a non-linear maximum likelihood method is usually adopted, in which the unobserved parts of demand and supply (whichever is greater) are integrated out.

The first application of testable excess demand model to the analysis of consumption markets in CPEs was made by Portes and Winter (1980). The consumption demand equation corresponds to the Houthakker-Taylor savings function, with current household savings, first difference in disposable income and lagged disposable income as explanatory variables. The hypothesis for consumption supply is that the planners will vary consumption goods supply around its trend value (viewed as long-run growth path) as a function of the deviation from trend of net material output (or agricultural output), real household liquid assets, and exogenous (investment plus defence) expenditure. To complete the model, a minimum condition is then introduced. Applying the Maddala-Nelson maximum likelihood method to the model yields quite surprising results for Poland, GDR, Czechoslovakia and Hungary: excess supply was the dominant regime in three out of four countries in 1954-1975. Their findings posed a great challenge to a fundamental proposition in the conventional wisdom about CPEs: the centrally planned economies are said to suffer from sustained, significant repressed inflation, use of the consumer sector as a buffer to absorb unforseen shocks, excessive household savings, rising subsidies required to maintain fixed prices, etc..

In the subsequent years, while the original Portes-Winter model was repeatedly used in Czechoslovakia, Portes and his associates have made substantial progress in its development. In 1987, Portes, Quandt, Winter and Yeo (1987) refined their econometric models and analyzed a variety of issues in CPEs. Their model differs from Portes-Winter one (1980) in the following main aspects: (a) a plan-adjustment equation determines the published plan for aggregate consumption goods; (b) those second-order quadratic trends used as proxies for plan variables in Portes-Winter model are replaced here by published plan series; (c) several variants of the models with different hypotheses regarding plan formation were discussed, estimated and tested; (d) instead of using the estimated or conditional (on the observed quantity of consumption goods) probability that consumption demand is in excess of consumption supply to assign each observation to an excess demand or supply regime, they determined the positive sign of average excess demand for a given year, if and only if the simulation number exceeds 50 out of 100 simulations for that year showing excess demand. Their discrete-switching disequilibrium model generates the results which again reject the chronic excess demand hypothesis for CPEs, though the statistical diagnostics for the model are satisfactory.

Consequently, the findings achieved by testable excess demand modellers were disputed, and their estimates of excess demand were questioned and described as unrealistic and 'absurd'. Kornai (1982), for example, raised two potentially serious objections to the work of the Portes school. The first argument is that at an aggregate level, the discrete-switching model is inappropriate because shortage and glut may coexist. Second he argues that after goods have been in short supply for some time, some consumers give up looking for them, and the persons who leave the goods market after futile shopping might be called 'discouraged consumers'. This actually raises the most fundamental and important issue: the aggregation problem. In answering this questioning, Burkett (1988) made an effort to estimate actual shortage and slack without assuming away their coexistence. He replaced the disputable minimum condition with the more realistic assumption that the quantity actually transacted on the aggregate consumption market is less than or equal to the minimum of demand and supply, due to the existence of slacks (unsaleable supplies) simultaneously with positive excess demand. This assumption was embodied in a simple hyperbolic relation for aggregate demand Q^d, aggregate supply Q^s and quantity Q^a agreed between buyers and sellers:

$$\frac{Q^d-Q^a}{Q^d}\frac{Q^s-Q^a}{Q^s}=\gamma'Z \qquad (2.31)$$

where γ' is a vector of coefficients and Z is a vector of predetermined variables that shift the hyperbola. The agreed quantity is equal to the observed quantity Q plus error term . Solving (2.31) with respect to Q^a and then Q yields:

$$Q=\frac{1}{2}(Q^d+Q^s)-\frac{1}{2}[(Q^d-Q^s)^2+4\gamma(Q^d)^2]^{1/2}+\mu \qquad (2.32)$$

Burkett then applied this technique to the consumer markets of five Eastern European countries, and found that the discrete-switching hypothesis cannot be rejected. He claimed that the advantage of using the hyperbolic relation rather than the minimum condition is that it simplifies estimation, especially when disturbances are serially correlated, and yields estimates of gross shortage and slack as well as net excess demand. The estimates indicates that the shortage ranged from 0.3% to 7.6% of consumer demand while slack ranged from 0.5% to 60.9% of supply. Potential consumer demand, purged of the discouraged consumer effect, commonly exceeded actual demand but seldom surpassed supply. Burkett concluded that the application of the techniques suggested by Kornai's theory of shortage can yield conclusions consistent with Portes' evidence of prevalent net excess supply. Charemza (1989) regards the Burkett's study as substantially closing the gap between Kornai's economics of shortage and recent disequilibrium econometrics.

Virtual price approach

The third group includes theoretical or econometric investigations of disequilibrium phenomena that do not clearly fall into chronic and testable excess demand modelling categories usually regarded as mainstream research on disequilibrium issues. This group may be classified as a virtual price approach. While the mainstream research continued to expand the frontiers of disequilibrium analysis in period 1976-1986, the virtual price approach developed in its own direction.

The concept of virtual prices is introduced and analyzed extensively in Neary and Roberts (1980). Their analysis started with assuming that the household faces rationing in some markets but is free to purchase goods in other markets. Based on this assumption the collection of goods may be partitioned into two subsets: $\tilde{x}$ being the vector of goods freely chosen but demanded in the face of constraint $\bar{y}$, and $\bar{y}$ being the vector of goods imposed. The household then has the consumption bundle $(\tilde{x},\bar{y})$. Next, they showed that $(\tilde{x},\bar{y})$ would be demanded by the household at some prices $(p,\bar{q})$ and income when faced no rationing constraints. Since the support prices for unrationed goods coincide with actual prices, the term virtual prices may be retained exclusively for the vector $\bar{q}$. With the introduced virtual prices $\bar{q}$, the constrained expenditure function $\tilde{E}$ is related to the unconstrained expenditure function E which can now be evaluated at the virtual prices:

$$\begin{aligned}\tilde{E}(p,q,u;\bar{y}) &= p\tilde{x}(p,q,u;\bar{y}) + q\bar{y} \\ &= px(p,\bar{q},u) + qy(p,\bar{q},u) \\ &= E(p,\bar{q},u) + (q-\bar{q})\bar{y}\end{aligned}$$

(2.33)

where $\tilde{x}(p,q,u;\bar{y})$ and $x(p,\bar{q},u)$ are the constrained and unconstrained Hicksian demand for goods x respectively, the former being evaluated at actual prices q and the latter at virtual prices $\bar{q}$; $y(p,\bar{q},u)$ is the unconstrained Hicksian demand for goods y which is evaluated at virtual prices $\bar{q}$; u is the given utility level. Given equation (2.33), it immediately follows that the virtual prices are the implicit function of $\bar{y}$, p and u:

$$\bar{y} = y(p,\bar{q},u)$$

(2.34)

Equation (2.34) gives the definition of virtual prices: they are those prices which would induce an unconstrained household to purchase the ration level $\bar{y}$. By comparing the marginal utility of $\bar{y}$ with the first-order conditions for a utility maximum obtained from an analysis using the primal approach, the relation between virtual prices and actual prices is as follows:

$$\bar{q} = q + \frac{\phi}{\lambda}$$

(2.35)

where ϕ is the vector of shadow prices of the $\bar{y}$ constraints, and λ is the marginal utility of income in the constrained situation. Equation (2.35) shows that $\bar{q}_j$ exceeds q_j when the household is (locally) constrained to consume less of commodity y_j than it wishes, and vice versa.

One of the important implications of the virtual price approach is that it enable a household' behaviour under rationing to be fully predicted from a knowledge of its unconstrained demand functions. Considering the case of a single rationed good, the unconstrained demand functions are:

$$p_i x_i = p_i \gamma_i + \beta_i (\tilde{E} - \Sigma p_j \gamma_j - q\gamma_0), \quad i=1,\cdots,n-1$$

$$qy = q\gamma_0 + \beta_0 (\tilde{E} - \Sigma p_j \gamma_j - q\gamma_0)$$

When commodity y is subject to a ration, the constrained demand function for the unrationed commodity x is

$$p_i \tilde{x}_i = p_i \gamma_i + \beta_i [\tilde{E} + (\bar{q}-q)\bar{y} - \Sigma p_j \gamma_j - \bar{q}\gamma_0], \quad i=1,\cdots,n-1$$

(2.36)

and the corresponding equation for goods y is

$$\overline{qy}=\overline{q}\gamma_0+\beta_0[\tilde{E}+(\overline{q}-q)\overline{y}-\Sigma p_j\gamma_j-\overline{q}\gamma_0] \tag{2.37}$$

Solving (2.37) for $\overline{q}$ yields:

$$\overline{q}=\frac{\beta_0}{(1-\beta_0)(\overline{y}-\gamma_0)}(\tilde{E}-\Sigma p_j\gamma_j-\overline{qy}) \tag{2.38}$$

Substituting (2.38) into (2.36) yields the rationed demand function for x, which depend linearly on the observable exogenous variable only:

$$p_i\tilde{x}_i=p_i\gamma_i+\frac{\beta_i}{1-\beta_0}(\tilde{E}-\Sigma p_j\gamma_j-\overline{qy}), \quad i=1,\cdots,n-1 \tag{2.39}$$

The notation and theory of virtual prices have been applied by some other economists in their studies. Wijnbergen (1985) uses virtual prices to analyze theoretically the intertemporal consequences of commodity market rationing. Some empirical applications of the virtual price approach can be found in Feltenstein and Farhadian (1987), Feltenstein et al (1990), and Feltenstein and Ha (1990). To avoid repetition, we will give a brief review of these empirical studies adopting the virtual price approach in the next section.

2.4 Some studies of the Chinese economy

In the Western disequilibrium literature, there are pitifully few studies about the Chinese economy, in comparison to the studies about the CPEs of the ex-Soviet Union and Eastern Europe. This may be due to the data problems. In 1986-1987 when macroeconomic data for China became available for a sufficiently long period to permit serious analysis, pioneering work of disequilibrium type was already appearing, taking into account some of the special characteristics of the Chinese economy. The study we are firstly interested in is the one by Feltenstein and Farhadian.

Actually Chow (1985) is the first study using the quantitative techniques of the Chinese data, but he estimates a permanent income hypothesis without allowing for the potential disequilibrium, as if the Chinese economy was a market-oriented one. Feltenstein, Lebow and Wijnbergen (1990, p. 235) rightly recognized that 'This is clearly inappropriate in the presence of substantial repressed inflation, as observed quantities will not be on the consumption demand curve'. Consequently they have sought to specify the relation between virtual and official prices, and then used the (unobservable) virtual prices to estimate a demand schedule as if the market was in equilibrium. The construction of the virtual price index is here backed by a theoretical derivation from an intertemporal model with goods rationing. It has the form of:

$$\log \overline{P} = \log P + \alpha \log \frac{M}{PR} \qquad (2.40)$$

where $\overline{P}$ and P are virtual and official price indices respectively, M is money stock, R is real retail sales, and α is a parameter to be estimated. Then they tested various savings functions using the virtual price index to deflate nominal savings and to include a real interest rate. For the case of no real interest rates included, savings functions are:

$$\frac{S}{\overline{P}} = b_0 + b_1 I^p + b_2 I^t \quad \Rightarrow \quad \frac{S}{P} = \left(\frac{M}{PR}\right)^\alpha (b_0 + b_1 I^p + b_2 I^t);$$

$$\frac{S}{\overline{P}} = b_0 + \left(\frac{S}{\overline{P}}\right)_{-1} + b_2(I - I_{-1}) \quad \Rightarrow \quad \frac{S}{P} = \left(\frac{M}{PR}\right)^\alpha \left[b_0 + b_1\left(\frac{S}{P}\right)_{-1} + b_2(I - I_{-1})\right];$$

$$\frac{S}{\overline{P}} = b_0 + b_1 I + b_2 I_{-1} + b_3 I_{-2} \quad \Rightarrow \quad \frac{S}{P} = \left(\frac{M}{PR}\right)^\alpha (b_0 + b_1 I + b_2 I_{-1} + b_3 I_{-2});$$

$$\frac{S}{\overline{P}} = b_0 + b_1 I \quad \Rightarrow \quad \frac{S}{P} = \left(\frac{M}{PR}\right)^\alpha (b_0 + b_1 I).$$

where S is per capita nominal savings and I is per capita real disposable income divided into permanent and transitory components I^p and I^t. These alternative savings functions are estimated on yearly data over the period 1955-1983 with and without constraint $\alpha=0$ (i.e., the official price index instead of virtual price index is used to deflate nominal savings). The empirical results show that the hypothesis $\alpha=0$ is decisively rejected in all specifications, in favour of the virtual price hypothesis. Later, they allow savings to depend on real interest rates in addition to wealth, the real interest rates $\overline{\rho}$ being given by

$$1 + \overline{\rho} = (1+i)\frac{\overline{P}}{P_{+1}}$$

$$\log(1+\overline{\rho}) = \log(1+\rho) + \alpha \log\left(\frac{M}{PR}\right)$$

where i is official nominal interest rates. Again the results suggest that the virtual price model far outperforms the official price level, and they find a negative and significant real interest rate effect on households' consumption behaviour in China. They concluded that there was no regime shift in household saving behaviour, as long as potential disequilibrium is taken into account. The implication of their model is that the higher savings in the post-reform period reflect the monetary overhang, and hence represent forced savings.

In 1987, Feltenstein and Farhadian (1987) studied the supply of and demand for money in China. They specify money supply and money demand equations and estimate them separately. In the specification of money demand equation, they use a similar virtual price technique, but give a slightly different version:

$$\log \overline{P} = \alpha \log P \qquad (2.41)$$
$$\overline{\pi} = \log \overline{P} - \log \overline{P}_{-1} = \alpha (\log P - \log P_{-1}) = \alpha \pi$$

The virtual price index stands in a constant log-linear relation to the official price index, that is, so the inflation rate of the former $\overline{\pi}$ is a constant multiple of the official inflation rate π. The money demand is then assumed to be explained by real income and the anticipated virtual inflation rate. The money demand equation so specified eventually becomes quite complicated and overidentified. The constant multiple α is, therefore, estimated by searching over a grid of values for the one which maximizes the log-likelihood function. The result, on the data from 1955-1981, was that $\alpha=2.5$, the virtual rate of inflation being 2.5 times higher than the official rate of inflation. The money supply equation is explained by the government deficit, the wage bill of state sector, and procurement payments to farmers, indicating that it reflects the government's monetary target and hence the target rate of inflation.

The above studies adopting a virtual price approach take the potential disequilibrium into account while maintaining the simplicity and clarity of equilibrium analysis. However, Portes and Santorum (1987) make two critical points on these studies. First, they query the exogeneity of money supply in China treated by Feltenstein-Farhadian model, and the separability between demand for and supply of money. Second, they point out that the specification of the relationship between virtual and official prices never permits that open inflation might eliminate excess demand; on the contrary, open inflation is in effect automatically magnified to show even more simultaneous repressed inflation. On doubting the endogeneity of money stock in China, Portes and Santorum first looked for causality relationships among such key variables as the money stock (both M_0 and M_2), disposable income and prices; second they estimated a well-specified equation for the money stock and tested the restrictions of price homogeneity, income homogeneity, and nominal and real adjustment. In the first step, they find bidirectional causality among M_2 and real income; but the bidirectional causality among M_0 and real income seems weaker, and there is a certain degree of independence of M_0 with respect to real income. In the second step, they get the results that the hypotheses of income homogeneity and price homogeneity with respect to M_0 cannot be rejected; M_0 behaves in a manner more suitable to building simple conventional models than does M_2.

When moving to the problems of consumption goods market in China, Portes and Santorum assess the extent of aggregate demand (supply) in a testable excess demand model. Following Burkett (1988), they allowed at macro level for the possible coexistence of micro markets in different states of excess demand or supply (shortages or slacks). For the purpose of comparison, this Burkett model and the model with Portes-Winter technique are both estimated for China over the period 1954-1983, with the result that the behaviour of Chinese households and planner was very similar to that shown in the earlier work on Eastern Europe. Also they report various indicators of tension on the consumption goods market in China: the official rate of inflation PI, the Feltenstein-Farhadian virtual price rate of inflation FPI, the Feltenstein-Lebow-Wijnbergen virtual price rate of inflation WPI, Burkett's index of relative shortage BSH, and the Portes-Winter index of percentage excess demand PWXD. The price indices FPI and WPI are much more erratic than the shortage (excess demand) indices BSH and PWXD. In any case, none of these indices suggests that excess demand dominated the entire period, but all suggest significant excess demand under the reform period 1979-1983.

It is also interesting to look at a differing point of view, in the context of savings behaviour in China, which is derived from a different approach. Qian (1988) questions the Feltenstein-Lebow-Wijnbergen study on two main points. First, the results of the Feltenstein-Lebow-Wijnbergen study are sensitive to the monetary aggregate selected: if M1 instead of M2 was used, the DW statistic would have been reduced from 1.86 to 1.27; second, their significant estimation of interest elasticity depends crucially on their assumption about households' expectations: households face rationing in a given year and expect rationing to be eliminated in the next year. It was doubted that this kind of expectation could survive every year for more than thirty years. Qian then makes an alternative hypothesis that with $s=Mv/PQ$ fixed, the increase in M/PQ is balanced by the decrease of v; that is, an increase in the demand for money. This implies that the increased savings in the post-reform period can be equally well explained by a shift in household saving behaviour-especially the MPS-over time, even without allowing for disequilibrium possibility. To illustrate this, alternative savings models, including absolute-income, permanent-income, asset-adjustment, and consumption models, were estimated, depending on the assumptions of shift in different parameters. For estimating urban household savings function the time series data are used for the period through 1985. The estimated shifting year for the absolute-income and permanent-income models is 1979 when economic reform was instituted, while for asset-adjustment model it is 1978. Turning to rural savings behaviour, cross-sectional data are used in the course of estimation. The findings are a higher propensity to save in the rural sectors than in urban sectors in the earlier 1980s. Qian argues, therefore, that his hypothesis is consistent with the theory of voluntary savings: there is no excess disequilibrium in the consumer-goods market during the recent years of the higher savings rate, and the recent high savings rate in China could be maintained in the future.

Recently, Feltenstein and Ha (1991) have used Chinese quarterly data for the period 1979-1988 to estimate a simple analytical model based on the virtual price approach. Their specification of the model is almost the same as the Feltenstein-Farhadian one previously reviewed, with the virtual prices (called 'true prices' in this paper) being formed by (2.40) rather than (2.41). The results strongly support their hypothesis of repressed inflation in China during 1980s. Consequently the controversies remain unsolved, between the two opinions about the source of high savings rate in China in the post-reform period.

2.5 The plan for this study

In the preceding three sections, we have briefly reviewed the aspects of the literature which are most relevant to the present study. Based on this review, we may work out a plan for the investigations which follow.

Before 1979, the Chinese economy shared basic features of CPEs of the ex-Soviet Union and Eastern Europe. Since 1979, the Chinese economy has undergone a series of far-reaching economic reforms. However, the path that this liberalization has taken has as yet not eliminated, but worsened, the disequilibrium. This has not only been recognised by the Chinese economists, but also confirmed by most studies by Western economists as reviewed in section 2.4. Given this, the disequilibrium framework is the most appropriate, and therefore will be employed in what follows. However, our approach will generally incorporate the basic features of the disequilibrium indicator model. We will deliberately assume the existence of chronic excess demand, except for the very few periods which demonstrate strong evidence of excess supply. In proxing the unobservable variables excess demand (supply), we will carefully select indicators, and treat them as being of an endogenous nature. The main reasons for not pursuing the testable excess demand approach are as follows. First, the testable excess demand models always generates surprisingly low (negative) excess demand estimates for all CPEs under investigation, which is hardly realistic and is sharp contradiction to the abundant evidence of chronic excess demand observed in CPEs (see Kemme

1989) as well as in China. In the case of permanent excess demand the parameters of the testable excess demand model are not identified (see Quandt 1989). Second, as Charemza has pointed out: 'it seems that even in the present era of rapidly growing computational possibilities, the only feasible way of introducing consumption disequilibrium to large econometric models would be through disequilibrium indicators' (see Charemza 1989, p. 294). Finally, the testable excess demand and virtual price approaches have been applied to the case of China. For the purpose of comparison, it is useful to try the disequilibrium indicator method which has not yet been adopted in the studies of the Chinese economy.

A striking fact is that the discussion of disequilibria and shortages in CPEs usually focuses on analysis of the consumption goods market, there being little literature on disequilibrium problems in the investment goods market. To our knowledge, there has been no disequilibrium model of the Chinese investment market and its relationship with consumption market tension. This is probably due in part to the lack of challenge similar to that offered by Richard Portes. As far as the investment sector is concerned, the permanence of excess demand is accepted by the partisans of the shortage school as well as by those of the disequilibrium school. For the case of China, the data problem may be the second reason. An even more important reason why the modelling of disequilibrium in the investment sector is relatively rare is the weakness of the theory of investment. Grosfeld (1989) has made preliminary attempts to address this problem, but her models seem applicable only in the context of traditional CPEs, not for China which has gradually moved from being centrally planned to being more market-oriented. Thus one of the main purposes and contributions of the present study is to derive a novel theoretical framework of investment demand capturing the new mechanisms resulted from the reforms. Based on this, a disequilibrium econometric model of investment market in the Chinese economy is constructed and estimated. We will thus analyze how the disequilibria in investment and consumption markets interact with each other.

As for the consumption and savings behaviour, our attention is paid mainly to the unsolved controversies mentioned in section 2.3 of this chapter. We believe that both the Qian's study and Feltenstein et al's study have taken extreme positions, and we try to make compromise between the two. To fulfil this intention, a novel approach proposed by A. Welfe (1989) is to be applied to the case of China. Specifically, the features in his consumption and saving models, i.e., a distinction between the forced and voluntary savings, the neutralization and activation of forced savings, and the modification of the classical budget constraint, will be incorporated in our models. In the optimization on the micro level, the effective demand functions in the Ito sense are considered. First, if the Dreze demand concept is applied there can be no discrepancy between effective demand and actual trades, which is counterintuitive. Second, Clower functions are in fact special cases of the Ito ones, with certain nonlinear restrictions. Thirdly, unlike Eastern European countries, China has been suffering the problems of excess labour supply due to the huge population; and households are restricted on labour supply, or there is certain degree of on-job-unemployment, even given the full employment policy pursued in China. Therefore in terms of disequilibrium regimes, the Chinese economy is perhaps best classified as 'classical unemployment'.

With the system consisting of models of the two major sectors in the economy, we are able to conduct some simulations to see the responses of the economy to economic policy shocks. Recently, the Chinese government has announced its objective mode for economic reform: 'the socialist market economy'. This implies that it will thoroughly abandon the direct plan-adjustment mechanism, and replace it with an indirect macro-regulation system. The fulfilment of this objective involves a systematic policy package of reform. Thus the aim is to construct a new model which can investigate the effects of such a package. The new model emerges from the womb of the historical one, but is characterized by the operation of the mechanism. This is done to see: (a) if further market-oriented reforms would considerably improve the behaviour of the economy in the sense that the economy would move from the norm of disequilibrium towards the norm of equilibrium; (b) what kind of policy package should be adopted to achieve the objectives successfully without causing drastic chaos in the economy.

3 Investment demand in the public-ownership economy: A game theory approach

3.1 Introduction

In modelling an economy, one needs first to understand the behaviour of the economy and the underlying relationships which determine and dominate that behaviour. Without well-founded theories to capture the characteristics and essence of the economy, the econometric modelling exercises would be purely *ad hoc*, and the policy conclusions based on the simulation of the constructed model could well be misleading.

The object of our analysis here is the Chinese economy in the 1980s, the first decade of economic reform. While economic reform has broadened the private sector, the public-ownership economy (POE) is still the dominant sector. The POE in China has been undoubtedly invigorated by the reform on the one hand, but also caused many new problems to the whole economy on the other. The POE in the post-reform period differs from the one in the centrally planned economies (CPEs) before reform, in the sense that the mechanism underlying the problems observed in CPEs, such as excess demand, forced savings, repressed inflation, shortage of commodities etc., has changed substantially. Therefore the economic theories concerning the traditional socialist economy have some limits in explaining the new phenomena occurring in the post-reform Chinese economy. Also the post-reform Chinese economy is certainly not a typical market economy. Macroeconomics developed on the basis of market economies in the Western countries can hardly be copied indiscriminately in modelling the Chinese economy, though this does not deny the application of the analytical methods and devices embodied in macroeconomics. Given the above considerations, this chapter attempts to propose a theory-consistent framework for the analysis of the investment demand in a POE which will serve as a theoretical foundation for the empirical studies in later chapters.

Before proceeding further, two issues need to be addressed. First, from the methodological point of view, there are two important approaches in economic research: a positive method and a normative method. Briefly speaking, the former aims at obtaining the knowledge about what the economy *actually is*, while the latter involves a judgement of what the economy *should be*. The theoretical framework presented in this chapter is concerned with the actual performance of the economy, and as such our approach follows the positive method. In other words, we intend to reveal the underlying processes of the Chinese economy in particular institutional arrangements, but do not judge if the system is reasonable. In our policy simulations, however, the normative approach will be unavoidable, because policy recommendations are necessarily based on the judgement of economic performance.

Second, the theoretical models in this chapter are short-run ones. In the short-run analysis of demand-supply relations, demand determination and analysis play a crucial role, since demand is more volatile in the short run while supply is more elastic in the long run. Thus in explaining economic fluctuations, rather than economic growth, it seems more plausible to begin the analysis with demand side, assuming that supply is given. Based on this point it follows that the emphasis of our analysis is on the socio-economic factors rather than on the material/technological factors.[1] This is because demand variables are mainly influenced, among other things, by social and economic relationships. We will see how the relationships of public ownership, the particular economic interests of all the agents and the interest contradictions between these agents determine aggregate demand and its structure in a particular way. Material/technological factors bring common features, while socio-economic factors bestow the endemic features on the determination process of economic variables in an economy.

3.2 Investment demand's determinant 1: contradiction between consumption and accumulation

Fan G. (1989) and Fan G. et al (1990) posed the question of what the particular mechanisms of inflation in the Chinese economy are and tried to answer it by constructing a new analytical framework. The main ideas presented in this section are built upon the basis of their work which is critically elaborated and developed to serve our own purposes here.

Income distribution and structure of aggregate demand

Central to the mainstream of macroeconomics since Keynes has been the notion that aggregate demand is determined by the expenditures of different groups in the economy. This approach to aggregate demand theory, beginning with income-expenditure relations over a life-cycle, presupposes the following special conditions of a capitalist or private sector economy: all the income goes, in primary distribution, to individuals as personal income, and the capital stock is generated by individuals who save (invest) during their working lives to finance their consumption during their retirements. Thus the composition of aggregate demand is determined by the composition of individuals' expenditures.

Nevertheless, in investigating a public-ownership economy,[2] we face different prerequisites: the primary distribution of national income divides it into two proportions, i.e., public income and personal income. In terms of the intrinsic provisions of POE, every individual is only a consumer but not a investor. Putting it another way, individuals can not carry out capital accumulation so as to become owners of new capital increments. Otherwise the dynamic process of capital accumulation will inevitably negate the POE itself. It is the state (central planner), that is, the unique agent of public property, who bears the responsibility of capital accumulation; in the economy as a whole, only the state and its local representatives exercise the functions of investment. As the agent responsible for capital accumulation, the state is legitimate in claiming directly a certain amount of income (profit-tax) from the primary distribution of national income. The income distribution firstly determines the composition of aggregate demand, since the public income mainly goes to investment and personal income mainly goes to consumption. Later it will be shown that the income distribution also determines the magnitude of aggregate demand through 'monetary augmentation of national income'. Therefore, while the theory of aggregate demand for a private-ownership economy can start directly from the *expenditure of income*, the analysis of the aggregate demand for a public-ownership economy must begin with *distribution of income*.

The proportion of income distribution is linked, in a special way, with the ratio between investment and consumption. On the one hand, changes in income distribution affect, through the expenditures of the corresponding parts of income, the ratio between investment and consumption. On the other hand, if individuals want more consumption, they have to strive to increase the share of personal income in the income distribution, and if the state intends accumulate more, it must obtain a bigger share of public income. Consumption and investment are two kinds of utilization of national income in physical form, but the income distribution underlying them reflects the particular social relations.

Let Y denote real national income, T public income, V personal income, and $b=T/V$ represent income distribution. Let Y^d denote aggregate demand, I investment expenditure, C consumption expenditure, and $a=I/C$ represent aggregate demand structure. For simplicity we at present assume that all the public income is collected to finance exclusively the expenditure on investment, and that there are no individual savings. In fact, according to the definitions of V and T, and based on the above analysis of the unique feature of income distribution of POE (i.e., the national income goes, in primary distribution, to both individuals as personal income and the state as public income), the income distribution proportion 'b' is always the first basic determinant of the aggregate demand structure 'a', whether or not there exist individuals' savings. Abstracting from individuals' savings enables us to concentrate on the fundamental relation between income distribution and demand structure. Now we have

$T=I;\ V=C;\ a=b.$

This relation is illustrated in Figure 3.1 where the aggregate income line overlaps the aggregate demand line and the income distribution line $0b$ goes on the top of the demand structure line $0a$. Figure 3.1 states clearly that the aggregate demand structure is determined by the income distribution. Relaxing some of the assumptions made above does not affect this basic conclusion. Although the basic model in Figure 3.1 is far from reality, it serves as a starting point for further analysis.

Letting $a=b$ does not ensure $Y^d=Y$. As long as the economy is not a barter economy, as long as money is involved in the operation of economy, aggregate demand will not necessarily be equal to real national income. Figure 3.2 shows the impact of excess money supply on aggregate demand. Y now represents real national income, $\underline{T}$ real public income, $\underline{V}$ real personal income and ΔM excess money supply. The excess money supply results in an increase in nominal national income and leads to aggregate demand exceeding real national output.[3] Now the aggregate demand line Y^dY^d no longer overlaps with the real income line $\underline{YY}$. It shifts upward (rightward) by ΔM, despite the income distribution proportion still being equal to the aggregate demand structure. This result is applied to all the economies which are in the full-employment state. However, the reasons behind the excess money supply vary with respect to different economies. In the following section we will see the particular mechanism of the 'monetary augmentation' of national income in the Chinese economy: it is the conflicts of interest inherent in the distribution of income that amplify the effects on aggregate demand.

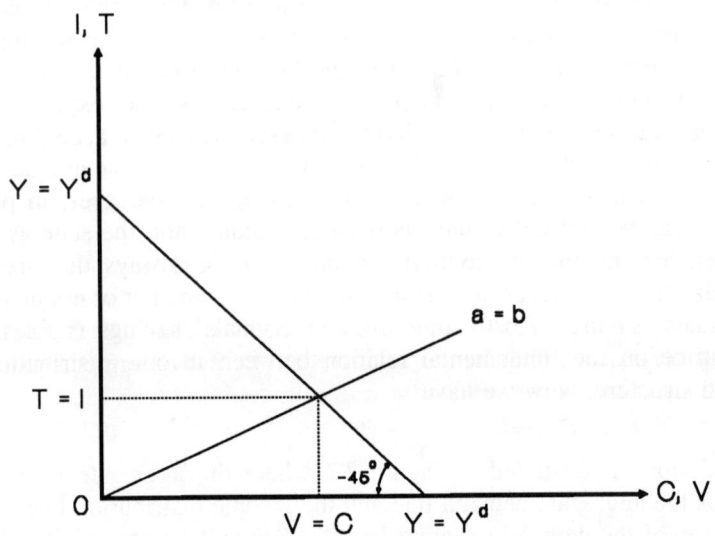

Figure 3.1 Income distribution and aggregate demand structure

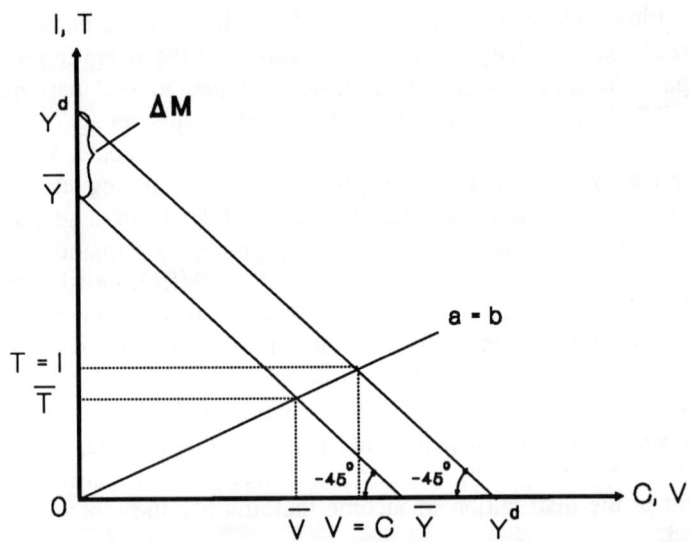

Figure 3.2 Effect of excess money supply on aggregate demand

Contradiction in income distribution and magnitude of aggregate demand

How is the phenomenon of excess money supply generated? What is the specific form of monetary augmentation of national income and its underlying behavioural setting? Fan G. et al (1990) have put forward a novel account by introducing a new concept of 'income illusion' (to be explained below). In the process of explication, they employ a linear functional form for production and a logarithmic utility form, and verified that optimum capital accumulation is positively related to the marginal productivity of capital. Since the 'income illusion' lowers the individuals' perceptions of the marginal productivity of capital, the disagreement between the individuals' and planner's optimum accumulation ratios arises. Under the multi-sovereignty mechanism (to be explained below), this disagreement will unavoidably cause aggregate demand to be in excess of aggregate supply.

This theory is inspiring overall, but lacks completeness. First, it does not consider the difference between individuals' discount rates and the planner's discount rate, and thus neglects another important reason for the disagreement. Second, the positive relation between the optimum capital level and the marginal productivity of capital depends on the specific functional forms chosen for production and utility. If we choose alternative functional forms, the marginal product of capital can disappear from the solution for the optimal capital level, or that relationship can become negative. So their conclusions lack generality. To overcome these two shortcomings, we will start our analysis by following the basic models introduced and developed in Blanchard and Fischer (1989).

(i) The individuals' optimum In analysing the individual optimum problems, we adopt the Ramsey infinite horizon optimizing model. Suppose that the population of all individuals in a society, N_t, grows at n. The labour force is equal to the population, with labour supplied inelastically. Output is produced using capital K_t, and labour N_t. There is no productivity growth. The output is either consumed or invested, that is, added to the capital stock. Formally,

$$Y=F(K_t,N_t)=C_t+\frac{dK_t}{dt} \qquad (3.1)$$

where Y_t is net output, and C_t is consumption. The production function $F(\cdot)$ is assumed to be homogeneous of degree one. In per capita terms

$$f(k_t)=c_t+\frac{dk_t}{dt}+nk_t \qquad (3.2)$$

where lowercase letters denote per capita values of variables. We assume $f(\cdot)$

to be strictly concave and to satisfy the following conditions, known as Inada conditions:

$$f(0)=0; \quad f'(0)=\infty; \quad f'(\infty)=0$$

We also assume that the economy starts with some capital so that it can get production off the ground:

$$k_0 > 0$$

The individuals' instantaneous utility $u(c_t)$ is non-negative and a concave increasing function of per capita consumption. Taking the case of continuous time, the individuals' welfare at time s, U_s, is the discounted integral:

$$U_s = \int_s^\infty u(c_t) e^{[-\theta(t-s)]} dt \qquad (3.3)$$

But for simplicity and without loss of generality, we only think of time as being discrete and consider the choice of individuals in allocating consumption between time t and $t+1$. So the representative individual has to find a solution to the following problem:

$$\max \quad U = u(c_t) + (1+\theta)^{-1} u(c_{t+1}) \qquad (3.4)$$

subject to

$$\begin{cases} f(k_{t-1}) = c_t + k_t - k_{t-1} + nk_t \\ f(k_t) = c_{t+1} + k_{t+1} - k_t + nk_{t+1} \end{cases}$$

The parameter θ is the rate of time preference, or the subjective discount rate, which is assumed to be strictly positive. After some mathematical manipulations, we can easily obtain the first-order condition for the individuals' maximum:

$$u'(c_t) - (1+\theta)^{-1}(1+n)^{-1}[1+f'(k_t)]u'(c_{t+1}) = 0 \qquad (3.5)$$

This condition is also known as Keynes-Ramsey rule. It implies that consumption increases, remains constant, or decreases depending on whether the marginal product of capital (net of population growth) exceeds, or equal to, or is less than the rate of time preference. This rule is quite fundamental and intuitive: the higher the marginal product of capital relative to the rate of time preference, the more it pays to depress the current level of consumption in order to enjoy higher consumption later.

Particularly when the optimum capital stock reaches such a point that the marginal product (net of population growth) is equal to the rate of time preference, the steady state occurs: both the per capita capital stock, k, and the level of consumption per capita, c, are constant over time. We denote the steady state values of these two variables as k^* and c^*. At this point there is a relationship known as the modified golden rule:

$$1+f'(k^*)=(1+\theta)(1+n) \qquad (3.6)$$

This relationship implies that the optimum capital level preferred by individuals in the steady state is determined by their tastes (subjective discount rate) and population growth.

So far we have considered individuals who live in a pure economy. In other words, the relationship (3.6) only reflects material/technological factors without special attention paid to institutional characteristics. There is no doubt that the modified golden rule is still effective in principle for POEs. However, when coming to the behaviour of a POE, one also needs to take into account the role played by the particular institutional arrangements.

What then characterizes the relationship (3.6) in the POE? Fan G. et al (1989) argue that the income illusion of individuals due to the POE would generate different 'parameters' on which their 'optimal choices' are made, though the choices are actually not optimal in terms of the true relation between capital accumulation and consumption increase.

In the POE, any individual, as an individual, functions only as a worker or labourer rather than as a capital owner. This implies the following two points. First, the individual does not and cannot carry out capital accumulation. Capital accumulation is completely external to him/her. Second, all his/her income takes the unitary form of labour income: wages-the payments for his/her labour, bonuses-the payments for his/her extra labour, pensions-the deferred payments for his/her labour during working ages. Consequently, the increase in individuals' consumption outwardly manifests itself as a result of an increase in productivity of labour, and has nothing to do with capital accumulation and capital productivity. The important role played by capital growth and utilization is concealed by the form which personal income takes, and disappears from the sight of individuals as labourers. Thus the capital return actually included in personal income *is perceived by individuals as* labour income as well. This phenomenon is termed by Fan G. et al as 'income illusion of the individuals in POE', or 'income illusion' for short.

Let ω be the 'income illusion coefficient', which reflect the degree to which individuals take capital productivity to be labour productivity. If $\omega=0$, that means that individuals have no income illusion at all. But according to our discussion, this is impossible due to the nature of a POE. The fact that all personal income takes the form of labour income will inevitably result in income illusion. On the other hand, there also cannot be a complete income illusion ($\omega=1$) in general terms. It is after all the fact as well that allowing for more accumulation at time t would increase consumption at time $t+1$, and this fact is more or less realized by individuals. Therefore we have $0<\omega<1$. Assume that both capital and labour increase by one unit. Applying the income illusion theory to the total differential of output per capita gives:

$$dy = f'(k)dk + f'(N)dN = f'(k) + f'(N)$$
$$= (1-\omega)f'(k) + [\omega f'(k) + f'(N)] = f'(k)_v + f'(N)_v \quad (3.7)$$

$$f'(k)_v = (1-\omega)f'(k) < f'(k) \quad (3.7a)$$

$$f'(N)_v = \omega f'(k) + f'(N) > f'(N) \quad (3.7b)$$

where $f'(k)_v$ is the '*illusive* marginal product of capital', and $f'(N)_v$ is the '*illusive* marginal product of labour'. Equations (3.7a) and (3.7b) state that, due to the income illusion, individuals attribute to labour a portion of the contribution being made by capital. Thus in the individuals' eyes, the capital productivity reduces to $(1-\omega)f'(k)$, while the labour productivity rises to $\omega f'(k)+f'(N)$. These consequences of income illusion can be more clearly signified in the special case where the production function is homogeneous of degree one. In this case, the per capita output is only dependent on the capital-labour ratio, and the derivative f'(N) in the total differential of the output should be equal to zero, so that:

$$f'(N)_v = \omega f'(k)$$

Despite no contribution being made by labour to an increase in per capita output, individuals still take a certain part of capital return as labour income. This illusive labour income is completely caused by the income illusion.

Replacing $f'(k^*)$ in (3.6) with $f'(k^*)_v$ in (3.7a) leads to:

$$1 + f'(k^*)_v = 1 + (1-\omega)f'(k_v^*) = (1+\theta)(1+n) \quad (3.8)$$

The *illusive* steady state level of capital k_v^* chosen by individuals is therefore determined by (3.8) which we term as the *illusive modified golden rule*. What does it imply? First, the material/technological relationship embodied in the modified golden rule (3.6) is still effective in a POE. Second, however, the material/technological relationship in the POE is distorted by the social/economic relationships of the POE, since ω is an institutional variable that reflects the social/economic relationships of the POE.

(ii) The planner's optimum Unlike individuals, a central planner,[4] as the agent of public ownership and the executive body for capital accumulation, fully and clearly realises the roles of capital accumulation in income growth; There are no such factors in the institutional arrangement that would distort or conceal the roles of capital accumulation from the central planner. A straightforward conclusion is that the central planner has no income illusion.

Again unlike an individual who cares, at least in his/her private decisions, only about himself/herself and not about future generations, the central planner, in principle, cares about all the generations. This is because, in principle, the central planner, as the agent of public ownership, knows clearly that public ownership implies that the material productive assets belong not only to the whole people, but also to all generations. Therefore in studying the central planner's optimal problems, the overlapping generation model with finite horizons turns out to be more appropriate. Given the above considerations, the central planner is assumed to care about the utility of T+1 current and future generations, and to discount the utility of future generations at rate Γ. This implies that a social welfare function, as the central planner's objective function, should be of the form:

$$U = (1+\theta)^{-1} u(c_{2,0}) + \sum_{t=0}^{t=T} (1+\Gamma)^{-t-1} [u(c_{1,t}) + (1+\theta)^{-1} u(c_{2,t+1})] \quad (3.9)$$

where $c_{1,t}$ denotes the consumption of a generation when *young* in period t, $c_{2,t+1}$ is the consumption of that generation when getting *old* in period $t+1$.[5] Other variables and parameters are defined as before.

The resource constraint faced by the central planner is considered as follows: the total supply of goods is allocated to the consumption of young and old living in the same period, and to investment to increase the capital stock for the next period, namely

$$k_t + f(k_t) = (1+n) k_{t+1} + c_{1,t} + (1+n)^{-1} c_{2,t} \quad (3.10)$$

Maximizing (3.9) subject to (3.10) gives the first-order conditions for the centrally planned optimum:

$$(1+\theta)^{-1} u'(c_{2,t}) - (1+\Gamma)^{-1}(1+n)^{-1} u'(c_{1,t}) = 0 \quad (3.11)$$

$$u'(c_{1,t-1}) - (1+\Gamma)^{-1}(1+n)^{-1}[1+f'(k_t)] u'(c_{1,t}) = 0 \quad (3.12)$$

Equation (3.11) is a condition for optimal allocation between the young and the old who are alive at the same time. Equation (3.12) is a condition for optimal inter-temporal allocation, and is similar to the Keynes-Ramsey rule (3.5) in the individuals' optimum discussed above.

What is the implication of the planner's optimum conditions? We focus on the steady state associated with (3.12). Let c_1^* and k^* denote the steady state values of c_1 and k. They satisfy

$$1 + f'(k^*) = (1+\Gamma)(1+n) \quad (3.13)$$

The steady state level of capital therefore satisfies the modified golden role at which the per capita consumption of all generations is maximized. Note the similarity of (3.13) to (3.6). In the present case, however, the level of steady state capital does not depend on θ, the individual discount rate, but on Γ, the planner's discount rate. We will hereafter term the relationship (3.13) as the *planned modified golden rule*. It has been stated before that Γ is the rate at which the central planner discounts the utility of future generations. In other words, Γ actually indicates how much the central planner cares about future generations. If he cares less about future generations, Γ is positive. If he cares equally about all generations, Γ is equal to zero. If he cares more about future generations, Γ is negative.[6] Clearly there is no reason for Γ and θ to be identical.

(iii) The interest conflicts between individuals and the planner To facilitate further discussion, we rewrite the illusive modified golden rule and the planned modified golden rule as (3.14) and (3.15) respectively below:

$$f'(k_v^*) = \frac{(1+\theta)(1+n)-1}{(1-\omega)} \tag{3.14}$$

$$f'(k^*) = (1+\Gamma)(1+n)-1 \tag{3.15}$$

The disagreement between these two rules is obvious, and is determined by two factors. The first one is the difference between θ, the individual discount rate, and Γ, the planner discount rate. The second one is the difference between ω and zero.

What are the economic implications of these two factors? How do they affect the decisions of individuals and the central planner on the resource allocation between consumption and accumulation? In answering these questions, we first analyze the two factors one by one, and then synthesize the results.

Let us consider the first factor by assuming the absence of the second one (i.e., ω-0=0 or ω=0). Thus (3.14) becomes

$$f'(k_v^*) = (1+\theta)(1+n)-1 \tag{3.16}$$

Comparing (3.15) and (3.16), one issue arises: since both Γ and θ are arbitrary parameters — that is, the planner discount rate is unrelated to the preferences as captured by the individuals' utility function — it is hardly surprising that k^* is generally not equal to the steady state level of capital k_v^* chosen by individuals. Theoretically, there are three noteworthy cases below.[7]

(1) $0<\theta<\Gamma$ so that $k^*<k_v^*$.[8] In this case, the central planner cares so little about future generations that he under-accumulates capital to over-satisfy the current generation of individuals. However, this is hardly possible in a POE. First this is against the nature of the central planner who functions as the

capital owner. Second, 'oversatisfaction' does not have much difference from 'unsatisfaction' (i.e., individuals are not in their optimal steady state by consuming c^*). Now that allowing individuals to consume more still cannot please them, why should the planner do this thankless job?

(2) $0 \leq \Gamma \leq \theta$ so that $k^* \geq k_v^*$. $[0,\theta]$ is the most likely value domain of Γ for the planner. Usually a Pareto-optimum-seeking planner should care equally about all generations, because if $\Gamma=0$ then $f'(k)=n$ which is known as the *golden rule* (Blanchard and Fischer (1989)). The golden rule is the condition on the capital stock that maximizes steady state consumption per capita.[9] But the 'impatient' individuals choose the capital stock reduced below the golden rule level by an amount that depends on their rate of time preference. They do not think that it is optimal to reduce current consumption in order to reach the higher golden rule consumption level. They might ask the planner to increase Γ till $\Gamma=\theta$ (i.e., reduce k^* till $k^*=k_v^*$) to meet their consumption desires. Whether the planner would agree to put lower weights on the future generations than on the current generation is another issue. One thing for sure is that before Γ reaches θ the planned capital stock k^* always exceeds the individuals' capital stock k_v^*.

(3) $-1<\Gamma \leq 0<\theta$ so that $k^* >> k_v^*$. The range $(-1,0]$ is the most likely domain of Γ for the central government. We have defined the central government as the sum of the central planner (economic body) and the political body. This implies that the central government's objective function involves the planner's objective function as well as political considerations. For simplicity, we assume that the political considerations are embodied in Γ. In other words, the central government is capable of interfering in the resource allocation by changing Γ to achieve its own objectives. The repeatedly observed phenomenon is that the government of POE pursues a high economic growth rate as its one of the most important targets.[10] This might be due to various considerations such as international, national, political, historical, social, military reasons etc.. This enthusiasm for high accumulation frequently makes Γ depart downward from the value 0 required by the golden rule. On the surface $\Gamma<0$ implies more care being given by the government to future generations, and the government does often make active propaganda, such as 'today's construction, tomorrow's better life', when it begins an ambitious investment plan. In fact, the government tries to sacrifice the individuals' interest for its own purposes. As Blanchard and Fischer (1989) have proved, the steady state of capital in excess of the golden rule are not Pareto optima: everyone can be made better off by reducing the capital stock. Such economies are often referred to as *dynamically inefficient*: they have overaccumulated capital. On the other hand, Γ can not go beyond -1, because when Γ approaches -1 (from 0), $f'(k^*)$ approaches 0 and k^*

approaches infinity.

Now we turn to the second factor by assuming the nonexistence of the first one (i.e., Γ-θ=0 or Γ=θ). Substituting θ in (3.14) by Γ and combining (3.14) with (3.15), we have the following relationship:

$$f'(k_v^*) = \frac{(1+\Gamma)(1+\theta)-1}{1-\omega} = \frac{f'(k^*)}{1-\omega} \qquad (3.17)$$

Here in fact we take an upper limit for Γ: the central planner completely respects the individuals' rates of time preference. Unfortunately, even if the central planner could not be more kind, the individuals' desired (but illusive) capital stock k_v^* is still below the planned capital stock k^*. The implications of relationship (3.17) is more straightforward and more evident than that embodied in both (3.15) and (3.16): due to the income illusion caused by the POE itself, that is, due to 1<ω<0, the following inequalities always hold:

$$\infty > f'(k_v^*) > f'(k^*) \; ; \; 0 < k_v^* < k^* \qquad (3.18)$$

Note that f'(k_v^*) is positively related to ω, the income illusion coefficient. The more illusions the individuals have about labour productivity (i.e., the bigger the ω is), the more a higher productivity of capital is illusively required to compensate and match the true one, and thus the less capital stock is desired by individuals. We have stated, however, that there cannot exist complete income illusion. In mathematical terms, when ω tends to 1, f'(k_v^*) tends to infinity, so that k_v^* tends to 0. This cannot be true in reality.

The above analysis can be synthesized by returning to (3.14) and (3.15). Let k^* denote the steady state capital stock chosen by the planner (government), k_v^* the steady state capital stock chosen by the individuals without income illusion, and $k_{v\omega}^*$ be the steady state capital stock by the individuals with income illusion. We have:

$$\because \theta \geq \Gamma > -1, \; \therefore (1+\theta)(1+n)-1 \geq (1+\Gamma)(1+n)-1; \; \therefore k^* \geq k_v^* \qquad (3.19)$$

$$\because 0<\omega<1, \; \therefore \frac{(1+\theta)(1+n)-1}{1-\omega} > (1+\theta)(1+n)-1; \; \therefore k_v^* > k_{v\omega}^* \qquad (3.20)$$

$$k^* - k_{v\omega}^* = (k^* - k_v^*) + (k_v^* - k_{v\omega}^*) > 0 \qquad (3.21)$$

Inequalities (3.19), (3.20) and (3.21) clearly indicate that the planner's desired capital stock k^* permanently exceeds the individuals' desired capital stock $k_{v\omega}^*$. This disagreement consists of two elements: $k^* - k_v^* \geq 0$, which is caused by departure of the planner's (government's) preferences from the individuals' preferences, and $k_v^* - k_{v\omega}^* > 0$, which is due to the individuals' income illusion. Note that the discrepancy θ-Γ≥0 is highly subjective or arbitrary for it actually reflects the planner's (government's) policy stance. Also for this reason it is possibly eliminated if the planner (government) happens to respect the individuals' preferences. However, the income illusion is institutionally determined. It cannot vanish unless a POE turns into a private ownership economy.

Fan G. et al (1990) only notice the role of income illusion but neglect that of preference differences in creating this contradiction. It seems in their studies that if there did not exist income illusion, the planner (not the government) and individuals would permanently agree with each other upon resource allocation. This is because they fail to distinguish the individuals' and the planner's objective functions, and simply assume a zero discount rate of future utility in the social welfare function, which is then viewed as the objective function for both the planner and individuals. Their assumption is only a special case ($\Gamma=\theta$), and the probability of $\Gamma=\theta$ could be extremely low. Thus one would be left with a sense of discomfort that their analysis based on such an assumption are of limited applicability and reliability. Besides, in the studies of Fan G. et al (1990), the role of income illusion in generating the illusive marginal product of capital, and hence the contradiction, depends on the specific functional forms they chose for utility and production.[11] We have shown here, however, that without any specification of utility and production functions, it can still be explained why an increase in the income illusion coefficient will widen the gap between the planner's and the individuals' desired capital stock. Thus our analysis has proved to be more complete and of more generality.

Let us go back to our main discussion. To be more realistic, we replace the central planner by the central government. Define a_g as the desired accumulation rate of the central government, and a_v as the desired accumulation rate of individuals. Substituting c^* into (3.10) (planner's accumulation equation) and $c_{v\omega}^*$ into (3.2) (individuals' accumulation equation), the terms a_g and a_v in steady state are implicitly given as (see Note 9 of this chapter):

$$a_g = \frac{f(k^*)-c^*}{f(k^*)} = n\frac{k^*(\Gamma)}{f[k^*(\Gamma)]} = a_g(\Gamma) \qquad (3.22)$$

and

$$a_v = \frac{f(k_{v\omega}^*)-c_{v\omega}^*}{f(k_{v\omega}^*)} = n\frac{k_{v\omega}^*(\theta,\omega)}{f[k_{v\omega}^*(\theta,\omega)]} = a_v(\theta,\omega) \qquad (3.23)$$

where $\dfrac{\partial a_g}{\partial \Gamma}<0$; $\dfrac{\partial a_v}{\partial \theta}<0$; $\dfrac{\partial a_v}{\partial \omega}<0$.

The relations in (3.22) and (3.23) are proved in an endnote.[12]

Taking the difference between a_g and a_v, the following inequality holds (see note 12 of this chapter):

$$a_g - a_v = [n\frac{k^*}{f(k^*)} - n\frac{k^*_{v\omega}}{f(k^*_{v\omega})}] = nA(\Gamma,\theta,\omega) \geq 0, \quad if \ \Gamma \leq \theta \land 0 \leq \omega < 1 \quad (3.24)$$

where $\quad \frac{\partial A}{\partial \Gamma} < 0; \ \frac{\partial A}{\partial \theta} > 0; \ \frac{\partial A}{\partial \omega} > 0.$

This suggests that all the analyses and conclusions about the conflicts between the planner's and the individuals' desired capital stock can be easily extended and applied to the conflicts between their desired accumulation rates.

The consequences of interest conflicts under two mechanisms

Following Fan G. et al (1990), we classify two types of mechanism in a POE: a State Sovereignty Mechanism (SSM), under which only the central government is in a position to determine resource allocation and economic variables; and a Multi-sovereignty Mechanism (MSM), under which some other agents (subunits, and individuals, but not necessary all of them at same time) are able to affect directly the determination of economic variables, such as primary income distribution, investment, output level, enterprises' expenditure, etc. Before the economic reform launched in 1979, the Chinese economy was dominated by the SSM. Since 1979, the SSM has been gradually replaced by the MSM.

The unavoidable difference reflected by (3.24) in the POE is, after all, only the difference between two subjective intentions, though it is due to both subjective and objective factors. To turn the subjective intentions into objective reality, one means, namely, decision-making power is indispensable. Under the SSM, income distribution is solely determined by the central government according to its preference, i.e., its desire to accumulate. In this circumstance, individuals have no alternative but to accept the set scheme of distribution. In Figure 3.3, a_g represents the government's accumulation line, and a_v exhibits the individuals' accumulation line. The government's desire to accumulate can be realized, and so a_g is drawn as a solid line. The individuals' desire to consume cannot come true, and so a_v is drawn as a dotted line. The national income is distributed, according to the central government's preference, into two parts: public income T for purchasing investment goods I, and personal income V for purchasing consumption goods C. Despite any dissatisfaction, individuals can do nothing but complain

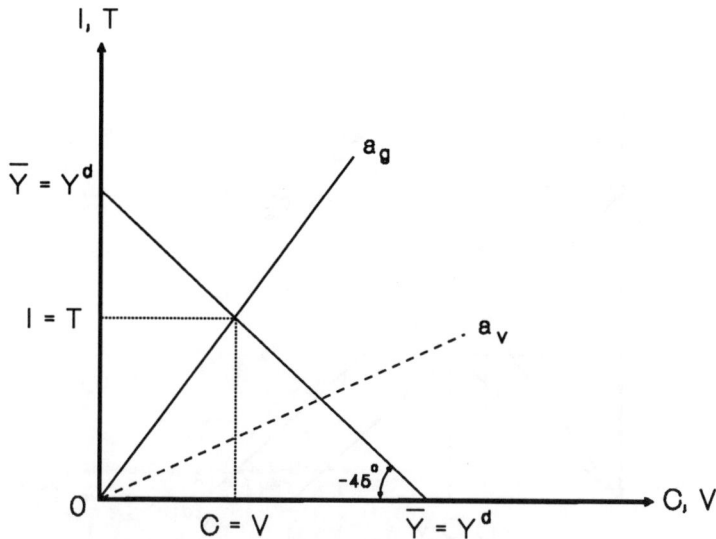

Figure 3.3 **The state sovereignty mechanism**

(sometimes even cannot complain). This situation is not bad at all, for at least there is no shortage or inflation ($Y^d=\bar{Y}$). What changes is only the structure of national income or aggregate demand: more investment, less consumption, and vice versa. However, this rarely happens in reality. We have stated that θ-Γ is highly subjective or arbitrary, and it reflects the government's policy stance which always inclines to high accumulation. Suppose that the government preference Γ suddenly declines for whatever reasons, in spite of the income distribution proportion already set according to the government's initial preference. Figure 3.4 encaptures diagrammatically the consequences of this sudden change of the central government's preference. The variable a_g is accordingly (because $\partial a_g/\partial \Gamma < 0$) increased to a_g' with an additional expenditure of investment (I'-T) to be made. How to finance the expenditure? One way is to reduce personal income V. Nevertheless, as long as the gross wage bill and wage rate are set, they are highly rigid downwards. The alternative way is to increase the money supply in the direction of investment (i.e., exclusively as accumulation funds). By the distribution of *nominal* income the central government can realize the redistribution of *real* income so as to keep the accumulation rate at its desired level. However, while the budget constraint could be soft, the resource constraint must be hard. The extra money supply immediately leads

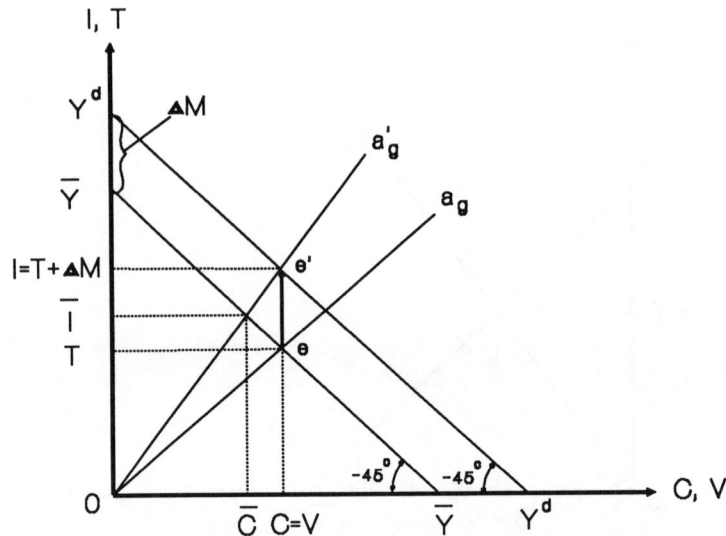

Figure 3.4 An increase of the central government's desire to accumulate

to the augmentation of aggregate demand, but cannot increase aggregate supply so rapidly as to catch up with the demand expansion. Aggregate excess demand $(Y^d-\bar{Y}=(I-\bar{I})+(C-\bar{C}))$ thus appears if the prices are sticky (which is the norm in POE), and both the investment and consumption markets suffer shortages $I-\bar{I}$ and $C-\bar{C}$ respectively because of the resource constraint $(\bar{I}+\bar{C}=\bar{Y})$.

What about the MSM? The MSM brought about by the economic reform ensures to subunits a large degree of autonomy in income distribution, and thus enables individuals to exert their influence on the primary income distribution in enterprises. They can pressure more directly the decision-making bodies to increase their incomes in the forms of: excessive bonus, reckless payments in kind, increased subsidies, expansion of floating wage scales and wage increases, and so on. Thus income distribution is no longer solely determined by the central government, but rather by both the central government and individuals. Figure 3.5 shows a picture of the MSM of this kind. The line b represents the realised accumulation rate or the realised distribution proportion. But why does it lie in between a_v and a_g? How is it determined? Would the MSM be better than the SSM? To answer these questions requires richer analysis. The discussion to follow will then try to figure out these problems by applying a game theory approach.

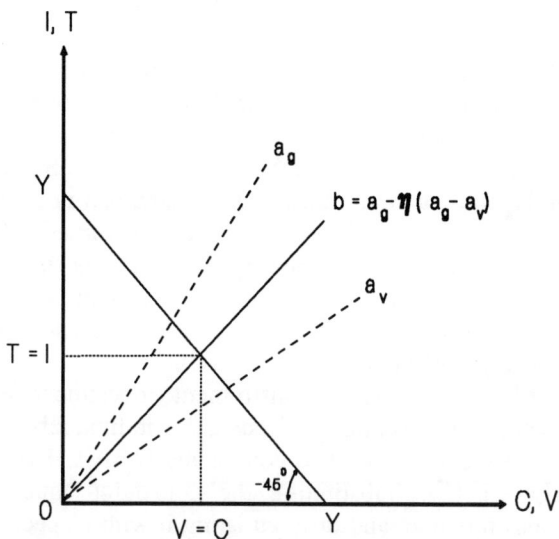

Figure 3.5   The multi-sovereignty mechanism

(i) A two-player game in the distribution of national income Consider the interaction of two players, referred to as the central government and individuals. Each player has a loss function J. The loss increases as instruments deviate from their desired level, and as accumulation rate deviates from its target:

$$J_g = (I - I_g^*)^2 + \Omega_g (H_g - H_g^*)^2, \tag{3.25}$$

$$\text{s.t. } H_g = \frac{a_g}{1 - a_g} C - I = A_g C - I; \quad H_g^* = A_g C_g^* - I_g^* \equiv 0.$$

$$J_v = (C - C_v^*)^2 + \Omega_v (H_v - H_v^*)^2, \tag{3.26}$$

$$\text{s.t. } H_v = \frac{1 - a_v}{a_v} I - C = A_v I - C; \quad H_v = A_v I_v^* - C_v^* \equiv 0.$$

The subscript 'g' refers to the central government and 'v' to individuals. The variable I (C) denotes investment (consumption), I_g^* (C_v^*) the corresponding target of the central government (individuals). The deviations of accumulation rate from its target are represented by $H_g - H_g^*$ ($H_v - H_v^*$). If the central government chooses such a value of I that $H_g = A_g C - I = H_g^*$ ($H_g^* = A_g C_g^* - I_g^* \equiv 0$), then $A = I/C = A_g = I_g^*/C_g^*$, i.e., the realized ratio of investment to consumption, A, is equal to the central government's desired one, A_g; and hence

$a=I/(I+C)=a_g=I_g^*/(I_g^*+C_g^*)$, i.e., the realized accumulation rate, a, is equal to the central government's desired one, a_g. If, on the other hand, the central government chooses such a value of I that $H_g=A_gC-I>H_g^*$ (or $H_g=A_gC-I<H_g^*$), then there must be the case where $a=I/(I+C)<a_g=I_g^*/(I_g^*+C_g^*)$ (or $a=I/(I+C)>a_g=I_g^*/(I_g^*+C_g^*)$), i.e., the realized accumulation rate is smaller (or larger) than the central government's desired one. The above discussion can be similarly applied to individuals, with the instrument variable I replaced by C, and the subscript 'g' of other variables replaced by 'v'. So, the deviations of H_g (H_v) from H_g^* (H_v^*) carry full information contained in the deviations of the realised accumulation rate, a, from the central government's (individuals') desired accumulation rate, a_g (a_v). But $H_g-H_g^*$ ($H_v-H_v^*$) is linear in I and C, while $a-a_g$ ($a-a_v$) is not. Thus the former is used to represent the latter. Ω_g (Ω_v) is the weight attached to accumulation rate deviations relative to investment (consumption) deviations.

Now each player possesses one instrument (investment funds I for the central government and consumption funds C for individuals) with which to minimize its loss function subject to constraints $H_g=A_gC-I$ ($H_v=A_vI-C$) and $H_g^*=A_gC_g^*-I_g^*$ ($H_v^*=A_vI_v^*-C_v^*$). Substituting the constraint equations into the corresponding loss function, and differentiating it with respect to instrument variable assuming that the other player's policy is given, yields the reaction functions for the two players respectively:

$$I=A_g\frac{\Omega_g}{1+\Omega_g}C-A_g\frac{\Omega_g}{1+\Omega_g}C_g^*+I_g^*=\alpha C-\alpha C_g^*+I_g^* \ ; \ \alpha=A_g\frac{\Omega_g}{1+\Omega_g}. \quad (3.27)$$

$$C=A_v\frac{\Omega_v}{1+\Omega_v}I-A_v\frac{\Omega_v}{1+\Omega_v}I_v^*+C_v^*=\beta I-\beta I_v^*+C_v^* \ ; \ \beta=A_v\frac{\Omega_v}{1+\Omega_v}. \quad (3.28)$$

These two reaction functions are depicted in Figure 3.6. They are run through the points (C_g^*, I_g^*) and (C_v^*, I_v^*) respectively, which are the centres of the two players's indifference contours representing their loss functions. In many studies (e.g. Eichengreen, 1985 and 1992), The centres of the players' indifference contours are usually taken as given, and their different locations are determined on the basis of some intuitive assumptions. Unlike these studies, we have, in the previous section, provided detailed accounts of how the points (C_g^*, I_g^*) and (C_v^*, I_v^*) are determined, and why (C_v^*, I_v^*) must lie to the southeast of (C_g^*, I_g^*). Equations (3.27) and (3.28) show that the slopes of the two reaction functions depend on the weights Ω_g and Ω_v respectively, given A_g and A_v. Take the central government for instance. If $\Omega_g \to 0$, then $\alpha \to 0$, and in the limit the central government's reaction function becomes $I=I_g^*$, a horizontal line with an intercept I_g^*. An implication of this case is that, if the central government does not at all worry about the deviations of the realised accumulation rate from its desired level, it will not take any actions against

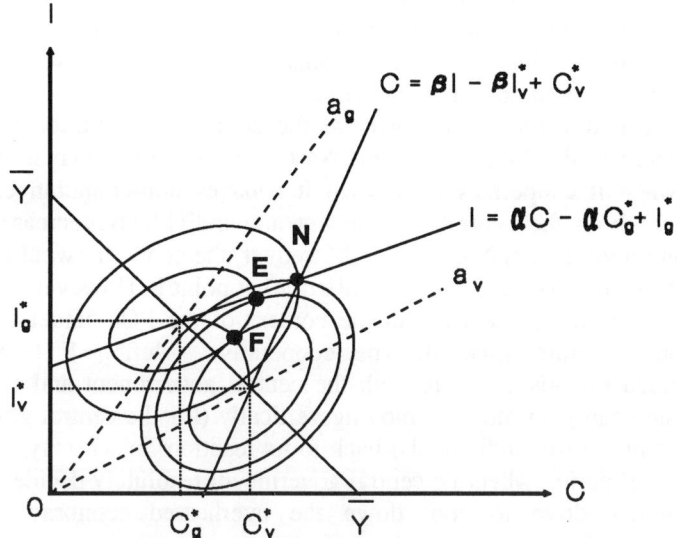

Figure 3.6 The central government's and individuals' reaction functions

individuals whatever moves they make for consumption. Suppose now that $\Omega_g \to \infty$. Since Ω_g is a weight *relative* to that placed on the investment deviations, this is equivalent to assuming that the latter tends to zero. In this case, $\alpha \to A_g$, and the central government's reaction function becomes $I = A_g C$, which overlaps its desired accumulation line a_g. This implies that the central government attempts to realise its desired accumulation rate at any costs due to the deviations of investment from its desired level. Both of the above two extreme cases are hardly likely to appear. A straightforward conclusion is that the central government's reaction function lies somewhere between the line a_g and the horizontal line $I = I_g^*$. Conducting the same analysis to the individuals' reaction function, we can also conclude that it lies somewhere between the line a_v and the vertical line $C = C_v^*$.

The equilibrium values of I and C under different solution concepts can now be determined. Figure 3.6 illustrates three points corresponding to three possible solutions. Point N is the Nash solution where two reaction functions intersect. At the cooperative solution F, the indifference contours of the central government and of individuals are tangent. But F only represents a particular point of tangency. If the losses of the two players are allowed to vary, there are an infinite number of Pareto-efficient cooperative solutions which compose the contract curve. Finally we consider the case where individuals act as the Stackelberg leader, and the central government follows. Substituting the central government's reaction function into the individuals' objective function and minimizing the loss yields the solution depicted at point E in Figure 3.6, where an individuals' indifference curve is tangent to the central government's reaction function.

Note that I and C are lower at the cooperative solution than at the Stackelberg leader-follower and the Nash solutions. Each player reaps more gains when it cooperates than when it behaves non-cooperatively, as the losses for both the central government and individuals decrease with the solution moving from N or E to F. Moreover, the economy would suffer the least degree of shortages (or open inflation) at point F. However, cooperative strategies are not sustainable in the context of the POE under MSM. The intuition is straightforward. The cooperative solution F brings about widespread dissatisfaction to both the central government and individuals: either side can gain more by moving vertically (for the central government) or horizontally (for individuals) back to its reaction line. It may occur in an exceptional period when the central government resolutely decides to launch an austerity drive to cool down the overheated economy. This will unavoidably involve, as we have observed in reality, tough and time-consuming bargaining between the central government and individuals (represented by subunits). Given the particular relationship in competition, every sector or enterprise or region will, for its own interest, ask the central government to 'tighten' other sectors, enterprises and regions, arguing that others' consumption funds are over-expanded, but its are not. Sometimes individuals may also attribute the overheated economy only to excessive investment, implying that the central government should 'tighten' itself. When agreements cannot be reached, the central government has to employ political power to enforce obedience upon opponents (individuals, subunits etc.) to its plans for rectifying economy, and the F point may well incline towards the side of the central government. Under these circumstances, SSM actually replaces MSM; and not surprisingly perhaps, in charge of economic rectifications are usually hardliners. This is why those reformers always complain about restoration of the old system during the rectification period. Therefore, under pressures from various sides, the economic rectification (represented here by the cooperative solution F) had never lasted for a long time. Can the cooperative solution then becomes a normal state in the Chinese economy? No. The competitions in the game are characterized by a lack of internal and external restraints. The internal restraint refers to the budget constraint which is, however, soft in the POE. The external restraint should be understood as a legal system. Nevertheless, as Holly and Hughes Hallett (1989, p. 211) put it, 'Legal systems are the most common mechanisms for enforcing and sustaining cooperative solutions but if there is widespread dissatisfaction with the law and if the law does not accord with what people regard as fair and reasonable then even the legal system may not work'; let alone there have not yet been such regulations or legal systems in China, by which the central government and individuals may feel bound so as to keep an agreement enforced in income distribution.

If cooperative strategies are not feasible, then which one of the non-cooperative solutions, the Nash solution or the Stackelberg leader-follower solution, is more likely to obtain? Indeed, both players benefit with movement from the Nash solution to the leader-follower solution. It is also clear that with upward-sloping reaction functions the follower reaps the greater gains: while both players benefit from less money having to be spent, only the follower benefits from a larger share in national income than the Nash solution would bring. As Cooper (1984) suggests, the fact that the follower reaps the larger benefits encourages both parties to engage in a game of 'chicken', each attempting to force the other to accept the role of leader. There may be extended periods when the Nash solution is observed as this game of 'chicken' is being played out. The above discussion arrives at a conclusion that the Nash non-cooperative solution is the most sustainable strategy in the context of a POE under the MSM, although it is not Pareto-optimal, and makes both players worse off than the other two solutions do. The Nash solutions for both I and C can be obtained as below:

$$I_N = \frac{1}{1-\alpha\beta}[\alpha(C_v^* - C_g^*) + I_g^* - \alpha\beta I_v^*] \tag{3.29}$$

$$C_N = \frac{1}{1-\alpha\beta}[\beta(I_g^* - I_v^*) + C_v^* - \alpha\beta C_g^*] \tag{3.30}$$

(ii) The Nash solution line Up to this point, we have assumed that the national income $\bar{Y}$ is given (a_g and a_v are always exogenously given), and hence (C_g^*, I_g^*) and (C_v^*, I_v^*), the centres of the two players' indifference contours, unchanged (because $I_g^* = a_g \bar{Y}$, $C_g^* = \bar{Y} - I_g^*$; and $I_v^* = a_v \bar{Y}$, $C_v^* = \bar{Y} - I_v^*$). Now we relax this assumption, and let $\bar{Y}$ rise form $\bar{Y}_1$ to $\bar{Y}_2$. In Figure 3.7, the first result of a rise in real national income is that the centres of these two players' indifference curves, (C_{1g}^*, I_{1g}^*) and (C_{1v}^*, I_{1v}^*), move along the accumulation lines a_g and a_v to the points (C_{2g}^*, I_{2g}^*) and (C_{2v}^*, I_{2v}^*) on the line $\bar{Y}_2\bar{Y}_2$. If all the other conditions remain the same, then we have two new reaction functions:

$$I = \alpha C - \alpha C_{2g}^* + I_{2g}^*$$

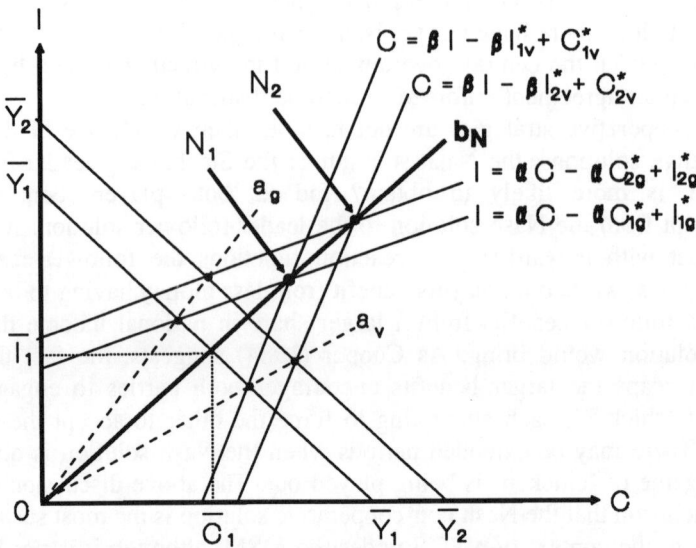

Figure 3.7 The Nash solution line

$$C = \beta I - \beta I_{2v}^* + C_{2v}^*$$

the first shifting upward by $(I_{2g}^* - I_{1g}^*) - \alpha(C_{2g}^* - C_{1g}^*) = [(1+\alpha)a_g - \alpha](\bar{Y}_2 - \bar{Y}_1)$, and the second shifting rightward by $(C_{2v}^* - C_{1v}^*) - \beta(I_{2v}^* - I_{1v}^*) = [1 - (1+\beta)a_v](Y_2 - Y_1)$. Note that, since the slopes of the new reaction functions do not change (still α and β), the new reaction lines parallel their old counterparts. They intersect at the new Nash solution N_2. It is easy to prove that the new and old Nash solutions, N_1 and N_2, must lie on the same straight line which passes through the original point O, given the above conditions. Thus, allowing only for variations in real national income, we have infinite number of the Nash solutions which compose b_N, referred to as the Nash solution line, depicted in Figure 3.7. Dividing I_N by C_N at any points of the line b_N, i.e., dividing equation (3.29) by (3.30), and multiplying both numerator and denominator by $1/\bar{Y}$, we calculate the slope of the Nash solution line as

$$b_N = \frac{I_N}{C_N} = \frac{(1+\alpha)a_g - \alpha(1+\beta)a_v}{1 - \alpha\beta + \beta(1+\alpha)a_g - (1+\beta)a_v} \quad (3.31)$$

which is un-correlated with real national income $\bar{Y}$. The signs of partial derivatives of b_N with respective to α, β, a_g and a_v are:

$$\frac{\partial b_N}{\partial \alpha} \geq 0; \quad \frac{\partial b_N}{\partial \beta} \leq 0; \quad \frac{\partial b_N}{\partial a_g} \geq 0; \quad \frac{\partial b_N}{\partial a_v} \geq 0.$$

Clearly, along the Nash solution line there is a general relation between I_N and C_N:

$$I_N = b_N C_N \tag{3.32}$$

This structural form will become the reduced form in (3.29), if one substitutes (3.30) and (3.31) into (3.32). For consumption, we assume that individuals make decisions based on 'rational' expectations of their opponent's actions. Since the game here is Nash, and 'As long as the game is Nash, then there are no incentives, in the absence of cooperation, for one of the players to depart from the Nash solution' (Holly and Hughes Hallett 1989, p. 195). Thus individuals would take I_N into account in forming their expectations:

$$C_N = \beta(I_N - I_v^*)^e + C_v^* \tag{3.33}$$

Using geometrical relations shown in Figure 3.7, this equation eventually becomes:

$$C_N = \frac{\beta}{1+\beta}(1+b_N)(C_N - \overline{C})^e + C_v^* \tag{3.34}$$

which will be employed in chapter 5 for further modelling of the consumption behaviour of households.

It is not surprising to find that, in the Nash non-cooperative game, nominal national income will expand at faster speed than real one. Let Y_N be nominal national income corresponding to the Nash solutions along the line b_N. Taking differences between Y_N and $\overline{Y}$, we have:

$$Y_N - \overline{Y} = I_N + C_N - \overline{Y} = \frac{(1+\alpha)(1+\beta)(a_g - a_v)}{1-\alpha\beta}\overline{Y} \tag{3.35}$$

Since $a_g - a_v > 0$, $1-\alpha\beta > 0$, $Y_N - \overline{Y}$ is positively related to $\overline{Y}$. This implies that, as real national income grows, the gap between nominal and real national incomes will widen. In other words, the economy is characterized by demand-determined shortages: however high the level of aggregate supply might be, aggregate demand will always exceed aggregate supply.

(iii) The multi-sovereignty mechanism The above studies have analyzed income distribution in strategic terms using game theory concepts. The behaviour of the central government and individuals is modelled as the Nash non-cooperative one. Therefore, the realised accumulation line b in Figure 3.5 is actually the Nash solution line b_N in Figure 3.7, and the slope of b, b',

should be b_N, namely,
$$b' = b_N = \frac{(1+\alpha)a_g - \alpha(1+\beta)a_v}{1-\alpha\beta + \beta(1+\alpha)a_g - (1+\beta)a_v}$$

From this equation, b itself can be derived below
$$b = \frac{b'}{1+b'} = \frac{(1+\alpha)a_g - \alpha(1+\beta)a_v}{1-\alpha\beta + (1+\alpha)(1+\beta)(a_g - a_v)} \quad (3.36)$$

After some mathematical manipulations, it reads as
$$b = a_g - \frac{(1+\beta)[(1+\alpha)a_g - \alpha]}{1-\alpha\beta + (1+\alpha)(1+\beta)(a_g - a_v)}(a_g - a_v) = a_g - \eta(a_g - a_v);$$
$$\eta = \frac{(1+\beta)[(1+\alpha)a_g - \alpha]}{1-\alpha\beta + (1+\alpha)(1+\beta)(a_g - a_v)}.$$

Here η depends, among other things, on α and β, the slopes of the two reaction curves. As Holly and Hughes Hallett (1989) suggest, the slope of each reaction curve is determined by both the responses of the economy (as represented by Ω_g or Ω_v, the strength of the effect of each instrument variable on the state of the underlying system) and by the tastes and preferences of each player, i.e., a_g or a_v. Thus the coefficient η may be seen as the degree to which the MSM favours individuals' sovereignty. η might also be the bargaining strength parameter in a cooperative game, but since cooperation between the central government and individuals occurs only in vary unusual circumstances, this consideration is ignored here. Given $\alpha/(1+\alpha) \leq a_g$ and $\beta/(1+\beta) \geq a_v$, one obtains that $0 \leq \eta \leq 1$, hence $a_v \leq b \leq a_g$. If $\eta \to 0$, then $b \to a_g$. Individuals have no influence at all on income distribution, and the realised distribution proportion is exactly the same as the central government would determine. This extreme case is a typical example of pure SSM in CPEs where the problem collapses to a single-player (the central government) game, and has been considerably weakened since 1979. If $\eta \to 1$, then $b \to a_v$. Individuals have a full voice in determining income distribution, and the realised distribution proportion is identical to the individuals' desired accumulation rate. This extreme case is a typical example of the pure individual sovereignty mechanism in a free market economy where the problem collapses to a single-player (individuals) game, and has not yet appeared in China. Thus when we talk about the MSM, the values of η must be in between 0 and 1, and the realised accumulation line b must lie between the lines a_v and a_g, while a two-player game is being played out.

Under the MSM, the process of realization of b in reality is as follows. Let us assume that, in the first round of conflicts, individuals acquire the personal income C_v^* which is above the total wage payments and wage rate set by the central government, and the corresponding distribution proportion is then lower than the central government's desire to accumulate. The central government will certainly not allow this to go unchecked, but what can it do? Retrieve the 'state sovereignty'? This seems against the reform. Reduce the already distributed personal income? This is not possible even under the SSM sometimes. The only feasible way seems to be to adopt the policies of deficit finance and deficit credit to realize its desired accumulation rate. However, while the central government has a full authority to issue money as before, it can no longer ensure that these newly added funds will go exclusively in the direction of investment. The subunits now with a certain degree of decision-making power ($\eta>0$) do not completely obey the central government as under the SSM. They, under the pressure of individuals, will divert a part of investment funds to individuals' personal income in the forms forenamed. This is illustrated in Figure 3.8 by two mutually vertical arrows starting from point v and ending up at point e. Then, the second round of conflict begins. Suppose that, after several rounds of conflict in a certain period, the distribution proportion is settled at the Nash equilibrium point N, with the personal income equal to C ($=C_v^*+\Delta M_v$) and the public income equal to I ($=I_v^*+\Delta M_g$), as shown in Figure 3.8. Although the realized distribution proportion fails to let individuals enjoy their desired consumption in real terms, it at least gives both sides 'fair' distribution of gains (losses), and thus alleviate the contradiction to a certain extent. This is why the central government often resort to this measure. But the cost is also high. Increasing money supply results in the augmentation of nominal national income, and hence the expansion of the aggregate demand. Like the case under SSM, the aggregate excess demand consists of two components, namely, excess investment demand and excess consumption demand:

$$Y^d - \bar{Y} = (I - \bar{I}) + (C - \bar{C}) = \Delta M_g + \Delta M_v$$

But the aggregate excess demand under the MSM may well exceed that under the SSM. This is clearly due to the non-cooperative nature of the MSM, and in this sense the MSM is worse than the SSM, though the SSM does not worry about distribution of any gains as it always assures a favourable one for the central government.

Now we can synthesize the analysis above in a simple mathematical relation. From Figure 3.8, and substituting the results of the preceding discussions for α, β, a_g and a_v, the following equation can be derived:

$$I = \frac{b}{1-b} C = \frac{(1+\alpha)a_g - \alpha(1+\beta)a_v}{1-\alpha\beta + \beta(1+\alpha)a_g - (1+\beta)a_v} C = I(C, \Gamma, \theta, \omega, \Omega_g, \Omega_v) \qquad (3.37)$$

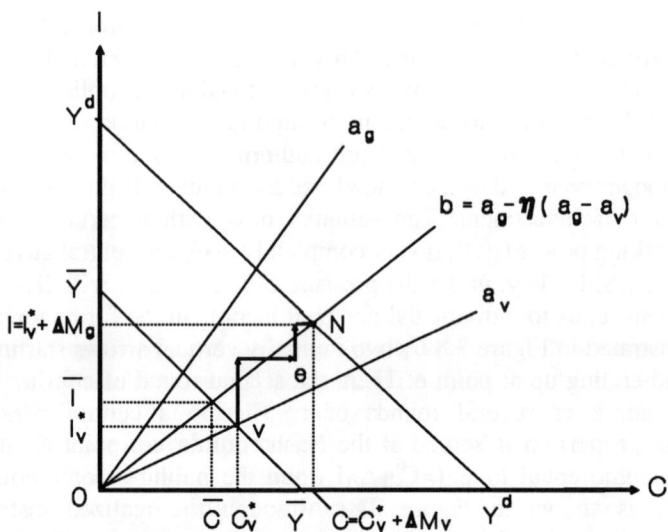

Figure 3.8 Conflicts between the central government and individuals in national income distribution under MSM

where $\dfrac{\partial I}{\partial C}>0$; $\dfrac{\partial I}{\partial \Gamma}<0$; $\dfrac{\partial I}{\partial \theta}<0$; $\dfrac{\partial I}{\partial \omega}<0$; $\dfrac{\partial I}{\partial \Omega_g}>0$; $\dfrac{\partial I}{\partial \Omega_v}<0$.

Equation (3.37) says that investment demand is a function of consumption demand C, the central government's policy stance Γ, individuals' time preference θ, the income illusion coefficient ω, and the weights Ω_g and Ω_v in the central government's and individuals' loss functions.

3.3 Investment demand's determinant 2: conflicts between sectors for investment resources

From section 3.2, we know that the resource allocation between accumulation and consumption eventually falls to proportion *b*, i.e., $\overline{I}$ for investment and $\overline{C}$ for consumption. Would everything then go off without a hitch once this (temporary) settlement is reached? The answer is simply no. If we divide the economy into two sectors: the investment goods sector and the consumption goods sector, the conflicts between central government and individuals on the ratio of accumulation to consumption will inevitably extend to the allocation of investment resources between these two sectors. In other words, the accumulation-consumption ratio and the sectoral proportion (industrial structure) are very closely associated with each other — like a shadow following a person. With strong desire to accumulate, the central government certainly intends to allocate more resources to the investment goods sector; With a strong desire to consume, individuals certainly hope to develop the consumption goods sector. This issue was neglected in the studies of Fan G. et al (1990), and is investigated in this section. The approach employed in this section is an analogue to that in the previous section, and thus only the main steps in the process of exposition are presented. Readers are referred back to the previous section for more details.

Two optimal choices by the central planner and subunits

Consider two sectors in the economy: one producing only investment goods and the other producing only consumption goods, and hence the name investment goods sector (IGS) and consumption goods sector (CGS). Since individuals are not investors in a POE, their representatives are assumed to be subunits (local government, enterprises etc.). The subunit's objective in making decisions regarding the allocation of the investment resources between IGS and CGS, is to maximize the function given by:

$$\Pi = \pi(i_t) + (1+r)^{-1}\pi(i_{t+1}) \qquad (3.38)$$

subject to the constraint:

$$i_t + (1+n)k_{It} - k_{It-1} = f(k_{It-1}); \qquad (3.39a)$$
$$i_{t+1} + (1+n)k_{It+1} - k_{It} = f(k_{It}) \qquad (3.39b)$$

where i is per capita investment in CGS, k_I per capita capital stock in IGS, $f(\cdot)$ per capita output of IGS, $\pi(\cdot)$ per capita net yield of CGS,[13] r the rate of return. Differentiating the corresponding Lagrangian Function with respect to i_t, i_{t+1} and k_t yields the first-order conditions for the subunits' optimum:

$$-\pi'(i_t)(1+n) + (1+r)^{-1}\pi'(i_{t+1})(1+f'(k_I)) = 0$$

In steady state, the subunits' optimal capital stock k_{Is}^* satisfies:

$$f'(k_{Is}^*) = (1+r)(1+n) - 1 \qquad (3.40)$$

We turn now to the behaviour of the central planner. Again it is assumed that the central planner not only cares about the net yield of CGS for the generation at time t, but also cares about the yields for all generations at time $t+1$, $t+2$, ..., $t+T$, by weighting them in his/her objective function:

$$\Pi = \sum_{j=0}^{T}(1+R)^{-j-1}\Pi_{t+j} = \sum_{j=0}^{T}(1+R)^{-j-1}[\pi(i_{1,t+j})+(1+r)^{-1}\pi(i_{2,t+j+1})]$$
$$= \cdots + [\pi(i_{1,t-1})+(1+r)^{-1}\pi(i_{2,t})] + (1+R)^{-1}[\pi(i_{1,t})+(1+r)^{-1}\pi(i_{2,t+1})] + \cdots \quad (3.41)$$

The resource constraints for such a central planner are:

$$i_{1,t-1}+(1+n)^{-1}i_{2,t-1}+(1+n)k_{It}-k_{It-1}=f(k_{It-1}); \quad (3.42a)$$
$$i_{1,t}+(1+n)^{-1}i_{2,t}+(1+n)k_{It+1}-k_{It}=f(k_{It}) \quad (3.42b)$$

Maximizing (3.41) subject to (3.42a) and (3.42b) leads to the first-order conditions for the central planned optimum:

$$-\pi'(i_{1,t-1})(1+n)+(1+R)^{-1}\pi'(i_{1,t})[1+f'(k_{It})]=0$$

In steady state, k_I^* satisfies:

$$f'(k_I^*)=(1+R)(1+n)-1 \quad (3.43)$$

Like the interest conflicts in the distribution of national income, the subunits and the planner have different modified golden rules regarding investment resource allocation. The problem comes from the difference between the subunits' rate of return and the planner's rate of discount. The subunits' rate of return r is non-negative, and is even higher in the circumstances where the price of consumption goods is more flexible than the price of investment goods. The planner's rate of discount R is highly subjective, and is usually equal to zero when he/she weights equally the net yields of CGS of all periods. Some times when effected by the central government, R could even become negative. Thus similar to the previous discussions,[14] we conclude that R<r and $k_I^* > k_{Is}^*$.

Next, substituting k_{Is}^*, i_s^* in the subunits' constraint (3.39), and k_I^*, i^* (define total per capita investment in CGS i_t as $i_{1t}+(1+n)^{-1}i_{2t}$ and denote steady state values of i by i^*; see Blanchard and Fischer 1989, p. 102) in the planner's constraints (3.42), and letting z_s denote the subunits' desired investment proportion, and z_g the central government's desired investment proportion, and the following expressions are obtained:

$$z_s = \frac{f(k_{Is}^*)-i_s^*}{f(k_{Is}^*)} = n\frac{k_{Is}^*(r)}{f[k_{Is}^*(r)]} = z_s(r); \quad \frac{\partial z_s}{\partial r}<0. \quad (3.44)$$

$$z_g = \frac{f(k_I^*)-i^*}{f(k_I^*)} = n\frac{k_I^*(R)}{f[k_I^*(R)]} = z_g(R); \quad \frac{\partial z_g}{\partial R}<0. \quad (3.45)$$

Taking the difference between z_g and z_s, the following inequalities hold:

$$z_g - z_s = n\left[\frac{k_I^*}{f(k_I^*)} - \frac{k_{Is}^*}{f(k_{Is}^*)}\right] = A_z(R,r) \geq 0, \quad \text{if } R \leq r; \quad (3.46)$$

where $\quad \dfrac{\partial A_z}{\partial R} < 0; \quad \dfrac{\partial A_z}{\partial r} > 0$

The allocation of investment resources may therefore be such that the central government, with its lower rate of discount (it cares more about consumption goods supply for future generations) than the subunits' rate of return, would like to place more emphasis on the development of investment goods sector than the subunits. This is actually the 'image' of conflicts between a_g and a_v projected on the 'screen' of investment resource allocation.

The subunits' effective right of the money supply

Before analysing the consequences of scrambling for investment resources, it would be useful to understand the special mechanism of money supply in a POE, because the 'monetary competition' between subunits is a major explanation to the expansion of investment demand under the multi-sovereignty mechanism.

The banking system of a POE is characterized by (1) the uniqueness of the state banking system, and (2) the subordinateness of the money-supplier to the money-demander. Within a POE there exists only and uniquely the state bank. The state bank consists of the central bank, many branches and the specialized banks, but this is a kind of division of labour between regions or between specialities; and the boundaries of property rights among these banks are not and cannot be clearly demarcated (because of the nature of the POE). There does not exist, within a POE, commercial banks which are economically independent, assume sole responsibilities for their profits or losses, and have full autonomy of operation. This characteristic is thus called uniqueness, and it inevitably bestows the well-known feature of a POE on banks: soft budget constraint. The second characteristic is actually the derivative of the first one: the central bank is subordinate to the central government, and the local bank to both the local government and the central bank. From the point of view of business the local bank is in principle subordinate to the central bank. However, the following reasons explain why a local bank is, *in fact to a certain degree*, subordinate to local government. First, the personnel appointments at the rank of governors or chief managers are decided by local governments, and the solutions to some problems occurring in local banks' routine duties and daily life rely on local governments. Second, the interests of a local bank show no difference from the interests of its locality. The more loans it issues, the more resources its locality is capable of purchasing, and the more prosperous that local economy will be. In turn, the local bank will make more profits through its saving and loan business. Third, from the point of view of function, a local bank is committed to ensure the supply of funds to its locality, to serve the economic construction of its locality, to meet the funds demanded for local economic development. But as we will see below, this is the usual noncooperative outcome. Under no cooperation, local banks (following the local governments' orders) over-provide loans because they do not account for impacts of their actions elsewhere, and fail to realise that the others will over-provide too.

It is the second characteristic of banking system that makes money-suppliers (local banks) *not* independent of money-demanders (local governments). However, the subordinateness of local banks to local governments does not necessarily cause excess money supply. There are other conditions needed: interest conflicts, indirect control methods. The first condition explains the incentive of local governments to issue more money. The second condition ensures that the local banks have a certain autonomy of operation. Under the state sovereignty mechanism, the central bank employs direct control methods. It determines the aggregate money supply according to the plan of overall balance of national economy worked out by the central planner (the central government), and then distributes vertically the planned quota of money supply (credit quota) to its local and specialized branches. Local banks can compete with each other regarding the planned quota, but they are not allowed to provide loans autonomously. Under the multi-sovereignty mechanism, the central bank adopts both direct control and indirect control methods (called the 'dual-track system'). The indirect control methods mean that the central bank let local branches have a autonomy to grant credits on the base of their saving deposits, and the amount of loans granted is not restricted by the planned quota. Although in the dual system this autonomy is confined within a certain scope, it gives local governments an effective right of money supply.

The formation of investment demand of investment goods sectors

Consider the case where the economy is under the multi-sovereignty mechanism. The two-player game between the central government and subunits here is exactly the same as analyzed in section 3.2. Each player has a loss function, J_k (for the central government) and J_c (for subunits) respectively, and these contain conflicting objectives. There are target variables, H_k and H_c, and also there are instrument variables available to these two players, I_k and I_c. More specifically, the loss functions for the central government and subunits are specified as:

$$J_k = (I_k - I_{kg}^*)^2 + \Omega_k (H_k - H_k^*)^2 \tag{3.47}$$

$$\text{s.t.} \quad H_k = \frac{z_g}{1-z_g} I_c - I_k = A_k I_c - I_k; \quad H_k^* = A_k I_{cg}^* - I_{kg}^*$$

$$J_c = (I_c - I_{cs}^*)^2 + \Omega_c (H_c - H_c^*)^2 \tag{3.48}$$

$$\text{s.t.} \quad H_c = \frac{1-z_s}{z_s} I_k - I_c = A_s I_k - I_c; \quad H_c^* = A_s I_{ks}^* - I_{cs}^*$$

The subscript 'k' represents the investment goods sector, 'g' the central government, 'c' the consumption goods sector, and 's' subunits. Ω_k and Ω_c are weights. For the same reasons given in section 3.2, we assume the most straightforward kind of non-cooperative strategy, a Nash game, being played out here. The only difference here is that two players compete for more investment resources, rather than for a bigger share in national income distribution. Therefore, to avoid unnecessary repetitions, we arrive straightforwardly at their reaction functions:

$$I_k = \frac{\Omega_k}{1+\Omega_k} \frac{z_g}{1-z_g} I_c - \frac{\Omega_k}{1+\Omega_k} \frac{z_g}{1-z_g} I_{cg}^* + I_{kg}^* = \alpha_k I_c - \alpha_k I_{cg}^* + I_{kg}^* \tag{3.49}$$

$$I_c = \frac{\Omega_c}{1+\Omega_c} \frac{1-z_s}{z_s} I_k - \frac{\Omega_c}{1+\Omega_c} \frac{1-z_s}{z_s} I_{ks}^* + I_{cs}^* = \alpha_c I_k - \alpha_c I_{ks}^* + I_{cs}^* \tag{3.50}$$

where

$$\alpha_k = \frac{\Omega_k}{1+\Omega_k} \frac{z_g}{1-z_g}; \quad \alpha_c = \frac{\Omega_c}{1+\Omega_c} \frac{1-z_s}{z_s}$$

The Nash solutions are:

$$I_k^N = \frac{1}{1-\alpha_k \alpha_c} [\alpha_k (I_{cs}^* - I_{cg}^*) + I_{kg}^* - \alpha_k \alpha_c I_{ks}^*]$$

$$= \frac{I}{1-\alpha_k \alpha_c} [\alpha_k (z_g - z_s) + z_g - \alpha_k \alpha_c z_s] \tag{3.51}$$

and

$$I_c^N = \frac{1}{1-\alpha_k \alpha_c} [\alpha_c (I_{kg}^* - I_{ks}^*) + I_{cs}^* - \alpha_k \alpha_c I_{cg}^*]$$

$$= \frac{I}{1-\alpha_k \alpha_c} [\alpha_c (z_g - z_s) + (1-z_s) - \alpha_k \alpha_c (1-z_g)] \tag{3.52}$$

Starting from this point, we draw Figure 3.9 to show the conflicts between

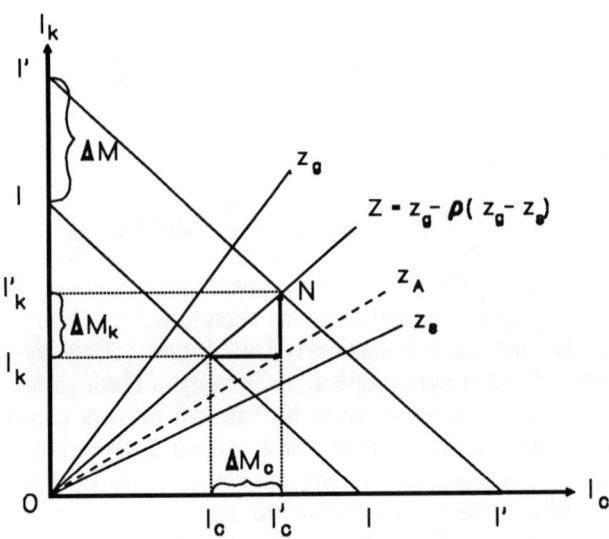

Figure 3.9 Conflicts between the central government and subunits for investment resources under MSM

the central government and subunits for investment resources, in which the realized investment-proportion line Z is the Nash solution line derived from two reaction functions and by allowing the initial investment resources to vary. The horizontal axis represents investment in the consumption goods sector I_c, and the vertical axis indicates investment in the investment goods sector I_k. The initial investment resources (here actually referring to investment funds) are given as I. Under the MSM, the realized investment proportion Z is neither the central government's desired one z_g, nor the subunits' desired one z_s, but rather something in between which depends upon the degree of to which the MSM favours to the subunits' sovereignty, ρ ($0<\rho<1$). Suppose that the initially allocated proportion of total investment funds I happens to be Z so that the consumption goods sector gets I_c and the investment goods sector acquires I_k. Subunits are not satisfied with I_c. With the effective right of money supply, they order the local banks to grant more loans to themselves (the enterprises or other units in the local) to expand their purchasing power and to finance their investment projects in the consumption goods sector. After several rounds of competition, these expanded credits are assumed to be ΔM_c so that $I'_c = I_c + \Delta M_c$ (which corresponds to the Nash solution point N), i.e., subunits reach their Nash equilibria. Nevertheless, the economy is not yet completely decentralized, and the central government would add at the same time an amount of funds ΔM_k on the top of I_k to finance the investment I_k' in the investment goods sector, so that its Nash equilibrium investment in IGS can be realised. It finally turns out that the 'resultant of forces' of theses two non-cooperative players pushes the allocation proportion back to its original level Z but with the augmented aggregate investment demand larger than the initial one. That is:

$$I'-I=\Delta M>0;\ I_k'-I_k=\Delta M_k>0;\ I_c'-I_c=\Delta M_c>0;\ \Delta M=\Delta M_k+\Delta M_c.$$

To derive the expression for aggregate investment demand, an auxiliary line z_A is added in Figure 3.9. According to this figure, the aggregate investment demand is sum of the original investment funds and the excess money supply resulting from the conflicts:

$$I'=I+\Delta M=I+\Delta M_k+\Delta M_c \tag{3.53}$$

Under MSM, the competitions for resources are usually provoked by the subunits in the first place. In other words, the central government is in a passive position while the subunits are in an aggressive position. Thus ΔM_k, ΔM_c are both expressed as function of I_c':

$$\Delta M_k=\frac{Z-z_A}{(1-Z)(1-z_A)}I_c';\quad \Delta M_c=\frac{Z-z_A}{Z(1-z_A)}I_c'.$$

So ΔM is given by

$$\Delta M=\frac{Z-z_A}{Z(1-Z)(1-z_A)}I_c' \tag{3.54}$$

But the slope of the line z_A is:

$$z_A'=\frac{I_k'}{I_c^N}=\frac{(1-\alpha_k\alpha_c)Z}{1-\alpha_k\alpha_c+\alpha_c(1+\alpha_k)z_g-(1+\alpha_c)z_s}$$

which leads to z_A below:

$$z_A=\frac{z_A'}{1+z_A'}=\frac{(1-\alpha_k\alpha_c)Z}{1-\alpha_k\alpha_c+\alpha_c(1+\alpha_k)z_g-(1+\alpha_c)z_s+(1-\alpha_k\alpha_c)Z} \tag{3.55}$$

Substituting (3.55) into (3.54) for ΔM, we have:

$$\Delta M=\frac{(1+\alpha_k)(1+\alpha_c)(z_g-z_s)}{1-\alpha_k\alpha_c+\alpha_c(1+\alpha_k)z_g-(1+\alpha_c)z_s}I_c' \tag{3.56}$$

where[15] $\dfrac{\partial\Delta M}{\partial z_g}>0;\quad \dfrac{\partial\Delta M}{\partial z_s}<0;\quad \dfrac{\partial\Delta M}{\partial \alpha_k}>0;\quad \dfrac{\partial\Delta M}{\partial \alpha_c}>0;\quad \dfrac{\partial\Delta M}{\partial I_c'}>0$

Adding up (3.37) and (3.56), and substituting Ω_k and z_g for α_k, Ω_c and z_s for α_c, r for z_s and R for z_g, one gets:

$$I' = \frac{(1+\alpha)a_g - \alpha(1+\beta)a_y}{1 - \alpha\beta + \beta(1+\alpha)a_g - (1+\beta)a_y} C + \frac{(1+\alpha_k)(1+\alpha_c)(z_g - z_s)}{1 - \alpha_k\alpha_c + \alpha_c(1+\alpha_k)z_g - (1+\alpha_c)z_s} I_c' \quad (3.57)$$

$$= I(C, \Gamma, \theta, \omega, \Omega_g, \Omega_y) + \Delta M(I_c', R, r, \Omega_k, \Omega_c)$$

Obviously,

$$\frac{\partial I'}{\partial I_c'} = \frac{\partial \Delta M}{\partial I_c'} > 0; \quad \frac{\partial I'}{\partial R} = \frac{\partial \Delta M}{\partial z_g} \frac{\partial z_g}{\partial R} < 0; \quad \frac{\partial I'}{\partial r} = \frac{\partial \Delta M}{\partial z_s} \frac{\partial z_s}{\partial r} > 0;$$

$$\frac{\partial I'}{\partial \Omega_k} = \frac{\partial \Delta M}{\partial \alpha_k} \frac{\partial \alpha_k}{\partial \Omega_k} > 0; \quad \frac{\partial I'}{\partial \Omega_c} = \frac{\partial \Delta M}{\partial \alpha_c} \frac{\partial \alpha_c}{\partial \Omega_c} > 0.$$

(3.57) is clearly a behavioural equation of aggregate investment demand, and it summarizes the theories about the POE so far expounded.

3.4 The investment behaviour of local governments

We have previously analyzed the fundamental contradictions in POEs regarding resource allocation, which underlie the causes of demand augmentation, and derived as a result the total investment demand function. In the process of explanation, the behaviour of subunits has been mentioned, but that was not a whole picture, because at that time attention was focused on the conflicts between the central government and subunits and its consequences. In this section, attention will be paid to the investment behaviour of local governments as representatives of subunits. In other words, we will study how $I_{c'}$ is formed, and what its determinants are.[16]

Local governments' financial constraints and objective functions

In a POE, the local national income of a region is also divided into two categories: public income and personal income. As usual we assume that individuals do not perform the duties of accumulation, and their personal income is mainly spent on consumption. Thus local governments, as the agents of public ownership in their localities, carry out investment within the public financial constraint. Let T denote public income, S public savings, CR credit granted, I investment expenditures, G non-investment expenditures. A local government faces the following fiscal constraint:

$$S_{-1} + T + CR = I + G + S \quad (3.58)$$

Actually equation (3.58) does not work as a *constraint*. It is simply an identity. The problem comes from CR. As was stated above, one of the characteristics of China's banking system is that the money suppliers (local banks) are not independent of money demanders (local governments). We are not at the moment interested in *what should be in principle*, but only care about *what actually happens in reality*: (1) When local economic authorities work out a investment plan and ask local banks to grant investment loans to support the plan, local banks often meet, or to a certain extent meet, these requirements; (2) The investments which go beyond the local governments' fiscal capability of payments are mainly financed by bank loans; (3) Local banks repeatedly exceed the credit line set in the central bank's plan. These facts indicate that local governments have an effective right of money supply. In the sense that CR can be varied to a certain degree according to the local governments' investment plan I, the financial constraint (3.58) is soft. Also in the light of this, we find that the major explanation for investment growth is the rapid expansion of credit.

Now we come to the local governments' objectives regarding investment. Let us suppose that a local government has its own 'utility' function like an individual. But the local governments' utility consists of different components: first, as a local agent of public ownership, it concerns the growth of public income (which is actually profits) brought about by capital accumulation (of fixed assets and money assets). Second, in accordance with the essential stipulations of public ownership (see note 2), the local government must try to mop up unemployment in its locality, and the fulfilment of this objective obviously requires more investment. The above considerations help to suggest the following objective function for a local government:

$$\pi = \pi_1(I, \Delta S) \cdot \pi_2[(L^s - L), I] \qquad (3.59)$$

where (L^s-L) denotes unemployment. For further algebraic manipulations it is convenient to express the $\pi_1(\cdot)$ as a Cobb-Douglas type function:

$$\pi_1 = I^\alpha (\Delta S)^\beta; \quad \alpha, \beta > 0.$$

The notional investment demand function can be obtained through maximization of the objective function (3.59) which states that $\pi_2(\cdot)=1$ under the fiscal constraint (3.58). Considering the Cobb-Douglas type of $\pi_1(\cdot)$ component the result is

$$\hat{I} = \frac{\alpha}{\alpha + \beta}(T + CR - G) \qquad (3.60)$$

As the result of maximization of the overall objective function (3.59), given $\pi_2 > 1$ ($\pi_2 < 1$), with a fiscal constraint, the employment-constrained investment function is derived. It is additionally assumed that the unemployment term is of linear form:

$$I^* = \frac{\alpha}{\alpha+\beta}(T+CR-G)+\gamma(L^S-L); \quad \gamma \geq 0 \qquad (3.61)$$

Investment conflicts between localities: local governments' expectations

For simplicity, we assume that in the POE there are two homogeneous localities A and B with equal preferences and equal numbers of workers etc. Both of them decide to make investments of their desired volumes I_A^* and I_B^*, and because they are homogeneous $I_A^* = I_B^*$. Desired investment means that it would maximize the locality's welfare (the local government's objective function), and any larger or smaller than the desired investment would decrease welfare. However, in a economy the total amount of economic resources available for investment in a certain period are limited. For this reason we may also assume that $I < I_A^* + I_B^*$. These assumptions then suggest a box diagram in Figure 3.10.

In Figure 3.10 we measure the investment quantities in region A and B on the horizontal axes $0_A\text{-}I_A$ and $0_B\text{-}I_B$, and their investment returns on the vertical axes $0_A\text{-}\pi_A$ (against $0_A\text{-}I_A$) and $0_B\text{-}\pi_B$ (against $0_B\text{-}I_B$). $0_A\text{-}I$ and $0_B\text{-}I$ on both horizontal axes represent total investment resources available for regions A and B. If A obtains its desired investment at I_A^* and hence the maximum returns $\pi_A(I_A^*)$, then B can only get $\bar{I}_B$ and hence $\pi_B(\bar{I}_B)$ which is much less than the optimum $\pi_B(I_B^*)$; and vice versa. This reflects the contradictions between local interests.

Note that the total investment return π is the sum of two regions' returns, namely:

$$\pi = \pi_A(I_A) + \pi_B(I_B)$$

Apparently the unique allocation point for the maximum total investment return is the tangent point between the two curves $\pi_A(I)$ and $\pi_B(I)$, corresponding to which A and B are allocated respectively I_A^0 and I_B^0, because at this point:

$$\pi^* = \pi_A(I_A^0) + \pi_B(I_B^0) > \pi = \pi_A(I_A) + \pi_B(I_B), \text{ if } I_A \neq I_A^0 \text{ ; } I_B \neq I_B^0.$$

Thus either region reaching its optimum position would make the whole social welfare *not* maximized, being deducted by $\Delta\pi$, the welfare loss:

$$\Delta\pi = \pi^*(I_A^0, I_B^0) - [\pi(\bar{I}_A) + \pi(I_B^*)] = \pi^*(I_A^0, I_B^0) - [\pi(I_A^*) + \pi(\bar{I}_B)]$$

The central planner, who is assumed to seek the optimum for the economy as a whole, will certainly choose to allocate the resources I between I_A^0 and

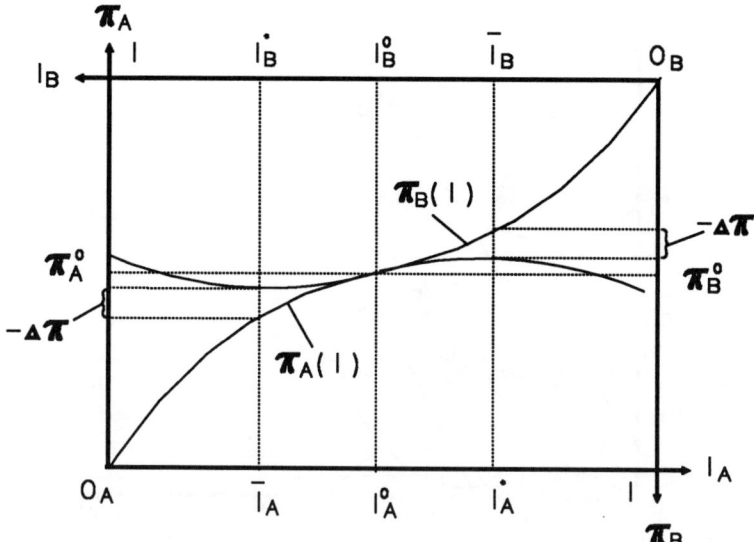

Figure 3.10 A box diagram of two localities' investments

I_B^0. Nevertheless, although the social welfare has been maximized, both A and B are yet locally unsatisfied, because:

$$\pi_A(I_A^0)<\pi_A(I_A^*); \quad \pi_B(I_B^0)<\pi_B(I_B^*).$$

Thus the contradictions between local interests and global interests arise. How does the central government deal with these contradictions? Can they be resolved?

The choices confronting the central government can be illustrated in Figure 3.11. Consider an economy of two regions A and B, each having a loss function, J_A and J_B respectively:

$$J_A=(I_A-I_A^*)^2+\Omega_A(H_A-H_A^*)^2, \quad s.t. \quad H_A=\phi_A I_B-I_A; \quad H_A^*=\phi_A \bar{I}_B-I_A^*$$
$$J_B=(I_B-I_B^*)^2+\Omega_B(H_B-H_B^*)^2, \quad s.t. \quad H_B=\phi_B I_B-I_A; \quad H_B^*=\phi_B \bar{I}_A-I_B^*$$

where $\phi_A=I_A^*/\bar{I}_B$ (>1) and $\phi_B=I_B^*/\bar{I}_A$ (>1). Suppose that the central government tries to be impartial, but it also wants the economy to suffer as lower costs as possible. In this case, it has to find a solution which minimizes the following global loss function:

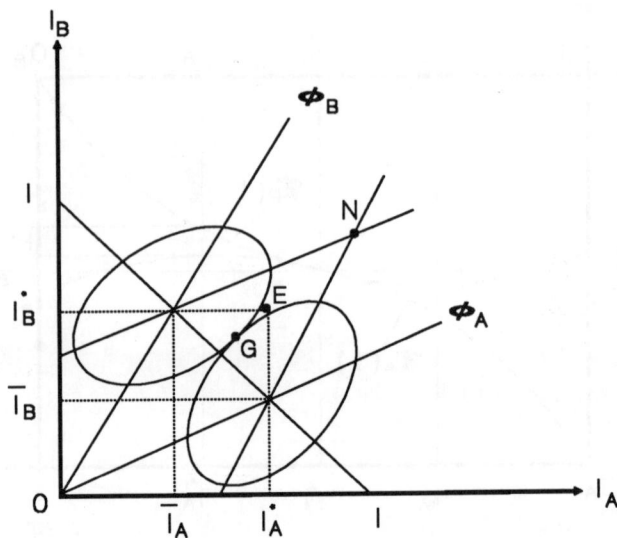

Figure 3.11 The planned allocative ratio of investment resources between regions

$J = J_A + J_B$

s.t. $H_A = \phi_A I_B - I_A$; $H_A^* = \phi_A \bar{I}_B - I_A^*$; $H_B = \phi_B I_A - I_B$; $H_B = \phi_B \bar{I}_A - I_B^*$

which puts an equal weight to the individual loss function. As we assumed earlier, these two regions are identical in all aspects, such that:

$I_A^* = I_B^* = I^*$; $\bar{I}_A = \bar{I}_B = \bar{I}$; $\Omega_A = \Omega_B = \Omega$; $\phi_A = \phi_B = \phi$.

In the symmetrical model like this, the global loss function becomes:

$J = (I_A - I^*)^2 + (I_B - I^*)^2 + \Omega\{[\phi(I_B - \bar{I}) - (I_A - I^*)]^2 + [\phi(I_A - \bar{I}) - (I_B - I^*)]^2\}$ (3.62)

Solving the first-order conditions $\partial J/\partial I_A = 0$ and $\partial J/\partial I_B = 0$ simultaneously, we find that

$$I_A = I_B = \frac{\alpha - 1}{2\alpha - 1 - \beta} I^* + \frac{\alpha - \beta}{2\alpha - 1 - \beta} \bar{I};$$ (3.63)

$$\alpha = \frac{\Omega}{1+\Omega}\phi; \quad \beta = \frac{\Omega}{1+\Omega}\phi^2.$$

This is a cooperative solution corresponding to point G in Figure 3.11, at which the losses of the two regions are equal. Note that, under SSM, localities do not have autonomy to determine their investments, and cooperations of this kind between regions are imposed by the central government. However, this solution is not sustainable. Local governments do not passively accept their 'fates'. In an annual 'plan meeting' convened by the central planning authority, they will seek various ways to influence or bargain with the central government; even when the meeting stands adjourned, they may go canvassing 'old chief' for their local interests, in order to move the point G towards their sides. Suppose now that region A has some agents (for example, its ex-governor of province is promoted as vice prime minister) in the central government, or it knows better than other regions how to use both facts and 'words' in persuading the central authority to approve its investment plan. As a result, A gains its desired investment quota I_A^*. Partiality cannot be tolerated, and therefore other regions will rally together to complain or to 'protest'. As often as not it is just out of the considerations for impartiality that the central government has to go to point E by supplementing investment $I_B^*-I_B$ in other regions, say, B as a representative. This is meant to force the central government to set $\phi=1<\phi_A=\phi_B$ in its collective loss function (3.62), thinking that the same weight has to be attached to I_A and I_B, both regions' investments (we are reluctant to call them as instruments here, as they cannot be fully controlled by regions), in their targets. In this case, the solutions in equation (3.63) immediately become $I_A=I^*=I_A^*$ and $I_B=I^*=I_B^*$ (because $\alpha=\beta$). Obviously, point E makes both regions A and B worse than point G, as a result of non-cooperations between regions. But under SSM, point E is possibly the worst outcome the economy could have, since the degree to which local governments can influence the central counterpart is highly limited. Otherwise there is no difference between the SSM and the MSM.

While the story ends at point E under the SSM, it starts from point E under the MSM. Learning lessons from reality, a region usually thinks in this way: it is stupid to behave honestly not increasing its purchasing power, while others cheat and keep granting more loans to themselves. Thus with the effective right of the money supply and soft budget constraints, and as locals do not trust each other, they launch rounds of competition, pushing the economy well beyond point E. This is shown in Figure 3.12. At E, each region can get better off by moving to its reaction line F_A and F_B respectively. As the noncooperative game is being played out, the economy will eventually reach the Nash equilibrium point N, but at this point it is overheated, with local investment demand well exceeding resources available. The so called 'extra-budgetary investment' in China may be identified in Figure 3.12 as the extra investment beyond the points corresponding to E, i.e., I_A^* and I_B^*, while the investment amounts below I_A^* and I_B^* can be thought of as the budgetary or planned investment. Suppose that region B is aware of this ultimate outcome. Thus I_B^d is the likely investment demand of B, but what value I_B^d would take and whether it can be fully achieved depend on many uncertain factors, such as other regions' behaviour (reaction function), the stability of the central government's economic policies, the macroeconomic situation etc..

With the geometrical relationships shown in Figure 3.12, we are now in a position to derive the expression for $I_B^d - I_B^*$ in terms of $I_B^d - I_B^s$ for the investigation of expectation formation coming later. According to the reaction function of region B, we define:

$$\alpha_A = \frac{I_B^d - I_B^*}{I_A^d - \bar{I}_A}$$

where $I_A^d - \bar{I}_A$ can be expressed as:

$$I_A^d - \bar{I}_A = \frac{\phi_N}{1+\phi_N}(I_B^d - I_B^s) - (I_B^d - I_B^*)$$

Combining these two relations yields

$$I_B^d - I_B^* = \frac{\alpha_A}{1+\alpha_A} \frac{1+\phi_N}{\phi_N}(I_B^d - I_B^s) \qquad (3.64)$$

The above discussion is focused on region B. But there is no reason why region A will not behave like this, given that A and B share the same properties of a POE. Consequently, these results can be applied to any regions including B and A in a POE.

Having analyzed the investment controversies between locals and between locals and the central authority, we are now able to consider the formation of a local government's current expectations about market situation for its investment decisions. As local governments are all 'birds of a feather', we decide to drop the subscripts A and B. The local governments' desired capital stock at time t should be

$$K_t^* = \int_0^t I(\tau)e^{-\delta(t-\tau)}d\tau + \int_{t-1}^t I^*(\tau)e^{-\delta(t-\tau)}d\tau \qquad (3.65)$$

However, due to other localities also scrambling for investment resources, a local governments' desired investment at t may only partly be realized. Because of uncertainty in competitions, the local government expects at t-1 the investment resources available for it at t to be $(I^s)^e$. The corresponding expected capital stock at t is therefore

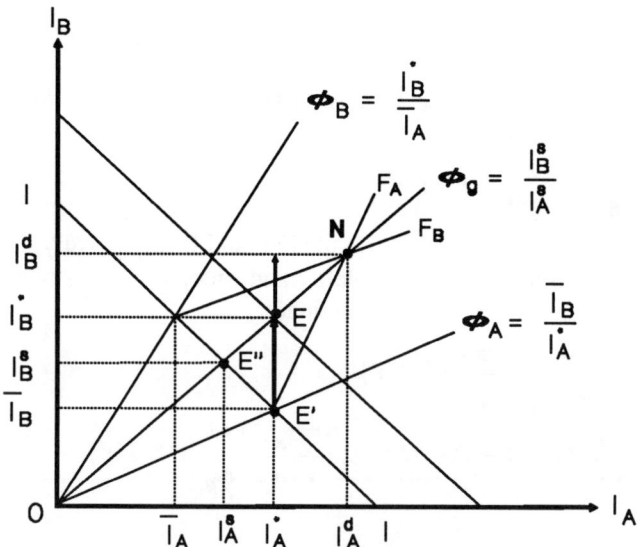

Figure 3.12 Conflicts between localities for investment

$$K_t^s = \int_0^{t-1} I(\tau)e^{-\delta(t-\tau)}d\tau + \int_{t-1}^{t} [I^s(\tau)]^e e^{-\delta(t-\tau)}d\tau \qquad (3.66)$$

The aim of expectation is nothing more than to take precautions. What would the local government do? In its view, the shortfall of realized investment arises simply because its purchasing power for investment goods is not sufficient enough. In other words, in order to achieve its optimal investment goods when it cannot get I* (due to its losses in competitions), it still has to prepare more money than initially needed, the extra money being I^d-I^*. Again because of uncertainty it would expect at t-1 the (eventually) necessary investment expenditures for t as below

$$K_t^d = \int_0^{t-1} I(\tau)e^{-\delta(t-\tau)}d\tau + \int_{t-1}^{t} [I^d(\tau)]^e e^{-\delta(t-\tau)}d\tau \qquad (3.67)$$

Here we make an additional assumption that the local government does not take into account any uncertain factors in choosing its desired investment I*, and leave the uncertain factors to be considered when forming its whole investment demand. This implies that the expectations about the desired investment should be the desired investment itself, i.e., $(I^*)^e=I^*$. By this assumption, it would not make any difference if we manipulate the integrated

function $(I^d)^e$ in the second integrating term in the following way:
$$(I^d)^e = I^* + (I^d)^e - I^* = I^* + (I^d)^e - (I^*)^e = I^* + (I^d - I^*)^e$$
Substitute this result into equation (3.67) which now becomes:
$$K^d = \int_0^{t-1} I(\tau)e^{-\delta(t-\tau)}d\tau + \int_{t-1}^{t} I^*(\tau)e^{-\delta(t-\tau)}d\tau + \int_{t-1}^{t} [I^d(\tau) - I^*(\tau)]^e e^{-\delta(t-\tau)}d\tau$$
$$= K_{-1} + \frac{e^\delta - 1}{\delta} I^* + \frac{e^\delta - 1}{\delta}(I^d - I^*)^e$$

Finally substituting (3.64) and (3.61) for I^d-I^* and I^* respectively in the above equation, and moving K_{-1} to the left hand side, the investment demand function of a local government is obtained:

$$I^d = \frac{e^\delta - 1}{\delta}[I^* + \frac{\alpha_A}{1+\alpha_A} \frac{1+\phi_N}{\phi_N}(I^d - I^s)^e]$$

$$= \frac{e^\delta - 1}{\delta}[\frac{\alpha}{\alpha+\beta}(T+CR-G) + \gamma(L^s - L) + \frac{\alpha_A}{1+\alpha_A}\frac{1+\phi_N}{\phi_N}(I^d - I^s)^e]$$
(3.68)

3.5 Investment demand and interest rates

The interest rate for investment credit is one of the costs of investment. Other conditions being equal, only if the gross returns of investment are larger than the investment costs, will the investment be carried out. Higher interest rates mean higher marginal costs and less profits to be earned, and thus reduces investment demand. This is the general relation between interest rates and investment described in the standard text book of economics. The question is: would this decreasing function of investment with respect to interest rates be relevant to the POE? This section is intended to answer the question.

First consider the centrally planned investment. If it is within the central government's fiscal ability to pay, the interest rate is no longer relevant. In the circumstances that the central government has to borrow money from public (by issuing 'construction bonds' and/or by getting a bank loan) to support its investment plan, it should in principle take the interest rate into account. The problem is, however, that the interest rate is either set by the government, or it is not endogenously determined by money demand/supply in financial markets (actually there are no such markets). In fact, it is usually in order to realise the planned accumulation rate and investment that the central government raises the 'planned interest rate' to attract more savings. In other words, the planned investment target determines the interest rate, not the other way round; the planned investment target itself is determined by other factors. Of course, the interest rate cannot be raised without limits. It is restricted by a ceiling which equals at most the expected returns on planned investment. Otherwise, the central government cannot afford to clear up its interest payment debts to public in the future. Below this ceiling, however, even large increases in interest rates will not affect the planned investment.

Unlike the central government, a local government (subunit) has no right to set interest rates, and what it can do is only to react to the changes in interest rates given exogenously. Some Chinese economists (for example, Zhou X. 1988, Bei D. 1988) thereupon argued that, in a POE, investment expansion, inappropriate resource allocation, and low efficiency are due to low interest rates; after economic reform the interest rate is still subject to control and therefore it does not reflect or regulate the demand for and supply of funds; and the interest rate ought to be raised to enter the range of high elasticity of investment demand. The underlying assumption of these arguments is that, once the interest rate reaches a certain level, investment demand will respond to it elastically, or the elasticity will become sufficiently high. These arguments forget one basic fact: in the pre-reform central planning system, although the nominal interest rate was very low, the real interest rate (or rental costs) of employing capital for state-owned enterprises could not be higher, as all profits had to be turned over to the state. Despite this, we still observed the 'almost insatiable demand' of enterprises for investment resources as described by Kornai (1980). Consequently, the assertion that there exists a range of interest rates in which the investment demand in a POE is elastic to interest rates is highly questionable.

Referring back to Figure 3.10, it is noticeable that, in a certain period the entire resources of a POE is definite (bound by a horizontal side I of the box), but the quantitative limit of the resources a subunit (region) can obtain is indefinite (variable within the box). This quantitative limit is independent of material/technological conditions, and of the boundary of property rights (because subunits are all in the same POE). If we regard the material productive resources as the *source of income*, then the softness of budget constraint of subunits can be more generally defined as the *indefiniteness of the sources of income of the subunits in the POE*. The interest rate is, in the final analysis, the price of a production factor. As a factor price, it plays a role in changing the relation between factor costs to regulate the employment proportion of resources with different degrees of scarcity. Higher interest rates result in higher rental costs of capital, which in turn lead people to use less capital. This substitution effect is true only in the circumstances where the source of income is definite (the budget constraint is hard). For a subunit

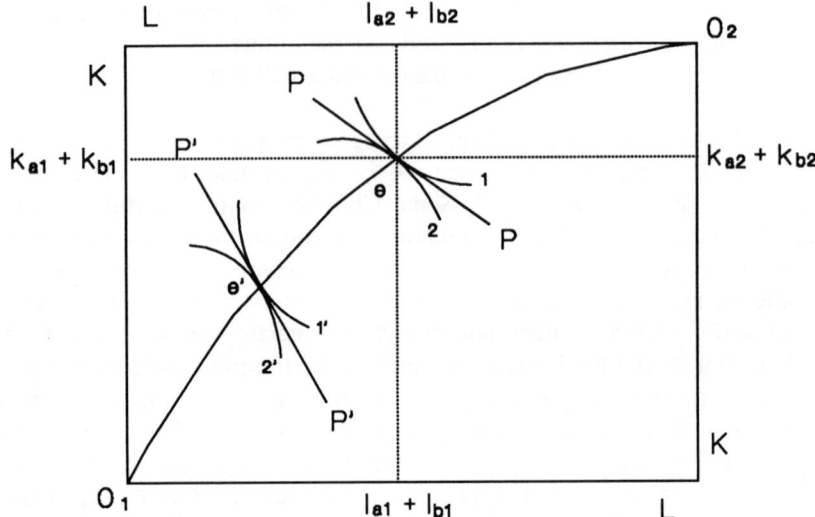

Figure 3.13 Definiteness of the whole POE's income sources

in a POE, however, investment does not mean, or is not viewed as, first of all, a kind of cost, but rather a source of income, or a way of occupying a larger share in the total scarce capital resources. The more scarce the capital resources are, the stronger the desire to have a larger share. Higher interest rates can restrain investment expenditures as costs conditional on the definite source of income, but cannot suppress the demand for capital as this source of income is indefinite.

To make this point more clearly, let us first look at box diagrams drawn in Figure 3.13. The lengths of the O_1L and O_1K axes represent total labour and capital services available for the whole POE. Curves representing the output of goods 1 are drawn relative to the origin O_1, and those representing the output of goods 2 relative to the origin O_2. $O_1 O_2$ is a production contract curve and point e is supposed to be Pareto optimal. This box tells us that, given the definite capital endowments K, the agent, as the owner of the entire K in the economy, allocates the capital resources between industries 1 and 2 in accordance with Pareto criterion. Thus the slope of the line PP gives the ratio of the price of labour services (i.e., wage rate) to that of capital services (i.e., interest rate) in a Pareto optimum equilibrium. If the economy happens to be in any other point, say e' than e, the agent may retrieve the optimal resource allocation by using a device, say, adjusting the relative factor prices P'P' to PP. In this sense the interest rate can play a role in regulating the

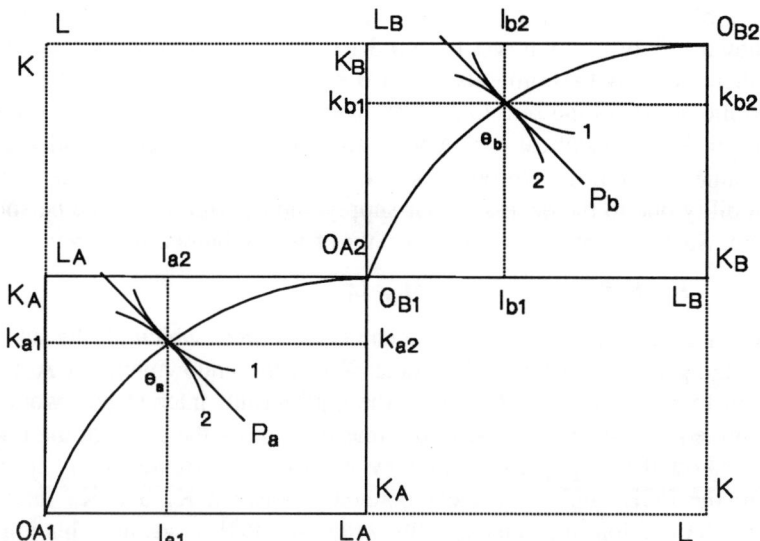

Figure 3.14 Indefiniteness of subunits' income sources (1)

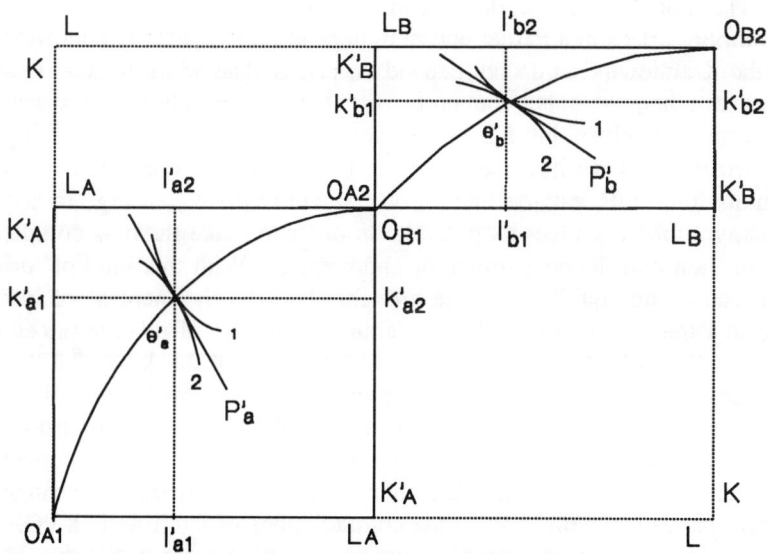

Figure 3.15 Indefiniteness of subunits' income sources (2)

demand for capital services.

What would happen if a subunit's endowments or income sources were changeable or even erratic? To answer this question let us look at a situation as shown jointly in Figures 3.14 and 3.15. Again for simplicity we assume that there are only two subunits A and B in the economy; these two subunits are homogenous in the sense that they have same amount of labour services $(0_A \, L_A = 0_B \, L_B)$, identical preferences, and all produce goods 1 and 2 using the same technology (production function). Also we assume labour immobility due to the excess labour supply and the rigidity of the personnel system. Since the economy consists only of two subunits, we have:

$$K_A + K_B = K_A' + K_B' = K; \quad L_A + L_B = L;$$

Now what seems to be scarce is the capital resources which all the subunits are longing for as a source of income. When the endowments of A and B happen to be K_A and K_B ($K_A = K_B$), the equilibrium interest rate would be determined by either the slope of the line $P_a P_a$ or by the slope of the line $P_b P_b$ (because they equal each other by assumption). However, by its very nature the POE implies no clear boundary between K_A and K_B. In other words, the relation of property rights within the POE is vague. This implies that K_A and K_B are indefinite and that there could be other possible values, for example, K_A' and K_B'. In this case, the original 'equilibrium' interest rate determined by $P_a P_a$ (or $P_b P_b$) would immediately disappear. In subunit A it becomes set by $P_a' P_a'$, and in B by $P_b' P_b'$.

The above considerations lead to the following conclusions. The equilibrium prices in a Pareto optimum depend on the given K endowments, but the K endowments do not depend on prices. The adjustment of relative prices can help to solve the problems of resources allocation when the endowments is given, but has no solution to the problem of determining the endowments. As we have seen before, the essence of contention between subunits in a POE rests on their strong 'quantity drive', an urge to acquire as many public resources as possible, in order to make them as component part of their own income source or endowments. With this kind of 'drive', there can be no equilibrium state brought about by the increase of interest rates to Pareto optimum levels. Any equilibrium state of relative prices will be immediately broken by investment competitions of this kind, and the rise in nominal interest rates will be immediately offset by the inflation rate resulting from the monetary competition and investment expansions of subunits. In the final analysis, it is the self-interest distribution (endowment distribution) which determines the change of relative prices, and changes in relative prices can neither solve the contradictions of interests in a POE nor solve a series of economic problems arising from these contradictions. In our opinion, therefore, however high the interest rate is, the investment demand

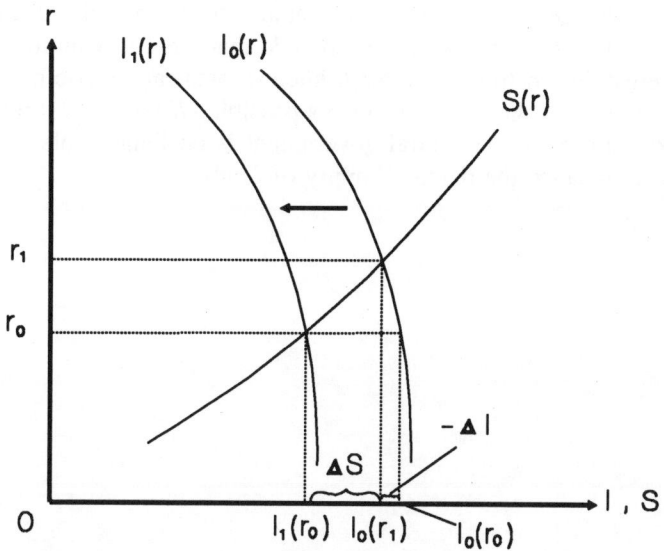

Figure 3.16 **Interest-rate rigidity of the POE's investment demand**

of economic agents in a POE has had a very low elasticity, if not being completely inelastic.

The interest-rate rigidity of investment demand is illustrated in Figure 3.16. The slope of the investment curve I(r) is quite steep. If the interest rate rises from r_1 to r_0, the investment demand would decrease by only -ΔI or $I(r_1)$-$I(r_0)$. So the interest rate device has fairly limited efficacy in regulating investment demand in the POE. This is why the central government usually adopts administrative means or other economic devices to suppress the investment demand of subunits. In Figure 3.16 this is meant to shift the investment curve $I_0(r)$ inward to the position of $I_1(r)$, rather than to move the investment demand along the curve $I_0(r)$. Besides, we also observe from Figure 3.16 that, in a POE the interest rate instrument has an asymmetric role in the relation between the demand and supply of funds: while it can effectively regulate savings and the supply of funds, it cannot effectively reduce investment and the demand for investment funds. When interest rates rise by r_0-r_1, savings increases by ΔS>>ΔI. This is not to deny that in a POE the demand and supply of funds can be balanced through interest rate adjustment, but this is a kind of one-way adjustment: supply-side adjustment. In the private-ownership economy, the adjustment of interest rate affects simultaneously both the demand and supply of funds, so financial markets can rapidly approach a state of equilibrium, and the magnitude of the change in interest rates need not be great. Unlike the private-ownership economy, the POE has to change interest rates substantially to balance the demand and supply of funds. Therefore we may conclude that there is a limited the role for the interest rate instrument to play: interest rates cannot rise indefinitely, being constrained by the debt repayments possible. When interest rates reach some maximum level, the central government is no longer able to use this instrument to balance the demand/supply of funds.

Notes

1. In this study, those factors such as production technology, capital equipment, resource conditions, labour force, capital accumulation, consumption preferences etc. are classified as material/technological factors. Those factors such as social economic relations, economic operation mechanisms, economic interest contradictions, economic management levels etc. are classified as socio-economic factors.
2. The public ownership is defined by a set of *internal* relations: (1) The equal and undifferentiated 'custody' or 'possession' rights of all or each piece of the means of production (non-labour factors of production or material productive assets, such as capital goods and natural resources) for all individuals who compose the economy; (2) Equal shares of non-labour income for all individuals, while any income differences are, or are supposed to be, attributed to, and only to, the labour contributions; (3) Sharing, by the whole economy, of the loss or risk of capital used in any single production unit; (4) Institutionally endowed right for all individuals who comprise the economy to work or to be 'employed'.
3. In the traditional Keynesian macroeconomics, it is aggregate demand that determines income. This theory is based on the assumption that there exists idle production capacity (labour and capital) in an economy. A POE is certainly not the case. As Kornai put it, the traditional socialist economy is characterized by resource constraints. Thus the theory that aggregate demand determines the total level of output is not applicable here.
4. Here the planner is defined as: the planner=the agent of ownership=the economic body=the government-political body.
5. Thus in period $t=T$, for example, there live two generations. The young are born in T, while the old were born in T-1. So the consumption of the young is $c_{1,T}$, and the consumption of the old is $c_{2,(T-1)+1}$ or $c_{2,T}$.
6. In Benthamite fashion, the central planner weights utility by the size of each generation so that $(1+\Gamma)=(1+n)^{-1}$. If the growth rate of population is positive, then Γ is negative.
7. Recall that θ is assumed to be strictly positive in discussions of individuals' optima.
8. It can easily be proved that k_1 is larger than, equal to, or less than k_2 iff $f'(k_1)$ is less than, equal to, or larger than $f'(k_2)$, provided that $f''(k)<0$ holds.
9. Define total consumption c_t as $c_{1,t}+(1+n)^{-1}c_{2,t}$ and denote steady state values of c and k by c^* and k^*, respectively. In steady state, with $dk/dt=0$, we have from (3.10) $c^*=f(k^*)-nk^*$, and the first-order condition

gives $f'(k^*)-n=0$. When the marginal product of capital is equal to the growth rate of population, the steady state consumption per capita is maximized.

10. The socialist countries such as the ex-USSR, the PRC and other Eastern European countries, all experienced a period in which the people's consumption was suppressed to a could-not-be-lower level, in order to obtain could-not-be-more capital accumulation and high growth rate. Brus W. (1972) names this stage as the 'socialist primitive accumulation'.

11. Fan G. et al (1990, p. 156) assume that the utility function is of logarithmic form, the production function is of linear form, and both the discount rate and the initial capital stock is zero. The maximization problem of both individuals and planner then becomes:

$$Max \ U=u(c_1)+u(c_2)=\ln c_1 +\ln c_2$$

subject to:

$$c_1+k_1=y_0$$

and

$$c_2=f(k_1)=rk_1+w$$

where all the variables are in per capita terms. The optimal solution for k is:

$$k_1^*=\frac{1}{2}(y_0-\frac{w}{r})$$

which is positively related to marginal product of capital r. If, however, an alternative production function of constant-return-to-scale is chosen here, the optimal solution for k becomes:

$$k_1^*=\frac{\alpha}{1+\alpha}y_0$$

which is independent of marginal product of capital $f'(k_1)$.

12. (a) Given

$$f'>0; \ f''<0; \ k^*>k_{v\omega}^*>0$$

and according to theorem of the mean, we have:

$$\frac{f(k_{v\omega}^*)-f(0)}{k_{v\omega}^*-0}=\frac{f(k_{v\omega}^*)}{k_{v\omega}^*}=f'(\xi_1) \quad (0<\xi_1<k_{v\omega}^*);$$

$$\frac{f(k^*)-f(k_{v\omega}^*)}{k^*-k_{v\omega}^*}=f'(\xi_2) \quad (k_{v\omega}^*<\xi_2<k^*).$$

Since f''(·)<0 and $\xi_1<\xi_2$, therefore f'(ξ_1)>f'(ξ_2), namely,

$$\frac{f(k_{v\omega}^*)}{k_{v\omega}^*}>\frac{f(k^*)-f(k_{v\omega}^*)}{k^*-k_{v\omega}^*}$$

Rearranging this inequality gives:

$$n\frac{k^*}{f(k^*)}>n\frac{k_{v\omega}^*}{f(k_{v\omega}^*)} \Rightarrow a_g>a_v.$$

(b) Define $g(k)=k/f(k)$. Again the theorem of the mean leads to:

$$\because \frac{k^*}{f(k^*)}-\frac{k_{v\omega}^*}{f(k_{v\omega}^*)}>0; \quad k^*-k_{v\omega}^*>0$$

$$\therefore g'(\xi)=\frac{g(k^*)-g(k_{v\omega}^*)}{k^*-k_{v\omega}^*}=\frac{\dfrac{k^*}{f(k^*)}-\dfrac{k_{v\omega}^*}{f(k_{v\omega}^*)}}{k^*-k_{v\omega}^*}>0$$

Replacing ξ by k, and without loosing generality, we get:

$$g'(k)=\frac{d}{dk}[\frac{k}{f(k)}]>0$$

(c) Differentiating (3.13) with respect to k^* yields

$$f''(k^*)=(1+n)\frac{d\Gamma}{dk^*}$$

$$\because f''(k^*)<0, \quad \therefore \frac{dk^*}{d\Gamma}=(\frac{d\Gamma}{dk^*})^{-1}=\frac{1+n}{f''(k^*)}<0.$$

Similarly

$$\frac{dk_{v\omega}^*}{d\theta}<0.$$

13. The basic assumption is that capital is of 'vintage' form so that, at a given time, investment i consists of new equipment whereas the capital

stock k_c is made up of successive layers of older equipment. Output is then in two parts: $\pi = y(k_c) + i^\alpha$ (see Allen 1982, p. 69).

14. All the reasons why $\Gamma < \theta$ can be applied here.
15. In the reduced form, ΔM is expressed as

$$\Delta M = \frac{(1+\alpha_k)(1+\alpha_c)(z_g - z_s)}{1 - \alpha_k \alpha_c} I$$

Taking logarithmic form, it becomes:

$$\log \Delta M = \log[(1+\alpha_k)(1+\alpha_c)(z_g - z_s)] - \log(1 - \alpha_k \alpha_c) + \log I$$

The following four inequalities hold:

$$\frac{1}{\Delta M} \frac{\partial \Delta M}{\partial z_g} = \frac{1}{z_g - z_s} + \frac{1}{1+\alpha_k} \frac{\partial \alpha_k}{\partial z_g} + \frac{\alpha_c}{1 - \alpha_k \alpha_c} \frac{\partial \alpha_k}{\partial z_g} > 0;$$

$$\because \frac{\partial \alpha_k}{\partial z_g} = \frac{\Omega_k}{1+\Omega_k} \frac{1}{(1-z_g)^2} > 0; \quad z_g - z_s > 0; \quad \alpha_k \alpha_c < 1.$$

and

$$\frac{1}{\Delta M} \frac{\partial \Delta M}{\partial z_s} = \frac{1}{(1+\alpha_c)} \frac{\partial \alpha_c}{\partial z_s} - \frac{1}{z_g - z_s} + \frac{\alpha_k}{1 - \alpha_k \alpha_c} \frac{\partial \alpha_c}{\partial z_s} < 0;$$

$$\because \frac{\partial \alpha_c}{\partial z_s} = -\frac{\Omega_c}{1+\Omega_c} \frac{1}{z_s^2} < 0.$$

and

$$\frac{1}{\Delta M} \frac{\partial \Delta M}{\partial \alpha_k} = \frac{1}{1+\alpha_k} + \frac{\alpha_c}{1 - \alpha_k \alpha_c} > 0;$$

and

$$\frac{1}{\Delta M} \frac{\partial \Delta M}{\partial \alpha_c} = \frac{1}{1+\alpha_c} + \frac{\alpha_k}{1 - \alpha_k \alpha_c} > 0.$$

16. Our reason for identifying I_c. (investment in the consumption goods sector or in the down-stream sector as will be termed in the later chapters dealing with empirical studies) with the investment of local governments is that, under MSM following the launching of economic reform, the decentralized investments whose proportions increased substantially were made mainly in down-stream sectors by local governments and by those state-owned enterprises and organizations under the local governments' control.

4 Econometric model of investment-production block and its estimation

4.1 Introduction

In this chapter, a complete disequilibrium-type demand/supply model of the investment and production sector is econometrically formulated and estimated for China using annual data. The estimation period is 1979-1989 for all but one equation (the production function is estimated for 1967-1989). There are two reasons for this difference in estimation period. First, since 1979 economic reform has brought about so many drastic changes in China's economic structure, especially in the investment sector, any extension of the investment model into the pre-reform period would have been highly questionable. In the pre-reform period, the state sovereignty mechanism gave no role for local governments, enterprises and individuals to play. It was the planner (the central government) who determined the economic (investment) variables. Thus in constructing the pre-reform investment model, it is sufficient to have one behavioral equation for the demand side, which represents the central planner's demand behaviour (the private sector was too small to be considered). Nevertheless, in the post-reform era, the multi-sovereignty mechanism led to a situation where subunits also became independent investment decision makers. Moreover, the non-state sector grew so rapidly that its investment behaviour can no longer be ignored. Therefore, we should have three, rather than one, investment demand equations which reflect *different* investment behaviour of three main economic agents (the central government, local governments and the non-state sector) respectively in the post-reform investment model. Corresponding to these changes, almost all the explanatory variables and auxiliary equations in the post-reform investment model do not and presumably should not appear in the pre-reform one. This further makes the post-reform investment model considerably different from the pre-reform one, not only in the number of variables (or parameter values) but also in the number of equations involved. Thus the post and pre-reform investment models would have to be estimated *separately* over two different periods, i.e., the pre-1979 and post-1979 periods respectively. In this sense, it is both economically implausible and econometrically intractable to extend the post-reform investment model back to the pre-reform period. However, the above considerations do not necessarily prevent the production function from being extended to the pre-reform period. What the economic reform had brought about is shifts in parameters of the production function, and it should not change the number of production function at aggregate level (one) and of explanatory variables involved (three in our case). Of course, the hypothesis of shifts in the production function will be tested. Unlike the investment block, there should be no estimation difficulties if we introduce dummy variables to capture the impacts of reforms and then estimate *one* equation over *two* different periods.

Second, statistical data on the most basic and important variables involved in the investment block (such as I, IL, IP etc.) were only available for the period under investigation. Those pre-1979 data were not officially collected (or published). When this empirical study started in 1991, the most updated data source we had at hand was the Statistical Year Book of China (1990) in which the data start from 1979, and are updated to 1989. Even for the period under investigation, there are, however, still one or two data points missing for a few variables, and they have to be constructed. For the production function, on the other hand, all the data needed covering both the pre-reform and post-reform periods are in good supply. They can be obtained either from official sources, or from other researchers' studies with some recalculations.

The reasons given here can also be applied to chapter 5, where we extend the consumption block to the pre-reform period as well, despite the studies of investment block are restricted to the post-reform period. The fact that the investment, production, consumption and price blocks have different estimation periods will not cause any problems in our policy simulations in chapter 6, since they all cover the same period from 1979 to 1989, and the parameter estimates in all blocks obtained for this period will be used there.

4.2 Structure of the model

The model consists of some behavioral equations together with disequilibrium indicators and identities. It is initially specified as follows:

(i) Investment block
$$DI=\alpha_1+\beta_1 DC+\gamma_1 DIL+\delta_1 DIP+\sigma_1 GEE+\epsilon_1 \tag{4.1}$$
$$DIL=\alpha_2+\beta_2 FUND+\gamma_2 UNE+\delta_2(DI-SI)^e+\sigma_2 Z1+\epsilon_2 \tag{4.2}$$
$$DIP=\alpha_3+\beta_3 RNRTP+\gamma_3 P^e_{+1}+\delta_3 INV_{-1}+\sigma_3 RI+\epsilon_3 \tag{4.3}$$
$$SI=\alpha_4+\beta_4 \Delta NI+\gamma_4(LOS_{-1}+LOF_{-1})+\delta_4 GEE+\sigma_4 IMP+\epsilon_4 \tag{4.4}$$
$$IMP=\alpha_5+\beta_5 NI_{-1}+\gamma_5 DEE_{-1}+\delta_5 OPE+\sigma_5 \Delta EXC+\epsilon_5 \tag{4.5}$$
$$FUND=\alpha_6+\beta_6(LOS+LOF)+\gamma_6 REB+\delta_6 Z3+\epsilon_6 \tag{4.6}$$
$$RTSP=\alpha_7+\beta_7(LOS+LOP)+\gamma_7 DC_{-1}+\delta_7 RPS+\sigma_7 Z1+\epsilon_7 \tag{4.7}$$
$$INV=\alpha_8+\beta_8 NI+\gamma_8 \Delta NI_{-1}+\delta_8 \Delta DEE+\epsilon_8 \tag{4.8}$$
$$RNRTP=RTSP-WLP-TP \tag{4.9}$$
$$DEE=DI-SI+DC-SC \tag{4.10}$$
$$RI=NRI-\frac{(P_{+1}-P)^e}{P} \tag{4.11}$$

(ii) Production block
$$\log(NI)=\alpha_9+\beta_{91}\log\overline{L}+\beta_{92}Z2\log\overline{L}+\gamma_{91}\log\overline{K}+\gamma_{92}Z2\log\overline{K}+\delta_{91}\log\overline{GEE}+\delta_{92}Z2\log\overline{GEE}+\epsilon_9 \tag{4.12}$$
$$K=K_{-1}+\Delta K \tag{4.13}$$
$$\Delta K=\alpha_{10}R+\beta_{10}R_{-1}+\gamma_{10}R_{-2}+\delta_{10}R_{-3}+\sigma_{10}R_{-4}+\phi_{10}R_{-5}+\epsilon_{10} \tag{4.14}$$
$$R=I-DPR \tag{4.15}$$

(iii) Disequilibrium indicators
$$I=\min\{DI, SI\} \tag{4.16}$$
$$P_{+1}-P=\frac{1}{\theta_{11}}(DIL-IL), \quad \text{if } DIL>IL \tag{4.17}$$
$$P_{+1}-P=\frac{1}{\theta_{12}}(DIP-IP), \quad \text{if } DIP>IP \tag{4.18}$$
$$P_{+1}-P=\frac{1}{\theta_{11}+\theta_{12}}(DI-I), \quad \text{if } DI>I \tag{4.19}$$
$$SI-I=\theta_{13}Z1, \quad \text{if } SI>I \tag{4.20}$$

(iv) List of variables

PK	Aggregate price index of investment goods; 1952=1.00 (**ZH, ARCO**)
DI	Aggregate investment demand in the economy, deflated by PK, in billion yuan
DIL	Investment demand of state-owned downstream sectors (as a proxy for investment demand of local governments), deflated by PK, in billion yuan
IL	ISS-IU; Actual investment in the state-owned downstream sectors, deflated by PK, in billion yuan
ISS	Actual investment in the state sectors, deflated by PK, in billion yuan (**SYBC**)
IU	Actual investment in the state-owned upstream sectors (including 1. agriculture; 2. heavy industry; 3. transportation, postal and telecommunication services), deflated by PK, in billion yuan (**SYBC, ARCO**)
DIP	Investment demand of non-state sectors, deflated by PK, in billion yuan
IP	I-ISS; Actual investment in the non-state sectors, deflated by PK, in billion yuan
SI	Aggregate investment supply in the economy, deflated by PK, in billion yuan
I	Total actual investment in fixed assets in the economy, deflated by PK, in billion yuan (**GU, SYBC**)
DC	Demand for consumption goods (retail sales) at constant prices in billion yuan (**SYBC**)
IMP	Total imports, deflated by PK, in billion yuan (**SYBC**)
RTSP	Retail sales of non-state sectors at constant prices in billion yuan (**SYBC**)
RNRTP	Proxy for net returns of non-state sectors at constant prices
P	Aggregate price index of retail sales; 1969=1.00 (**SYBC**)
UNE	Total unemployment in urban areas in tens of thousands (**SYBC**)
WLP	Wage and salary income in non-state sectors + self-employment income of non-farmers at constant prices in billion yuan (**SYBC**)
TP	Tax revenue of government from non-state sectors at constant prices in billion yuan (**SYBC**)
OPE	IMP/NI as proxy for the degree of openness of the economy.
REB	Ratio of extra-budgetary revenue to budgetary revenue, as proxy for the degree to which the economic decision-making power is decentralized (**SYBC**)
RPS	Indicator of the degree to which non-state sectors grow, proxied by the ratio of retail sales of non-state sectors to that of state sectors

	(SYBC)
DEE	Total excess demand in domestic markets at constant prices in billion yuan
ΔDEE	DEE-DEE$_{-1}$
RI	Real interest rates on households' time deposits
NRI	Nominal interest rates on households time deposits (**ACFB, LIHU, ARCO**)
FUND	Total extra-budgetary funds, deflated by PK, in billion yuan (**SYBC, ARCO**)
NI	Index of national income; 1952=100 (**SYBC**)
ΔNI	NI-NI$_{-1}$
K	Total fixed assets in the economy, deflated by PK, in billion yuan (**ZH, ARCO**); $\bar{K}=(K+K_{-1})/2$
ΔK	Effective increase in fixed assets, deflated by PK, in billion yuan
R	Accumulation of fixed assets, deflated by PK, in billion yuan (**SYBC**)
INV	Changes in inventory stocks (accumulation of circulating assets), deflated by PK, in billion yuan (**SYBC**)
GEE	Government expenditures on economic construction, deflated by PK, in billion yuan (**SYBC**); $\overline{GEE}=(GEE+GEE_{-1})/2$
EXC	Exchange rate, yuan/dollar (**ACFT, ARCO**)
ΔEXC	EXC-EXC$_{-1}$
LOS	Working capital loans to state sectors, deflated by PK, in billion yuan (1. industrial production loans; 2. industrial supply and marketing enterprises and material supply department loans; 3. commercial enterprise loans; 4. construction enterprise loans), (**ACFB**)
LOF	Fixed assets loans to state sectors, deflated by PK, in billion yuan (**ACFB**)
LOP	Loans to non-state sectors, deflated by PK, in billion yuan (collective-owned enterprise loans and individual business loans), (**ACFB**)
DPR	I-R; Depreciation of total fixed assets, deflated by PK, in billion yuan
L	Total employees in the economy, tens of thousands (**SYBC**); $\bar{L}=(L+L_{-1})/2$
Z1	Dummy variable (Z1=1, 1989; Z1=0, otherwise)
Z2	Dummy variable (Z2=0, 1968-1978; Z2=1, 1979-1989)
Z3	Dummy variable (Z3=1, 1980-82,89; Z3=0, otherwise)
ε	Error terms of behavioral equations

α,β,γ,δ,σ,φ,θ Structural parameters of the model
(For the abbreviations **SYBC, ACFB, ACFT, ARCO, ZH** and **GU**, please

refer to Appendix 4A.)

In the above system, the following variables are, at the present stage, treated as exogenous: DC, UNE, WLP, TP, RPS, GEE, NRI, OPE, EXC, REB, LOS, LOF, LOP, L, as well as DPR. Nevertheless, the variable DC, although treated as exogenous in the investment-production block, is regarded as endogenous when the model is extended to include a consumption block. Similarly, several types of endogenous variables can be distinguished, as a consequence of the disequilibrium assumption. The variables DI, DIL and DIP are unobservable when the relevant agents fail to realize their desired levels of investment. On the other hand, the variable SI is not observed in the presence of excess supply of investment goods. (DI-SI)^e is a variable which can be classified as 'twice unobservable': first because it is an expectations variable, and second because expectations are formed on an unobservable variable (DI-SI).

4.3 Specification of the behavioural equations in the model

The aggregate investment demand is explained by (4.1) as a behavioural equation rather than as an identity. Referring back to chapter 3, we can rewrite the theoretical model of aggregate investment demand (3.57) below:

$$I' = \frac{(1+\alpha)a_g - \alpha(1+\beta)a_v}{1-\alpha\beta + \beta(1+\alpha)a_g - (1+\beta)a_v} C + \frac{(1+\alpha_k)(1+\alpha_c)(z_g - z_s)}{1-\alpha_k\alpha_c + \alpha_c(1+\alpha_k)z_g - (1+\alpha_c)z_s} I_c'$$

$$= I'(C, \Gamma, \theta, \omega, \Omega_g, \Omega_v, I_c, R, r, \Omega_k, \Omega_c)$$

where

$$\frac{\partial I'}{\partial C} > 0, \frac{\partial I'}{\partial \Gamma} < 0, \frac{\partial I'}{\partial \theta} < 0, \frac{\partial I'}{\partial \omega} < 0, \frac{\partial I'}{\partial \Omega_g} > 0, \frac{\partial I'}{\partial \Omega_v} < 0$$

$$\frac{\partial I'}{\partial I_c'} > 0, \frac{\partial I'}{\partial R} < 0, \frac{\partial I'}{\partial r} > 0, \frac{\partial I'}{\partial \Omega_k} > 0, \frac{\partial I'}{\partial \Omega_c} > 0$$

It tells us that, due to various interest conflicts, the multi-sovereignty mechanism and non-cooperation between economic agents, aggregate investment demand is a function of consumption demand, the investment demand of the consumption goods sectors, both the central government's policy stance and individuals' and subunits' preferences, and the strength of the effect of each instrument variable on the state of the underlying system (see section 3.2). According to this theoretical conclusion, DC is certainly the first candidate as a regressor, the sign of which should be positive. As for the investment demand of the consumption goods sectors, it is represented by DIL and DIP separately, because state-owned downstream sectors and non-state sectors are mainly engaged in producing consumption goods, and we believe that the role of DIL should be stronger than that of DIP in conflicts for investment resources. Equation (3.57) has also postulated positive signs for DIL and DIP. The central government's preference variables (Γ and R) are highly subjective reflecting its policy stance, and are thus embodied in GEE. As we stated in chapter 3, the lower the values Γ and R take, the higher capital accumulation rate the central government desires; and therefore, the more GEE it will have to spend in the direction of economic construction. So we expect that $\partial DI/\partial GEE>0$, though $\partial I/\partial \Gamma <0$ and $\partial I/\partial R<0$ in (3.57). Other variables, such as the individual discount rate (θ) and income illusion (ω), the strength of the effect of each instrument variable on the state of the underlying system (Ω_g, Ω_v, Ω_k and Ω_c), and the subunits' discount rate r, are all assumed to be institutionally determined. Since institutional arrangements change slowly in the short-run, they are regarded as relatively constant in this exercise, and should be reflected in the intercept. Hence equation (4.1) turns the theoretical model (3.57) into an econometric model which enables us to test the theoretical hypotheses.

Although the formation of aggregate investment demand has been theoretically explained in the previous chapter, a brief account of historical observations about the central government's investment behaviour will clarify its working. First, when working out an overall plan for the economy, the central government usually gives a top priority to its desired accumulation rate. Before reform, this priority was relatively easily realized since it was only the central government which has authority to determine all the economic variables. The economic reform, aimed first to delegate power to a lower level, enables individuals to acquire a larger share of national income for consumption purposes by pressing sub-units' decision-making body. So consumption funds have kept increasing during the 1980s. Before the economy reaches an excessively overheated state, the central government has always added more investment funds to fulfil its desire. There has been no other alternative measures for the central government to take, unless it decides to retrieve all the powers given to sub-units, but that would oppose the direction of reform. So controversies have often arisen between hardliners who blame the reform for leading to an out of control economy, and reformers who advocate further reform to establish self-check mechanisms concerned with consumption funds in subunits. Second, upstream sectors (including agriculture, heavy industry, transportation, postal and telecommunication services) are, from the central government's point of view, the infrastructure and lifeline of the national economy, and therefore have been all along under its control, in regard to their activities of investment, production, marketing, and price-setting etc.. After launching the economic reform, the decentralized investments (whose proportion has been getting increasingly important) were made by local governments and enterprises mainly in downstream sectors for quick returns. This has led to severe imbalances and bottlenecks in industrial structure. Shortages appearing inside the system compelled the central government to plan intensive investment in upstream sectors, trying to restore and maintain balance. Even self-raised investment funds of upstream sectors were brought into line with the central plan (see the Chinese Economic System Reform Research Institute (CESRRI), 1988). Consequently, the selection of the four variables in equation (4.1) has historical merit as well.

Equation (4.2), a behavioural relation of investment for local governments, is formulated on the basis of the theoretical study in section 3.4. Recall equation (3.68) which is rewritten as follows for convenience:

$$I^d = \frac{e^\delta - 1}{\delta}[\frac{\alpha}{\alpha + \beta}(T + CR - G) + \gamma(L^s - L) + \frac{\alpha_A}{1 + \alpha_A}\frac{1 + \phi_N}{\phi_N}(I^d - I^s)^e]$$

This relation says that the investment demand of local governments[1] is positively related to the investment funds available, T+CR-G, excess labour supply, L^s-L, in localities and expectations of shortage in the investment goods markets. Coming to the econometric formulation, we replace the variable I^d by DIL. This is because exactly how much local governments spend annually on investment is unfortunately unknown due to lack of relevant data. The alternative way to conduct an empirical study of local governments' investment behaviour is to examine investment in state-owned downstream sectors. The reasons have been mentioned earlier. T+CR-G is a theoretical variable and is not observed. We use the variable FUND in its place. This can be justified in the following ways. First, as many previous studies have shown, local governments are initiators of extrabudgetary investment (see, for example, Reynolds 1987; Zhong 1990). Second, statistical data shows that the ratio of extrabudgetary investment funds to total investment expenditures in state sectors grew from 43% in 1979 to 87% in 1989. This implies that T+CR-G, the local governments' investment funds, has increasingly become of an extrabudgetary nature. Thus we assume that there is a close relation between T+CR-G and FUND. The excess labour supply L^s-L is not intended to be explained in our model, and thus is replaced by UNE which is exogenous. It reflects the effect of the local governments' intention to mop up the unemployment level on their investment decisions. In accordance with equation (3.68), current expectations about the market situation should also be considered, which leads to introduction into (4.2) of the expectations variable (DI-SI)^e. The signs of these three regressors should all be positive. Dummy variable Z1 (Z1=1 for

1989; zero otherwise) expresses the effect of the drastic austerity measures adopted by the central government in 1989 onward to bring in the soaring economy for a hard landing, and so its sign is negative.

Equation (4.3) states that the investment demand of non-state sectors is affected positively by net returns and future expectations of output prices, and negatively by inventory stocks and the real interest rate. The observations on net returns of non-state enterprises are not directly available, and their retail sales minus wage costs and taxes are used instead in the estimation process. Circulating assets accumulation, according to the Statistical Yearbook of China, refers to the increase in inventory stocks in the whole economy each year, and thus acts as a barometer of the macroeconomic climate for the investor. The real interest rate is expected to have a negative influence on investment demand, because unlike state-owned sectors non-state sectors are mainly market-guided and subject to a hard budget constraint.

Equation (4.4) is a hypothesis about aggregate investment on the supply side. It is assumed that aggregate investment supply is subject to the requirement of economic growth, injection of working capital loans as well as fixed assets loans in the previous period into the economy, government's expenditures on economic construction and imports. Prior to economic reform, investment supply usually corresponded to a bargaining position of the planning authority and was primarily determined by the planned growth rate. This has changed gradually since 1979. On the one hand, a sizable fraction of investment goods are produced by those state-owned enterprises which have not yet been completely freed from administrative interference by the government. The actual growth of domestic production ΔNI is, therefore, a factor determining production decisions of the investment goods producers. On the other hand, since state-owned enterprises are given a certain discretion to organize production activity, they respond as well to the demand signals generated by the money supply in the previous year ($LOS_{-1}+LOF_{-1}$) and government expenditures GEE. But government expenditures on economic construction immediately stimulate the supply, while working capital and fixed assets loans are assumed to have a lagged impact on the supply. Imports IMP are taken as an additional regressor in the investment supply equation, because they are mainly investment goods (investment goods account for between 70% and 86% of total imports in the 1980s).

So far we have provided detailed accounts of specification for the main equations concerning investment demand and supply. To complete the model for policy simulations in chapter 6, the sub-model of the investment block is extended to include four more auxiliary behavioral equations (4.5)-(4.8) which link the investment model to the consumption model, and endogenous variables to some policy instruments and institutional variables. In equation

(4.5) imports depend positively on lagged national income, NI_{-1}, lagged total excess demand in domestic markets, DEE_{-1}, and the degree of openness of the economy treated as an exogenously institutional variable, but negatively on changes in the official exchange rate. Equation (4.6) tells us that the extrabudgetary funds FUND is a positive function of total credits advanced to the state sectors (LOS+LOF), and the degree of decentralization, which is proxied by the ratio of extrabudgetary funds to budgetary funds, REB, and is also treated as an exogenously institutional indicator. In addition, China has experienced two periods of economic rectification: 1980-1982 and 1989-1991, in which the central government retrieved the economic decision-making powers from a lower level. Thus a dummy variable Z3 (Z3=1 for 1980-1982 and 1989; z3=0 otherwise) is introduced to capture the negative impacts of these austerity drives on the local governments' extrabudgetary funds. Equation (4.7) assumes that the retail sales of non-state sectors (RTSP) is positively affected by working capital loans granted to both state and non-state sectors (LOS+LOP), the consumption demand in the previous period (DC_{-1}) and the degree of privatization RPS. Moreover in the second austerity drive which was more strenuously pursued than the first one, no parts of the economy including the non-state economy were unaffected, and thus a dummy variable Z1 is again added to the equation. Finally, in the function of inventory accumulation (4.8), we test its possible role as a buffer to absorb shocks. We could reasonably relate the changes in inventory stocks positively to current national output NI and the lagged increase in national output ΔNI_{-1}, but inversely to the difference between the current and lagged total excess demand.

So much for the investment block. Let us now turn to the production block. It contains only four functions: one for gross national production (4.12), one for the effective increase in fixed assets (4.14), and two identities (4.13) and (4.15) defining fixed assets formation and fixed assets accumulation.

The gross national product corresponds to the total output derived from internal sources. It is expressed by a Barro-Grossman type production function (Barro and Grossman, 1976). Concerning the equation (4.12), the roles of L and K^2 in the production process are easily understood and do not need further explanation. The addition of government expenditures on economic construction in the equation expresses the aim of it to intervene in a positive way in the production process by exogenous stimulation of material and technological progress (see also Charemza and Gronicki, 1988). So the coefficient of $\log(\overline{GEE})$ is expected to have a positive sign. Since the equation will be estimated over 1967-1989, it is natural to assume structural changes resulting from economic reform. We would expect that the elasticities of labour and government expenditures on economic construction decrease, while the elasticity of fixed assets increases. First, the pre-reform Chinese economy was, to a large extent, labour-intensive, while since 1979 the capital-intensive industries have grown rapidly as a result of the introduction of foreign capital and technology and of massive investment in the capital-intensive enterprises. This explains why the labour elasticity should decrease while the capital elasticity should increase. Second, the ability of the government to intervene in the economy was considerably weakened as the economy moved from being centrally planned to being market-oriented. So the elasticity of GEE should fall as well.

The part of the model (equation (4.14)) describing the effective increase in fixed assets will be taken directly from some Chinese economists' studies. We will return to their estimates of the capital stock in the Chinese economy later in section 4.5.

4.4 Disequilibrium indicators

It is necessary and useful to discuss the disequilibrium indicator before moving on to the model estimation, for when demand (supply) variables are not observed, the role of disequilibrium indicators becomes essential in the respecification of the econometric model to be estimated. According to Charemza and Gronicki (1988), disequilibrium indicators can be defined as variables which could be used as proxies for excess demand (i.e., a difference between demand and supply); respecification means substituting the observable proxy for the unobservable variable without substantial loss in information about the model's structure. By the definition of disequilibrium indicator we understand that a disequilibrium indicator should be either the result of excess demand, or inversely the cause which leads to excess demand *inter alia*. In this study the former notion is adopted.

Perhaps dealing with disequilibrium indicators is the most complicated problem here. First it is usually connected with a question of whether it is possible to state *a priori* the sign of a particular excess demand. As can be seen in chapter 2, testable excess demand approach advocates the statistical testing of equilibrium versus disequilibrium hypothesis. If the equilibrium hypothesis is rejected it is possible to evaluate the sign of excess demand by calculating the probability that demand is greater than supply, or simply by subtraction of supply from demand estimates. However, this procedure has generated results which fail to be consistent with the abundant evidence of chronic excess demand observed in those CPEs. An alternative way allows *a priori* admittance of sign of excess demand based either on theoretical considerations or on independent expert's opinions. Charemza and Gronicki

(1988) argued that this is practically the only feasible way where the same type (sign) of disequilibrium is expected, especially if a relatively large model is considered. In our study the latter procedure is applied, though the sign of excess demand is not the same for the period under investigation. We assume *a priori* that in China in the period 1979-1989, demand generally exceeded supply in the first ten years, while supply is larger than demand in the last year. This assumption can be derived from various economic theories and empirical studies of the Chinese economy made by Chinese economists and economic authorities. The former instance that demand exceeds supply is normal phenomenon in a socialist country (see, for example, Kornai 1980 and 1982), while the latter instance that supply exceeds demand is an exceptional circumstance which could occur when the austerity drive is drastic and *effective*. The Chinese economy in 1989 is without doubt in the latter state (see, for example, Guo 1991, Liu 1991, Sun 1990 and Yang 1990).

Second, it involves a question of how to select appropriate variables as a disequilibrium indicator. For an economy with freely negotiated prices the simplest disequilibrium indicator is the Walrasian law of demand and supply: prices are willing to rise as excess demand increases, and to fall as it declines. In literature (e.g. Fair and Jaffee 1971, Fair Kelejian 1974, and Maddala and Nelson 1974), the model considered under the title 'Quantitative Method' reflects such an idea. It is:

$$D_t = X'_{1t}\beta_1 + \alpha_1 P_t + \mu_{1t},$$
$$S_t = X'_{2t}\beta_2 + \alpha_2 P_t + \mu_{2t},$$
$$\Delta P_t = P_t - P_{t-1} = \gamma(D_t - S_t), \quad \gamma > 0.$$

where D_t and S_t are the demand and supply variables, X'_{1t} and X'_{2t} are vectors of exogenous variables, and P_t is the level of prices. Here we understand that prices and excess demand should be the ones corresponding to the same market. For example, when excess investment demand (represented by $D_t - S_t$ in the above model) increases (decreases), it is the investment goods prices (i.e., P_t in the above model) that are willing to rise (fall). Obviously this is not the case in the context of the Chinese economy. The answer to this question seems to rely on an in-depth understanding of economic mechanisms in China.

The main access for enterprises to compensate for their loss resulting from some constraints in purchasing investment goods is to shift their loss to users of their products by raising output prices. A request to raise output prices by a state-owned enterprise is usually supported by the higher administrative organs, because the fiscal levy of local governments depends mainly on enterprises' sales revenue and profits, though the prices are only allowed to rise to a limited extent for other reasons. Non-state enterprises respond to the presence of rationing in a similar way, but they have more discretion to raise output prices because they are more market-dependent. As far as downstream sectors of either public-ownership or non-public ownership are concerned, their products are primarily consumption goods, and accordingly their output are measured at the aggregate level by the retail price index. Concurrent with investment expansion causing excess investment demand, is usually consumption funds expansion causing excess consumption demand which in turn creates a favourable sellers market in which enterprises can raise their output prices (see Xia and Li, 1987). In this manner, shortages appearing in investment markets will spill over to consumption markets, and will be mirrored in an increase in retail prices. Nevertheless, retail prices may not rise instantaneously to compensate for enterprises's loss. The time needed for them (especially for the state-owned enterprises) to negotiate and bargain with price-management authorities, and for the requests for raising prices to be approved, are probably key parts of the answer. The above considerations lead to the conclusion that increase in retail prices rather than in investment goods prices, in the next year rather than in current year, can be proxies for positive excess investment demand. Adapting the model of 'Quantitative Method' to take into account of the above considerations, we postulate the following equations as shown (4.17), (4.18) and (4.19):

$$\Delta P_{t+1} = P_{t+1} - P_t = \frac{1}{\theta_{11}}(DIL_t - IL_t), \quad \text{if } DIL_t > IL_t$$

$$\Delta P_{t+1} = P_{t+1} - P_t = \frac{1}{\theta_{12}}(DIP_t - IP_t), \quad \text{if } DIP_t > IP_t$$

$$\Delta P_{t+1} = P_{t+1} - P_t = \frac{1}{\theta_{11} + \theta_{12}}(DI_t - I_t), \quad \text{if } DI_t - I_t > 0$$

where the variable P_t is not investment goods prices, but rather the retail prices which are used in this book to represent consumption goods prices.[3]

But this is not the end of story. When the investment goods market switches regime from excess demand to excess supply, as it obviously did in China in 1989, the assumption that the adjustment of retail prices in the subsequent year should be negative becomes inconsistent with reality, for P_t actually rose by 0.044 (see Table 4.1). Note, however, that the increase in P_t in 1990 was much less than in the previous year when ΔP_t reaches its peak 0.3171 of the 1980s. If this peak illustrates the fact that excess investment demand peaked in 1988 as has been widely recognized by the Chinese government and economists, then the sharp decrease of ΔP_t in 1990 ought to be understood as a result of the presence of excess investment supply in 1989 owing to the austerity measures taken by the government in that year. But

Table 4.1
Price indices of retail sales

t	P_t	ΔP_t
1978	1.0311	—
1979	1.0516	0.0205
1980	1.1146	0.0629
1981	1.1411	0.0265
1982	1.1631	0.0220
1983	1.1806	0.0174
1984	1.2140	0.0334
1985	1.3209	0.1069
1986	1.3998	0.0789
1987	1.5023	0.1024
1988	1.7800	0.2777
1989	2.0971	0.3171
1990	2.1411	0.0440

Note: t=year. P_t=price indices of retail sales in year t. ΔP_t=differences between the current P_t and previous P_{t-1}

why should not ΔP_{90} be negative in response to $(DI-SI)_{89}<0$? The reasons lie in the shortcomings of the existing economic system such as rigidity of prices and wages, public ownership of most enterprises, and an immature market system etc.. Since in the period investigated the excess investment supply appeared only in the last year, it seems sensible to choose dummy variable Z1 as an indicator for excess investment supply in equation (4.19). Actually Z1 expresses the attempts of the government at cutting down aggregate domestic demand in 1989, which gave rise to a switch of disequilibrium regime in the investment market. This treatment is not, of course, appropriate if the model is extended beyond 1989, or if the excess supply regime lasts for more than one period. In this circumstance some other variables need to be found as proxies for excess disequilibrium, but for the time being, this consideration is ignored.

4.5 Estimation results

Respecification and estimation

Our estimation of the model begins with equations (4.2) and (4.3), since the calculation of the data on DI relies on the estimated results of these two equations. In equation (4.2), the dependent variable DIL is not observed for 1979-1988 as DIL>IL. Moreover, the expectation variable in (4.2) is related to the unobservable (DI-SI). To replace them by observable proxies, relations (4.17) and (4.19) are used. After transformation into the forms:

$$IL = DIL - \theta_{11}(P_{+1} - P) \qquad (4.21)$$

$$(DI-SI)^e = (\theta_{11} + \theta_{12})(P_{+1} - P)^e \qquad (4.22)$$

and imposition of a restriction h, the respecified form of (4.2) becomes:

$$IL = \alpha_2 + \beta_2 FUND + \gamma_2 UNE + \delta_2(\theta_{11} + \theta_{12})(P_{+1}-P)^e - \theta_{11}h(P_{+1}-P) + e_2 \qquad (4.23)$$

where $h = \begin{cases} 1, & \text{for} \quad 1979\text{-}1988; \\ 0, & \text{for} \quad 1989. \end{cases}$

The equation is estimated using the two-step estimators of RE models based on the substitution method. But the endogeneity of the disequilibrium indicator[4] requires the application of some variants of this general procedure. In the first step, estimates of $(P_{+1}-P)^e$ are computed by OLS regression of $P_{+1}-P$ on lagged exogenous variables. In the second step these estimates are substituted back into the RE model, as if the data on $(P_{+1}-P)^e$ are given, and the equation is estimated by an instrumental variables procedure, while for the disequilibrium indicator the instruments are current exogenous variables and one predetermined variable. The results are:

$$IL = -256.6033 + 0.5628 FUND + 0.4522 UNE + 360.1284(P_{+1}-P)^e$$
$$(-3.4162) \quad (11.206) \qquad (4.1313) \qquad (1.9785)$$

$$ -250.0157 Z1 - 512.2256 h(P_{+1}-P)$$
$$(-6.0188) \quad\; (-3.1866)$$

$$\bar{R}^2 = 0.9903 \quad SE = 15.7568 \quad \chi_S^2(5) = 5.0000 \quad \chi_R^2(1) = 0.8676$$
$$\chi_F^2(1) = 1.0721 \quad \chi_N^2(2) = 0.2529 \quad \chi_H^2(1) = 0.8171$$

$$(4.24)$$

The statistic tests given are: the adjusted coefficient of determination $\bar{R}^2$, the standard error of regression SE. In addition we have provided all the diagnostic tests in LM version (since F-version tests are not applicable for the case of IV method): χ^2_S is Sargan's statistic for a general test of misspecification of the model and the instruments, χ^2_R for a test of residual serial correlation, χ^2_F for a test of functional form misspecification, χ^2_N for a test of non-normality of errors and χ^2_H for a test of heteroscedasticity. In the brackets below the estimated parameters t-ratios are given. (All the statistics reported later concerning the estimated results of other behavioral equations have the same definitions as reported here, unless otherwise stated).

The dependent variable DIP is not observed as well for 1979-1988 as DIP>IP. Similarly by replacing the unobservable variable with the relation in (4.18), the respecified form of (4.3) is

$$IP = DIP - \theta_{12} h(P_{+1} - P) + e_3$$
$$= \alpha_3 + \beta_3 RNRTP + \gamma_3 P_{+1}^e + \delta_3 INV_{-1} + \sigma_3 RI - \theta_{12} h(P_{+1} - P) + e_3 \qquad (4.25)$$

where $h = \begin{cases} 1 & \text{for } 1979-1988; \\ 0 & \text{for } 1989. \end{cases}$

With the data on $(P_{+1}-P)^e$ obtained in the first step of estimating (4.24), we can calculate RI using equation (4.11). Concerning P^e_{+1}, its one-year-ahead predictor is obtained by regressing P_{+1} on the exogenous and predetermined variables (including P; see endnote 4) at time t. Applying a similar procedure to that in estimating (4.23) to (4.25) gives:

$$IP = -204.8875 + 0.5256 RNRTP + 268.348 P_{+1}^e - 0.2421 INV_{-1}$$
$$(-5.5654) \quad (9.813) \qquad (5.0637) \qquad (-2.8674)$$

$$-1268.8 RI - 397.3529 h(P_{+1} - P)$$
$$(-4.8895) \quad (-2.2641)$$

$\bar{R}^2 = 0.9975 \qquad SE = 21.8431 \qquad \chi_S^2(4) = 5.0000 \qquad \chi_R^2(1) = 2.8222$

$\chi_F^2(1) = 2.1002 \qquad \chi_N^2(2) = 0.1209 \qquad \chi_H^2(1) = 0.3954$

$$(4.26)$$

Given the estimates of θ_{11} and θ_{12} the data on DIL, DIP and DI can now be calculated by using the relations (4.17)-(4.19):

$$DIL = IL + \theta_{11} h(P_{+1} - P) = IL + 512.2256 h(P_{+1} - P) \qquad (4.27)$$
$$DIP = IP + \theta_{12} h(P_{+1} - P) = IP + 397.3529 h(P_{+1} - P) \qquad (4.28)$$
$$DI = I + (\theta_{11} + \theta_{12}) h(P_{+1} - P) = I + 909.5785 h(P_{+1} - P) \qquad (4.29)$$

Note that the aggregate investment demand should be the sum of the investment demand of state-owned upstream sectors DIU, state-owned downstream sectors DIL and non-state sectors DIP, namely,

DI=DIU+DIL+DIP. Equation (4.29) actually implies that DIU=IU. In other words, we have assumed that total excess investment demand results from state-owned downstream sectors and non-state sectors, while state-owned upstream sectors face no rationing. This is because the central government possesses all the necessary means, such as the power of money supply and material distribution, and even administrative orders, to implement its investment plans for the state-owned upstream sectors. Another unobservable variable in aggregate investment demand function is DC. We will come to the estimation of DC in chapter 5, but for the time being its estimates are taken for granted. Having solved the above data problems, we are now in a position to estimate equation (4.1). Since the explanatory variables DC, DIL and DIP are endogenous, an instrumental variables method is adopted, which leads to the following results:

$DI = -323.177 + 0.2310DC + 1.176DIL + 0.8381DIP + 0.5563GEE$
$(-3.3043)(3.2336)(5.1967)(4.1258)(4.7629)$

$\overline{R}^2 = 0.9983 \quad SE = 32.5854 \quad \chi_S^2(5) = 4.3569 \quad \chi_R^2(1) = 1.1519$
$\chi_F^2(1) = 0.0920 \quad \chi_N^2(2) = 1.3999 \quad \chi_H^2(1) = 1.178$

(4.30)

In the investment supply function (4.4) SI is not observed for 1989, though it is observable for 1979-1988. The respecified form of the equation is obtained in a similar manner to that described above:

$$I = \alpha_4 + \beta_4 \Delta NI + \gamma_4(LOS_{-1} + LOF_{-1}) + \delta_4 GEE + \sigma_4 IMP - \theta_{13}(1-h)Z1 + e_4 \quad (4.31)$$

where $h = \begin{cases} 1 & \text{for } 1979\text{-}1988; \\ 0 & \text{for } 1989. \end{cases}$

This equation is estimated again by an IV method with the final results:

$I = -113.2164 + 2.9959 \Delta NI + 0.2719(LOS_{-1} + LOF_{-1}) + 0.5437GEE$
$(-1.9435)(6.2742)(11.891)(6.2308)$

$+0.5397IMP - 249.6938Z1$
$(6.8380)(-5.2244)$

$\overline{R}^2 = 0.9991 \quad SE = 22.2376 \quad \chi_S^2(2) = 0.4299 \quad \chi_R^2(1) = 2.5347$
$\chi_F^2(1) = 3.0976 \quad \chi_N^2(2) = 2.1484 \quad \chi_H^2(1) = 0.4873$

(4.32)

The remaining behavioral equations in the investment block involve no contemporaneously endogenous variables on their right hand sides, and thus we decide to simply apply OLS to them. The final estimates for (4.5)-(4.8) are given respectively as:

$$IMP = -581.384 + 0.6057NI_{-1} + 0.2097DEE_{-1} + 1021.8OPE$$
$$(-22.8714)\ (6.9460)\quad\ (3.4493)\quad\ \ (18.0523)$$

$$-128.9237\Delta EXC$$
$$(-4.9621)$$

$\overline{R}^2 = 0.9987\quad SE = 15.9352\quad F_R(1,5) = 1.3231\quad F_F(1,5) = 0.6664$
$\chi_N^2(2) = 0.8274\quad F_H(1,9) = 1.0752$

(4.33)

$$FUND = -152.9204 + 0.1915(LOS + LOF) + 6.5004REB - 90.8896Z3$$
$$(-1.7028)\quad\ (9.2920)\quad\quad\quad (3.4186)\quad\ (-2.8464)$$

$\overline{R}^2 = 0.9853\quad\quad SE = 49.3072\quad\quad F_R(1,6) = 0.0377$
$F_F(1,6) = 3.1538\quad \chi_N^2(2) = 0.5791\quad F_H(1,9) = 0.2720$

(4.34)

$$RTSP = -517.7217 + 0.1978(LOS + LOP) + 0.2820DC_{-1} + 614.6028RPS$$
$$(-4.7687)\ (2.0722)\quad\quad\quad (2.8441)\quad\ (2.8055)$$

$$-339.4357Z1$$
$$(-5.3909)$$

$\overline{R}^2 = 0.9962\quad SE = 39.7691\quad F_R(1,5) = 0.0472$
$F_F(1,5) = 0.8186\quad \chi_N^2(2) = 0.4817\quad F_H(1,9) = 0.2835E-3$

(4.35)

$$INV = 3.4136\Delta NI_{-1} + 0.2969NI - 0.4362\Delta DEE$$
$$(2.5246)\quad\quad (2.5781)\ (-4.384)$$

$\overline{R}^2 = 0.932\quad SE = 59.6808\quad F_R(1,7) = 1.9782$
$F_F(1,7) = 1.0027\quad \chi_N^2(2) = 0.8958\quad F_H(1,9) = 0.0693$

(4.36)

The t ratio for intercept α_8 in equation (4.8) was initially estimated as -0.13489, and therefore we decided to drop it and to re-estimate the equation excluding α_8. This has generated estimation results in (4.36). F_R, F_F and F_H correspond respectively to χ_R^2, χ_F^2 and χ_H^2 defined above, but in F-version.

Regarding the production block, the IV method is applied to equation (4.12) since the variable K is considered to be endogenous. The initial estimation results are:

$$\log(NI) = -13.8197 + 1.6718\log(\overline{L}) - 0.2861Z2\log(\overline{L})$$
$$(-2.5976) \quad (2.738) \quad\quad (-2.7725)$$

$$-0.0138\log(\overline{K}) + 0.4968Z2\log(\overline{K})$$
$$(-0.1315) \quad\quad (3.0949)$$

$$+0.3625\log(\overline{GEE}) - 0.2145Z2\log(\overline{GEE}) \quad\quad (4.37a)$$
$$(5.2141) \quad\quad (-2.4388)$$

The estimate of γ_{91} (-0.0138) is insignificantly different from zero, and moreover it has the wrong sign. In view of this, we have decided to re-estimate this production function by dropping $\log(\overline{K})$ while keeping $Z2\log(\overline{K})$, obtaining:

$$\log(NI) = -13.1892 + 1.5989\log(\overline{L}) - 0.2967Z2\log(\overline{L})$$
$$(-6.1655)(6.733) \quad\quad (-4.8452)$$

$$+0.5118Z2\log(\overline{K}) + 0.3656\log(\overline{GEE}) - 0.2181Z2\log(\overline{GEE})$$
$$(4.7585) \quad\quad (5.7964) \quad\quad (-2.6851)$$

$$\overline{R}^2 = 0.9976 \quad SE = 0.0248 \quad \chi_S^2(1) = 0.1985 \quad \chi_R^2(1) = 0.4073$$
$$\chi_F^2(1) = 0.9569 \quad \chi_N^2(2) = 0.9434 \quad \chi_H^2(1) = 1.134$$

$$(4.37b)$$

where $\overline{L} = \dfrac{L + L_{-1}}{2}$; $\overline{K} = \dfrac{K + K_{-1}}{2}$; $\overline{GEE} = \dfrac{GEE + GEE_{-1}}{2}$.

The problem arose of lack of time series observations on either total capital stocks or total fixed assets in any past issues of the Statistical Year Book of China, while we were proceeding to the estimation of the production function. However, a Chinese economist Zhang (1991) recently published a paper in which the level of total capital stock for the period 1952-1990 was estimated. He assumes that the ratio of capital stock to national income was 3 in 1952 so that $KO_{1952} = 200$ billion yuan at the prices of 1952, and the effective increase of capital stocks ΔKO is a distributed lags function of accumulation level RO over up to five previous years. The coefficients of five lags he gave are: 26% of accumulation forming effective production capacity in the first (current) year, 26% in the second year, 20% in the third year, 12% in the fourth tear, 9% in the fifth year and 7% in the sixth year. That is:

$$\Delta KO = 0.26RO + 0.26RO_{-1} + 0.20RO_{-2}$$
$$+ 0.12RO_{-3} + 0.09RO_{-4} + 0.07RO_{-5} \qquad (4.38)$$

As for how these results are obtained, he refers readers to Wu and Zhang (1989). Unfortunately, we could not find that publication, and as there are no other more accurate estimates of KO, we can only employ Zhang's results at present. Note, however, that KO is total capital stocks rather than total fixed assets K. According to the relation between total capital stocks KO, fixed assets K and total circulating assets KC (i.e., $\Delta KO = \Delta K + \Delta KC$), and the relation between total accumulation RO, fixed assets accumulation R and circulating assets accumulation RC (i.e., RO=R+RC), we have based on (4.38):

$$\Delta K = 0.26R + 0.26R_{-1} + 0.20R_{-2} + 0.12R_{-3} + 0.09R_{-4} + 0.07R_{-5} \qquad (4.39)$$

The data on total fixed assets calculated by this equation were used in estimating the aggregate production function (4.37b).

Some discussion of the results

By now the estimation of the model of the investment-production block has been completed. Before empirical results are discussed, however, two econometric issues should be examined: the treatment of expectations, and the estimation technique for disequilibrium models. First, we consider the procedure used to estimate the expectation variables of the model (current excess investment demand proxied by one-period-ahead inflation rate, and one-period-ahead retail prices). Expectations are assumed 'rational' or 'consistent' with the underlying model. Two widely adopted approaches to implementing this assumption empirically are known as the substitution method (SM) and the errors-in-variables method (EVM). The SM procedure consists in estimating unrestricted reduced-form equations for the relevant expectation variables and using the predicted values as proxies for expectations. The EVM method, on the other hand, replaces the expectation variable with the realized (observed) one, and then apply IV to the estimating equation to assure consistent estimates. The EVM procedure has many advantages over the SM approach (see Wickens 1982 and 1986, Pagan 1984 and Pesaran 1987). However, in the model described above, the expected and realized values of the same variable (($P_{+1}-P)^e$ and $(P_{+1}-P)$) appear; and the coefficients of these variables cannot be separately identified, if the EVM method is used. Therefore, the SM approach has to be adopted instead.

The second econometric issue relates to estimation technique for disequilibrium models. In literature (see, for example, Fair and Jaffee 1972, Fair and Kelejian 1974, Amemiya 1974, Goldfeld and Quandt 1975), two-stage least squares (2SLS) technique and the maximum likelihood estimator are discussed. As Amemiya (1974) argued, the fact that the disequilibrium indicator contains zero values does not in any way violate the conditions for consistency of 2SLS estimator, if an appropriate predictor of disequilibrium indicator is obtained. As for the problem of efficiency of a 2SLS estimator, it arises only if the same parameter in a disequilibrium indicator equation appears in both demand and supply equations. In this study, however, we have allowed asymmetric disequilibrium indicators, and the adjustment coefficients differ from excess demand regime to excess supply regime. Therefore, the problem of efficiency resulting from the above constraint that the same parameter appears in both demand and supply equations is not especially relevant to our case here. The maximum likelihood method, on the other hand, will become computationally intractable and more complicated, in the two cases where μ_t^D (error terms in a demand function) and μ_t^S (error terms in a supply function) are serially correlated, and where μ_t^D and μ_t^S are contemporaneously correlated but serially uncorrelated. In view of these facts, we decided to apply 2SLS (or IV) method in the estimation of disequilibrium models.

Overall, the estimation results look quite satisfactory. High t-ratios as well as high $\bar{R}^2$ coefficients confirm the initial specification of the model, and all variables have the expected *a priori* sign. We have, where available (e.g., equations (4.33)-(4.36) for the tests of serial correlation, functional form misspecification and heteroscedasticity), tried to report diagnostic statistics in F-version, because on the basis of Monte Calor results Kiviet (1986) has shown that, in small samples, the F version is generally preferable to the LM version. But in other cases where the F-version statistics are not applicable, the LM-version ones have to be presented. The diagnostic statistics (LM or F version) in almost all the above estimated equations are below their critical values at the 10% level,[5] indicating that we cannot reject the hypotheses of absence of serial correlation, non-normality, functional form misspecification and heteroscedasticity at the 10% level of significance. The only two exception are $\chi_R^2(1)=2.8222$ in equation (4.26) and $\chi_F^2(1)=3.0976$ in equation (4.32). However, these two LM statistics are yet both below $\chi_{0.95}^2(1)=3.84$, suggesting that we cannot reject, at the 5% level of significance, the hypotheses that the residual is serially independent in (4.26), and that the linear functional form is correctly chosen in (4.32). For those equations ((4.24), (4.26), (4.30) and (4.32)) estimated by an IV procedure, the Sargan's statistics were additionally reported. Again, since they are all below their critical values at the 10% level, we are unable to reject the hypothesis of no misspecification of the model and instruments at the 10% level of significance. Of course, we cannot over-claim econometric robustness and precision of the results obtained above, because of the small sample size. Although regression may be viewed as being used for a kind of calibration, we can at least infer from the data some evidences in favour of those theoretical assumptions made earlier and employed in the specification of the econometric model here.[6]

Below we provide detailed discussion of the empirical results of behavioral equations in the investment-production block. Parameters measuring the conflicting effects on aggregate investment demand of consumption demand, investment demand in the down-stream sector and the policy stance of the central government are all highly significant (see equation (4.30)). In magnitude, these coefficients are plausible, although we cannot find similar estimates in literature to compare with, since the investment theories proposed in chapter 3 for econometrical studies here are novel and capture the unique feature of the 1980s Chinese economy. If (4.30) is expressed in terms of DIU, the investment demand of upstream sectors under the control of the central government, i.e.,

DIU=DI-DIL-DIP
  $= -323.177 + 0.231DC + 0.176DIL - 0.1619DIP + 0.5563GEE$

the results will then show large impacts of the central government's policy stance, GEE, and consumption demand, DC, on aggregate investment demand, indicating sharp conflicts in the POE for distribution of national income. Also the impact of local governments' investment demand is not negligible, conforming to the theoretical hypothesis of conflicts between the central authority and local authorities in the POE for investment resources. Interesting enough, the non-state sector's investment demand seems to have a negative impact on the upstream sector's investment demand; the central government is ready to make a concession to the non-state sector, presumably because it is more market-dependent and utilizes resources more efficiently.

All the variables in the local governments' and non-state sector's investment demand functions are significant and of the right sign (see (3.24) and (3.25)). In particular, the high t values, negative sign and the reasonable size (see Table 4.2 for estimates of excess investment demand) of the coefficients of P_{+1}-P confirm our specifications of disequilibrium indicators. The local government's investment demand is mainly affected by extra-budgetary funds FUND (β_2=0.5628) and unemployment level UNE (γ_2=0.4522). However, as a result of conflicts between regions for investment resources (see section 3.3), the effect of their expectations of excess investment demand is also fairly high, since the estimated coefficient δ_2 (in equation (4.23) is

$$\delta_2 = \frac{\delta_2(\theta_{11}+\theta_{12})}{\theta_{11}+\theta_{12}} = \frac{360.1284}{512.2256+397.3529} = 0.3959$$

The non-state sector's investment demand shows significant and positive response to the variable RNRTP representing its net returns ($\beta_3=0.5256$), and a certain positive response to the expectations of retail prices for period t+1, P^e_{+1} ($\gamma_3=268.348$). Changes in inventory stocks (lagged one year), on the other hand, affect the investment demand negatively and significantly, with the parameter $\delta_3=-0.2421$. Nevertheless, the non-state sector's investment demand function provided less satisfactory results than the other two investment demand functions. The coefficient σ_3 on the variable RI, the real interest rate, is a bit too high, though it has the right sign. This might be due to the fact that we have chosen interest rates on households's time deposits, which are officially set and too low. According to Fan G et al (1993), the state banking system grants more than 80% of its total loans to the state-sectors, and it is a dominant banking system in China. As a result of this kind of 'discrimination', the 'black' or 'grey' financial markets have emerged and developed, as major capital sources for the non-state sectors. Therefore, the true interest rates that the non-state sectors face are mainly the loans interest rates in these financial markets, which are much higher than the officially set loan interest rates, and even higher than the household deposits interest rates. Unfortunately such data are not available. However, the fact that the estimate of σ_3 has the correct sign and is not utterly implausible may be taken as evidence of somehow strong response of the non-state sector to the interest rate changes, implying that the econometric results do not invalidate the use of the model for policy analysis.

The estimated investment supply function (4.32) fits the data well, with all coefficients bearing the expected signs, reasonable magnitudes and very high t ratios. The fitted equation exhibits a significant response to the government expenditures on economic construction ($\delta_4=0.5437$), while lagged values of domestic credits, in the forms of working capital and fixed assets loans to the state sector, tend to have relative small impact ($\gamma_4=0.2719$). This suggests that fiscal policy stimulates more supply, but takes less time to become effective, than monetary policy. Besides, the large estimate of import parameter, σ_4 (=0.5397), indicates that investment supply was maintained, to a noticeable extent, by imports during the 1980s. The coefficients in the re-estimated production function (4.37b) are all statistically significant and bear the right signs, unlike its initial estimation results in (4.37a). How do we explain these results? Prior to 1979 the Chinese economy was dominated by labour-intensive industries, and the economic growth mainly depended on the input of labour factors. Thus, for the pre-reform period, the estimated labour elasticity of output is 1.6718, while the capital elasticity of output is

Table 4.2
Estimates of excess investment demand/supply

t	I	$(DI-SI)_1$	$(DI-SI)_1/I$	$(DI-SI)_2$	$(DI-SI)_2/I$
1979	1020.0	57.63	5.65%	3.0	0.3%
1980	980.0	24.76	2.53%	11.3	1.15%
1981	1057.0	20.03	1.89%	15.0	1.42%
1982	1230.4	17.07	1.39%	2.7	0.22%
1983	1430.1	33.50	2.34%	25.5	1.78%
1984	1832.9	111.06	6.06%	66.5	3.63%
1985	2543.2	87.36	3.43%	115.0	4.52%
1986	3019.6	120.25	3.98%	226.8	7.51%
1987	3940.9	346.94	8.80%	463.2	11.75%
1988	4496.5	450.99	10.03%	915.2	20.35%
1989	4137.7	-429.52	-10.38%	——	——

Note: *t=year. I=total investment. $(DI-SI)_1$=our estimates of excess investment demand/supply. $(DI-SI)_2$=Sun's estimates of excess investment demand/supply. All the figures concerning investment are in billion yuan at the price level of 1979*

negligible. During the 1980s, the share of capital-intensive enterprises in the economy rose substantially. As a result, the contribution of capital increments to economic growth increased. This is reflected in the estimate of labour elasticity of output being reduced to 1.3022, and in the estimate of capital elasticity of output being increased to 0.5118. In addition, we find that the coefficient of government construction spending also reduced from 0.3656 to 0.1475 after 1979. This is surely the result of decentralization in economic reforms.

Finally, the auxiliary equations (4.33)-(4.36) display good statistical properties, the right signs of all coefficients, and yield interesting results as well. Very briefly, imports are well driven by disequilibria in domestic markets, and closely related to the degree of openness of the economy; extrabudgetary funds significantly respond to domestic credits and the degree to which the economic decision-making power is decentralized; retail sales of non-state sectors depends mainly on the lagged consumption demand and current domestic credits, and the ownership reforms also contribute a lot to the increase in retail sales of non-state sectors; changes in inventory stocks do act as a buffer to absorb shocks, since they respond positively to fluctuation in output, but negatively and significantly to changes in domestic shortages.

Given the estimates of local governments and non-state sectors investment demand, and of aggregate investment supply, we have a general accounting equation for disequilibrium relation at an aggregate level:

$$DI-SI=909.5785h(P_{+1}-P)-249.6938(1-h)Z1$$

Imputing all the relevant data into this equation, estimates of excess investment demand/supply (denoted as $(DI-SI)_1$) are computed in Table 4.2, together with Sun's estimates (denoted as $(DI-SI)_2$. See Sun 1990). Sun's estimates of excess investment demand are not based on an econometric model, but on the following simple (but arbitrary) calculation. He assumes *a priori* that the reasonable deflators for GNP increase at 2.5%, and using the differences between this 'reasonable' and those actual figures and the ratios between investment and GNP, he is able to calculate the aggregate excess demand and hence obtain excess investment demand. His method seems to be rather arbitrary and *ad hoc*, and also it appears that he underestimated the excess investment demand in the first half of 1980s, while overestimating that in the second. Even so, we still decide to use his results for comparison, since we do not have any other ones. Both our and Sun's estimates have shown that during the 1980s, the shortage in investment markets was getting worse, and in 1988 excess investment demand reached its maximum volume. This then forced the government to adopt the three-year 'tightening policy' starting from the subsequent year, which is the most drastic one in the post-reform period.

4.6 Conclusions

In preceding sections we have specified and estimated a complete disequilibrium model for the investment and production block. The estimation results are quite good, which show that our theoretical hypotheses propounded in the previous chapter and embodied in the structural relations of the model are fitted and thus supported by the historical data: the contradictions inherent in the POE and the MSM mechanism are major factors contributing to the investment expansion during the last decade. These assumptions are mainly incorporated in the behavioral nature of aggregate investment demand which reacts to the other main endogenous variables, and in the introduction of expectations into the local governments' investment demand function. The conflicts within the state sector persistently pull up demand and thus create a favourable sellers market for the non-state sector, hence even the non-state sector has not taken into account the prices of investment goods in forming their demand. Our empirical results show that the investment demand expansion became more and more serious especially in the years from 1984-1988. This is consistent with the real situation observed then.

Notes

1. Here the term 'local governments' has a broad meaning. It actually refers to local governments, state-owned enterprises and institutions under their controls.
2. Following Hulyak (1989), in the course of estimation the mid-year stocks $\bar{K}$ and $\bar{L}$ instead of K and L are used, and so is the average GEE of two years.
3. According to the *Statistic Yearbook of China*, retail sales have two categories: consumption goods (services) and agricultural production materials, with the former accounting for more 80% of total retail sales. Therefore, the level of retail prices is principally determined by the level of consumption goods prices.
4. Consider the equation $P_{t+1}-P_t=\gamma(D_t-S_t)$. This change affects the date for which price is endogenous, i.e., P_{t+1} is endogenous while P_t is predetermined. See Ito (1980) and Quandt Richard E (1988).
5. $\chi^2_{0.90}(1)=2.71, \chi^2_{0.90}(2)=4.61, \chi^2_{0.90}(3)=6.25, \chi^2_{0.90}(4)=7.78, \chi^2_{0.90}(5)=9.24$, $F_{0.90}(1,5)=4.06, F_{0.90}(1,6)=3.78, F_{0.90}(1,7)=3.59, F_{0.90}(1,9)=3.36$.
6. See Pierre-Richard Agenor (1990), in which 13 annual data points (1974-1986) were used to estimate macroeconomic model for a developing country with a sizable parallel market for foreign exchange. The parameters estimates were then used to analyze the effects of alternative policy measures on the economy under the assumption of rational forward-looking expectations.

Appendix 4A - Sources of data

This Appendix presents the sources of statistical data used in this chapter. The following abbreviations (given in brackets in the list of variables in section 4.2) are used to indicate whether the data are from the original source or are reconstructed.

SYBC *Zhongguo Tongji Nianjian (The Statistical Year Book of China)*, Beijing, PRC.
ACFB *Zhongguo Jinrong Nianjian (Almanac of China's Finance and Banking)*, Beijing, PRC.
ACFT *Zhongguo Duiwai Jingji Maoyi Niajian (Almanac of China's Foreign Trade)*, Beijing, PRC.
GU   Guo (1990)
ZH   Zhang (1991)
LIHU Li and Hu (1990)
ARCO the author's reconstruction of original series or of one year data.

5 Consumption and savings

5.1 Introduction

A preview

Consumption market modelling is, without doubt, the best developed area of disequilibrium analysis of CPEs; it is also, however, the most disputed area (see chapter 2). The controversies in disequilibrium consumption modelling are mainly caused by the different approaches and assumptions employed, so that the empirical results generated by these models often appear to be in conflict. With respect to the consumption market in the Chinese economy, we work upon the assumption that it has been chronically afflicted by the problem of excess demand over the period under investigation. This assumption is not only consistent with a variety of theories and observations, but also supported by a majority of studies by both Chinese economists and some Western economists. Thus a disequilibrium indicator modelling approach is adopted here to measure the degree of consumption market rationing. Concerning the modelling of savings, we will assume, as Welfe (1989) does, that shortages result in less money being spent than desired by consumers; this unspent money, or more precisely, forced savings add (partly or fully) to current income, so increasing demand even more. To capture this phenomenon, we will try to modify the classical budget constraint when deriving the consumption demand and savings models. With this kind of approach, a distinction can be easily made between forced savings and voluntary savings. Our purpose of distinguishing between these two kinds of savings is to question either the argument that the higher rate of entire savings is merely a result of repressed inflation and thus forced, or the belief that it is simply caused by behavioral change and therefore voluntary (see chapter 2). The analysis of this chapter concludes that both repressed inflation and behavioral change contributed to the sharp rise in household savings in the 1980s.

Some historical evidence

Before starting our main discussion, it is useful to look at the consumption experience of households in the period from 1968-1989. This is illustrated in Figures 5.1 and 5.2. In Figure 5.1, there are four macroeconomic indicators (in nominal terms, with 1969=100): indices of household money holdings (SID) (containing household cash holdings and savings deposits), of household cash holdings (MID), of household consumption expenditures (CID) and of retail prices (PID). To have a closer look at the behaviour of prices over the period 1968-1989, we replicate PID in Figure 5.2 with a smaller scale. From these two Figures we can see that there is a striking contrast between the pre-1979 and post-1979 periods. Before 1979, household money holdings and consumption expenditures grew almost at same speed, and the price level remained unchanged. After 1979, however, the growth paths of household money holdings and consumption expenditures began to diverge, and the gap between these two paths was getting increasingly large. Meanwhile, the price level was no longer as rigid as before, and rose persistently as well (see Figure 5.2), but less rapidly than money holdings (see Figure 5.1). Then the following questions arise: Does the more rapid increase of household money holdings in the post-reform period compared to the pre-reform period reflect an underlying structural shift and behavioral change? Or is it merely a monetary phenomenon, resulting from increased repressed inflation? There have been, as we saw in the literature review (chapter 2), two different approaches to answering these questions. In Qian's study (1988), for example, the author allows for a shift in household savings behaviour, especially in the marginal propensity to save, over time, but does not take the possibility of disequilibrium into account. Using this approach he is able to explain the rapidly increased money holdings and concludes that these money holdings represent voluntary savings. In contrast, Feltenstein and Farhadian (1987), Feltenstein et al (1990) and Feltenstein and Ha (1991) stress the potential disequilibrium in the Chinese economy. They adopt what they term the 'virtual price (or true price sometimes)' defined as that price level which would induce the observed quantity of consumption and savings in the absence of rationing. They conclude that there was no change in household saving behaviour as long as the potential disequilibrium is allowed for. The implication of their studies is that the higher savings rate in the 1980s reflects the excessive monetary expansion and the increased degree of repressed inflation, and hence represents forced savings. This disagreement,

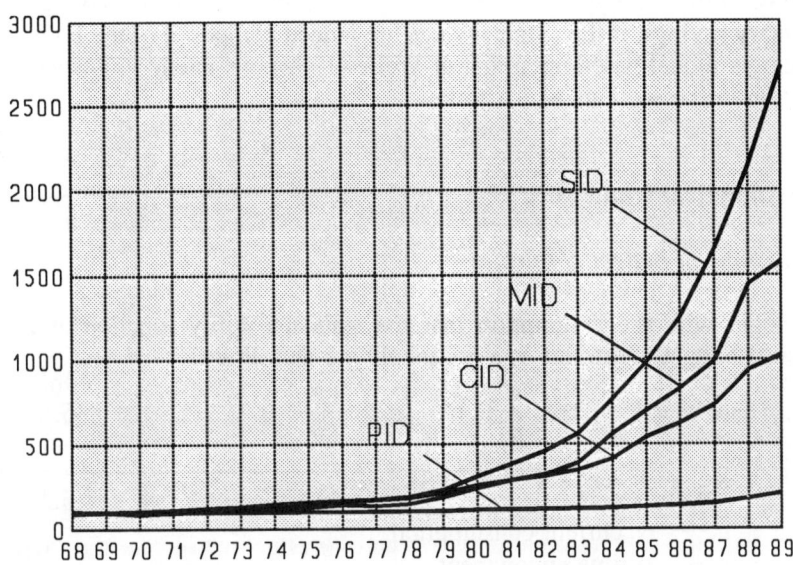

Figure 5.1 Macroeconomic indicators of China 1968-1989

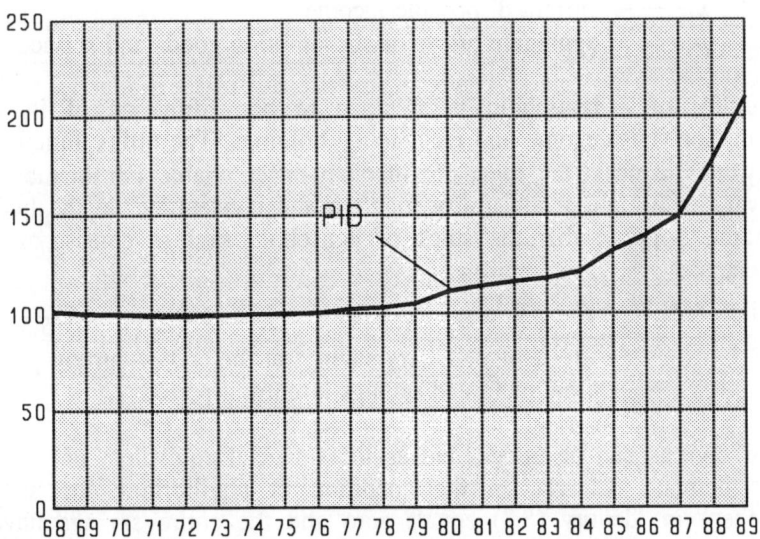

Figure 5.2 Index of retail prices

we feel, arises because no distinction is made between forced and voluntary savings. Accordingly we pose the third question: Is it possible to encompass these two different hypotheses by distinguishing between forced savings and voluntary savings, if the entire savings are indeed composed of the both? By building a model based upon that of Welfe (1989), we intend to answer this question in the sections which follow.

5.2 Analytical framework

Discussions of budget constraint

We begin with the assumption that the standard utility function and the classical budget constraint of a household are as follows:

$$u = u\left(\frac{c}{p}, t-l, \frac{s}{p}\right) \tag{5.1}$$

$$s_{-1} + y = c + s \tag{5.2}$$

where
    c —— current consumption
    t —— time endowment
    l —— labour time
    s_{-1} —— stock of total savings at the end of the previous period
    s —— stock of total savings at the end of the current period
    y —— current disposable income
    p —— aggregate prices of consumption goods and services

The utility of a household is assumed to be a function of its real consumption, leisure time and real money holdings. The utility function is strictly quasi-concave and twice continuously differentiable. For the moment, however, let us ignore the utility function and concentrate on the budget constraint. Suppose that the stock of household savings consist of two components:

$$s = vs + fs \tag{5.3}$$

where
    vs —— stock of voluntary savings at the end of current period
    fs —— flow of forced savings in current period

Forced savings can be understood as the financial equivalent of positive excess demand. Clearly, in the condition of equilibrium, the second component in identity (5.3) equals zero and the entire savings have a voluntary character. Now we assume, however, that, because of insufficient supply of goods, and after all possible transfers of demand, households have accumulated forced savings at the end of the preceding period. In the current period they may neutralize a fraction of them and utilize the rest to enrich their purchasing power. Thus the previous period's forced savings are divided into neutralized and activated forced savings:

$$fs_{-1} = \eta fs_{-1} + \varphi fs_{-1} \qquad (5.4)$$

where $\eta \in [0,1]$ —— coefficient of neutralization of forced savings
$\varphi = 1-\eta$ —— coefficient of activation of forced savings

The neutralization of forced savings means that households will treat them as voluntary savings, planning to utilize them for the purchase of goods in the future, or keeping them in banks as a financial reserve, or just as a result of giving up search for goods. $\eta=1$, where households neutralize the entire forced savings, will occur when they expect shortages to be temporary, and expect the open inflation rate to be low so as not to undervalue their savings. The reason for the activation of forced savings is that they constitute financial security for postponed demand especially for the durable goods. The more intense the households expect the shortage in the durable goods market to be, the more of the forced savings they will try to keep for panic purchasing. Thus the classical budget constraint should be modified to become the 'effective' one as follows:

$$ye = y + \varphi fs_{-1} + \xi vs_{-1}$$

or

$$ye = y + \varphi fs_{-1} \quad if \ 0 \leq \varphi \leq 1, \ \xi = 0 \qquad (5.5)$$

and

$$ye = y + fs_{-1} + \xi vs_{-1} \quad if \ 0 < \xi \leq 1, \ \varphi = 1 \qquad (5.6)$$

where ye —— activated income
$\xi \in [0,1]$ —— coefficient of utilization of voluntary savings

This implies that the how many elements (maximum three) the activated income consists of depends on the degree to which the forced and/or the voluntary savings are activated (utilized). If only an activated fraction of forced savings is added into current disposable income, the effective budget constraint is (5.5), and the activated income consists of two elements: y and φfs_{-1}. Theoretically, it is possible that the stock of voluntary savings may some times decrease as well. One may point out two reasons for this. First, this might be due to inflation combined with relatively low interest rates. Second, if real income decreases, and households want to keep their standard of living unchanged, then the voluntary savings will be partly drawn on.

When a fraction of voluntary savings is added to current disposable income, the effective budget constraint will become identity (5.6).

It should be noted, however, that the neutralization of forced savings and the utilization of voluntary savings exclude each other. In other words, if households decide to incorporate part of forced savings into voluntary savings, or in the present case η is larger than zero and φ is less than one, then they will not simultaneously use voluntary savings for the purchase of goods. So ξ is equal to zero. On the other hand, if households decide to utilize voluntary savings, that is, ξ is larger than zero, then they will not simultaneously neutralize forced savings. Thus η is equal to zero.

Actually the process of neutralization is not constant over time, but we treat it as such here to keep things simple, and thus the further estimated values of φ and η express their mean tendencies. In addition, it is assumed that only in very few years, did households draw on a fraction of voluntary savings. Therefore by smoothing the dissaving process over time, the mean value of φ is still expected to be less than one, and hence the mean value of ξ remains zero. Under these assumptions the identity (5.5) rather than (5.6) will be used as the effective budget constraint in what follows.

Now households have the activated income ye at their disposable to devote to the purchase of goods and to increase savings (because China lacks financial markets at that time). From identities (5.2)-(5.5) one can easily derive identity (5.7):

$$y + \varphi fs_{-1} = c + \Delta ns = \bar{c} + fs + \Delta ns \qquad (5.7)$$

where $\Delta ns = \Delta vs - \eta fs_{-1}$ ——— an increase in the stock of normal savings
Δvs ——— an increase in the stock of voluntary savings
c ——— households' desired consumption expenditures
$\bar{c}$ ——— transacted amount of consumption

If the increase in normal savings is defined as the increase in voluntary savings minus the neutralized part of last year's forced savings, then the activated income is distributed between desired consumption and an increase in normal savings, or equivalently between the realized consumption, forced savings and the increase in normal savings in the presence of rationing. How do we understand normal savings? This requires distinctions to be made between Δns and Δvs, and Δns and fs. First, voluntary savings contain normal savings as well as neutralized forced savings. If there is no fs then $\Delta vs = \Delta ns$. But as normal savings constitute the main part of voluntary savings, they have a voluntary character. Second, normal savings are directly independent of the actual market situation in either the previous or current period. In the identity (5.7) c plus Δns expresses the *ex ante* allocation of activated income, whereas $\bar{c}$ plus fs plus Δns should be understood as the *ex post* allocation.

This implies that before transactions can take place in consumption markets, a household has an original plan for saving which is the result of their normal propensity to save, although as will be indicated later the size of normal savings is, among other things, influenced negatively by households' anticipations of market situation. The forced savings, however, appear only after transaction. Third, the normal savings are accumulated with several motives such as durable goods, dependents, marriage, retirement, legacy etc., while forced savings are directly the results of worsening of market situation.

Corresponding to the modified budget constraint namely the effective budget constraint (5.7), a modified utility function is proposed, that is, the utility of a household is the function of its real consumption, leisure time and additional normal savings in real terms:

$$u = u\left(\frac{c}{p}, T-l, \frac{\Delta ns}{p}\right) \tag{5.8}$$

The utility function (5.8) differs from (5.1) in two aspects. First, the third argument here is normal savings rather than total savings. Second, the normal savings is expressed as flows rather than as stocks. This utility function will serve as a foundation for formulating the actual utility function in order to derive the models of consumption demand and of normal savings in the next section.

Derivation of consumption and saving models

In the utility function (5.8) there were no assumptions about the impacts of shortages, prices and interest rates on household behaviour. In their studies of the Polish economy, Charemza and Gronicki (1988) consider the consequences of households' expectations about the future consumption disequilibrium for its utility, and propose a utility function with dynamic implications. We follow their work, but assume here that consumption demand and normal savings are affected by expectations of *present* excess demand. Prior to reform when the official price level was extremely stable, the expected increase of excess demand simply implies a predicted worsening of the market situation. After reform was instituted, the price increases were increasingly responsive to the excess demand in the previous year, and the expectations of present excess demand may be considered as the expectations of future open inflation. Accordingly, in the case of expected increase of excess demand, households tend to stock up despite their forced savings. Besides, the introduction of the variable, expected excess consumption demand, into the utility function can be justified by, or is consistent with, the analysis of strategic behaviour of the central government and individuals in chapter 3. Equation (3.34) there suggested that the individuals' Nash equilibrium consumption consists eventually of elements $(C_N - \bar{C})^e$ and C_v^*, the expectations of excess consumption demand and desired consumption. This previously obtained theoretical result is thus incorporated in the more detailed discussion of consumption behaviour here. In addition to the expected excess demand, the price is supposed to have negative influence on consumption demand and the real interest rate to have positive influence on normal savings. The above considerations help to suggest the following actual utility function,[1] together with restrictions:

$$u = u_1(\frac{c}{p}, T-l, \frac{\Delta ns}{p}) \cdot u_2[\frac{(c^d - c^s)^e}{p}, p, \frac{c}{p}] \cdot u_3[\frac{(c^d - c^s)^e}{p}, ri, \frac{\Delta ns}{p}] \quad (5.9)$$

$$wl + nli - nc + \varphi fs_{-1} = c + \Delta ns \quad (5.10)$$

$$l = \bar{l} \quad (5.11)$$

where
- wl —— total wage income in the wide sense
- nli —— non-labour income
- nc —— non-consumption spending
- ri —— real interest rates
- p —— aggregate price index
- l —— labour restriction

The new variables are defined above with old ones defined as before. Equation (5.10) is an effective budget constraint in which the activated income is expressed as wage income in broad sense plus non-labour income minus non-consumption spending. wl contains (1) wage, bonus and salary income in both state and private sectors; (2) self-employment income of both non-farm and farm; (3) other earnings. nli is sum of net credits advanced to households and income other than earnings and credits balances. nc includes (1) tax payment of households to the state; (2) purchase of means of production by farms; (3) other expenditures of households. fs_{-1} needs to be estimated. For further algebraic manipulations it is convenient to express the $u_1(.)$ in a Cobb-Douglas form:

$$u_1 = \left(\frac{c}{p}\right)^\alpha (T-l)^\beta \left(\frac{\Delta ns}{p}\right)^\gamma, \quad \alpha, \beta, \gamma > 0.$$

In the optimization on the micro level, the effective demand functions in the Ito sense (Ito, 1980) are considered. First, if the Dreze demand concept (see Dreze 1975, Younes 1975, Grandmont and Laroque 1976, Hahn 1978) is applied, there can be no discrepancy between effective demand and actual trades, which is counterintuitive. Second, Clower functions (see Clower 1965, Barro and Grossman 1976, and Benassy 1975) are in fact special cases of the

Ito ones, with certain nonlinear restrictions. Thirdly, unlike Eastern European countries, China has been suffering the problems of excess labour supply due to the huge population; and households are restricted on labour supply, or there is certain degree of on-job-unemployment, even given the full employment policy pursued in China.

To specify the effective consumption demand function, it is necessary to consider the quantity restrictions which households are subject to. Based on the above considerations, it seems reasonable to assume that households respect the restriction on their labour supply, $\bar{l}$, along with the budget constraint in formulating their optimization problem. Accordingly equation (5.11) is added into the system. As Quandt (1988) noted, when a consumer knows that his labour offer will be rationed to an amount $\bar{l}$ which is less than his notional supply, he may maximize (5.9) subject to (5.10) and (5.11) with respect to real consumption and normal savings. Solving the first-order conditions, we have the following results:

$$\frac{\tilde{c}}{p} = \frac{\alpha}{\alpha+\beta+\gamma}\left(\frac{wT+nli-nc+\varphi fs_{-1}}{p}\right) \tag{5.12}$$

$$\frac{\hat{c}}{p} = \frac{\tilde{c}}{p} + \frac{\alpha}{\alpha+\gamma}\frac{w}{p}(\bar{l}-\tilde{l}) \tag{5.13}$$

$$\frac{c^d}{p} = \frac{\hat{c}}{p} + \delta\frac{(c^d-c^s)^e}{p} - \tau p \tag{5.14}$$

$$\frac{\Delta \tilde{ns}}{p} = \frac{\gamma}{\alpha+\beta+\gamma}\left(\frac{wT+nli-nc+\varphi fs_{-1}}{p}\right) \tag{5.15}$$

$$\frac{\Delta \hat{ns}}{p} = \frac{\Delta \tilde{ns}}{p} + \frac{\gamma}{\alpha+\gamma}\frac{w}{p}(\bar{l}-\tilde{l}) \tag{5.16}$$

$$\frac{\Delta ns}{p} = \frac{\Delta \hat{ns}}{p} - \phi\frac{(c^d-c^s)^e}{p} + \theta ri \tag{5.17}$$

where $\dfrac{\tilde{c}}{p}$ ——— Walrasian consumption demand

$\dfrac{\hat{c}}{p}$ ——— effective consumption demand

$\dfrac{c^d}{p}$ ——— actual effective consumption demand

$\dfrac{\Delta \tilde{ns}}{p}$ ——— Walrasian saving demand

$\dfrac{\Delta \hat{n}\hat{s}}{p}$ —— effective saving demand

$\dfrac{\Delta ns}{p}$ —— actual effective saving demand

fs —— $c^d - c^s \geq 0$

$\delta, \tau, \phi, \theta > 0$ —— parameters

The Walrasian consumption and saving demand functions (5.12) and (5.15) are obtained through maximization of the utility function (5.9) with the condition that

$$u_2 = u_3 = 1$$

under the budget constraint (5.10). The effective demand functions (5.13) and (5.16) are obtained by adding one more constraint, namely the quantity rationing in labour markets, into the optimization problem. Finally, maximizing the overall utility function (5.9), given $u_2(\cdot), u_3(\cdot) > 1$ (or $u_2(\cdot), u_3(\cdot) < 1$) corresponding to the optimized variables in question, with respect to the budget constraint and labour offer ration, yields the actual effective consumption and saving demand functions (5.14) and (5.17). Those factors, i.e., expectations, prices and real rates of interest, are assumed to be of linear form. In the effective demand functions, the second component expresses the impact of disequilibrium in labour markets on consumption and saving demand, or in other words, the effective demand equals the Walrasian (notional) demand plus spill-over terms. Substituting (5.12), (5.13) into (5.14), and using the relation for the Walrasian labour supply, namely,

$$\dfrac{w}{p}\tilde{l} = \dfrac{\alpha+\gamma}{\alpha+\beta+\gamma}\left(\dfrac{wT}{p}\right) - \dfrac{\beta}{\alpha+\beta+\gamma}\left(\dfrac{nli - nc + \varphi fs_{-1}}{p}\right)$$

for $w\tilde{l}/p$, we have:

$$\dfrac{c^d}{p} = \dfrac{\alpha}{\alpha+\gamma}\left(\dfrac{w\bar{l}+nli-nc+\varphi fs_{-1}}{p}\right) + \delta\dfrac{(c^d-c^s)^e}{p} - \tau p \qquad (5.18)$$

Similarly the saving demand function can be written as:

$$\dfrac{\Delta ns}{p} = \dfrac{\gamma}{\alpha+\gamma}\left(\dfrac{w\bar{l}+nli-nc+\varphi fs_{-1}}{p}\right) + \theta ri - \phi\dfrac{(c^d-c^s)^e}{p} \qquad (5.19)$$

Equations (5.18) and (5.19) will serve as a base for forming the econometric models in section 5.3.

Consumption supply function

The equation of consumption supply that we will estimate is specified below:

$$\frac{c^s}{p} = b_0 + b_1 \psi \frac{ct}{p} + b_2(1-\psi)\left(\frac{c^d}{p}\right)_{-1} + b_4 ag_{-1} + b_5 lyxy + \varepsilon_3 \qquad (5.20)$$

$$\psi = \exp(-b_3 Z2t), \qquad Z2 = \begin{cases} 0, & t < 1979 \\ 1, & t \geq 1979 \end{cases}$$

where
- c^s —— nominal value of supply of consumption goods
- ct —— a second-order exponential time trend in consumption
- ag —— index of gross agricultural output; 1952=100
- $lyxy$ —— $(liid - liidt)/liidt$
- $liid$ —— index of gross output of light industry; 1952=100
- $liidt$ —— a second-order exponential time trend in $liid$
- $b_i > 0$ (i=1,2,3,4,5) —— parameters

Prior to economic reform, in China as in other socialist countries, the supply of consumption goods depended largely on the behaviour of the central planner. Therefore supply can be regarded as a function of planned consumption. However, long and consistent time series data for plan targets of consumption are not available for China. In this case, we decided to follow Portes and Winter (1980). They have proposed a solution whereby plan targets can be proxied by time trends, since time trend value is considered as the steady growth objective with which planners form their plans. This solution was also employed by Burkett (1988) in a Eastern European context where plan targets were not available as well. Thus in the equation (5.20), ct is used to proxy the unavailable series for plan targets. Since 1979, the economic reform has resulted in the decentralization of decision-making power in state-owned downstream sectors, and in the rapid development of non-state sectors, so that the role of market mechanism has gradually come into play. As a result, consumption goods supply appeared to be increasingly less responsive to mandatory plans but more to lagged consumption demand. Here the variable, lagged consumption demand, provides the quantity signals in consumption markets. These quantity signals, in the absence of complete price signals, act as market mechanism in regulating the behaviour of consumption goods producers. However, the replacement of the planning mechanism by the market mechanism is a gradual process. To capture this phenomenon, we have introduced a parameter ψ, the value of which varies with time, and a dummy variable Z2 (as used in the production function, in chapter 4) indicating the effect of reform. Here the time variable t in ψ represents the progress of economic reforms which led to the changing role of the central planning. Before 1979, Z2 equals zero, ψ is one and 1-ψ is zero. Hence the lagged consumption demand representing market forces disappears from the supply function, while the plan variable affects supply through the parameter b_1. After 1979, Z2 equals one. ψ and hence b_1 times ψ declines following exponential path. Consequently the planned consumption gradually reduces its influence on the supply. On the other hand, 1-ψ and b_2 times 1-ψ grows also following an exponential time path. So lagged consumption demand gradually imposes more and more influence on the supply. In addition to the above variables, the consumption goods supply is also thought to respond to the lagged gross agricultural output and the fluctuation in the gross output of light industry.

Disequilibrium indicators

Chapter 4 discussed the issue of disequilibrium indicators, and tried to select the appropriate disequilibrium indicator variables in investment markets. Since actual consumption demand or supply are not observed, we encounter a similar problem for the estimation of the consumption model. Below we focus on the selection of disequilibrium indicators for consumption markets.

According to the studies by Fan et al (1990), the increases in household current deposits in China should be more understood as increases in forced savings, while the increases in time deposits can be, to a large extent, treated as increases in voluntary savings. Following this suggestion, we assume that the growth of household current deposits is the result of and proportional to excess demand, namely

$$\frac{\Delta mc}{p} = h1 \frac{c^d - c^s}{p}, \qquad \text{iff } c^d - c^s > 0 \qquad (5.21)$$

where mc ——— household current saving deposits
Δmc ——— $mc - mc_{-1}$
$h1 > 0$ ——— parameter

Equation (5.21) says that, if real household current deposits increase, this must be the result of excess demand or forced savings, because the inequality that c^d minus c^s is larger than zero is a necessary and sufficient condition. One cannot, however, say that a fall in household current deposits mean that the consumption market must be in excess supply. This is because there is another possibility (other than excess supply) that, after all the transfers of demand, the balance in markets is just reached. So the decrease in real household current deposits does not necessarily signify an excess supply regime. To have disequilibrium indicators for both regimes, equation (5.22) is proposed:

$$\frac{ct}{p} - \frac{c_{-1}}{p_{-1}} = h2\frac{c^d - c^s}{p}, \quad \text{iif } c^d - c^s < 0 \tag{5.22}$$

where $h2 > 0$ —— parameter

This relation assumes a plan adjustment mechanism for the excess supply regime. When the central government wants to cut down the consumption demand, say, for the purposes of fighting inflation or rectifying the overheated economy, planned consumption will be less than previously realized consumption. As mentioned before, the time series of plan targets are not available, and thus the time trend in consumption is used instead as a proxy.

Obviously, as the adjustment mechanism varies from the excess demand regime to the excess supply regime, the disequilibrium indicators proposed above are of asymmetric property. Based on (5.21) and (5.22) the respecified consumption demand and supply functions are formulated separately below as:

$$\frac{c}{p} = \frac{c^d}{p} - \frac{R1}{h1}\frac{\Delta mc}{p}, \quad R1 = \begin{cases} 1, & \text{if } \frac{\Delta mc}{p} > 0 \quad (c^d > c^s) \\ 0, & \text{otherwise} \quad (c^d \leq c^s) \end{cases} \tag{5.23}$$

$$\frac{c}{p} = \frac{c^s}{p} + \frac{R2}{h2}\left(\frac{ct}{p} - \frac{c_{-1}}{p_{-1}}\right), \quad R2 = \begin{cases} 1, & \text{if } \frac{ct}{p} - \frac{c_{-1}}{p_{-1}} < 0 \quad (c^d < c^s) \\ 0, & \text{otherwise} \quad (c^d \geq c^s) \end{cases} \tag{5.24}$$

$$c = \min\{c^d, c^s\} \tag{5.25}$$

Equation (5.25) is the minimum condition which states that the quantities transacted are equal to the short side of demand and supply in consumption markets. Thus in (5.23), when c^d is larger than c^s, $R1$ is one, and the quantities transacted c fall onto the supply schedule c^s; when c^d is less than or equal to c^s, $R1$ is zero, and c falls onto the demand (and supply) schedule c^d (c^s). Analogously similar results can also be applied to equation (5.24). It should be noted that $R1$ and $R2$ cannot simultaneously equal one, because two regimes exclude each other. But they can simultaneously equal zero when the market is in equilibrium.

5.3 Econometric model and estimation results

The formation of the econometric model

Having discussed the theoretical model in the preceding sections, we are now able to put forward an econometric model for estimation. To simplify matters, we drop the price variables and employ capital letters to express variables in real terms.

Let us first deal with the consumption demand model. Substituting (5.18) for consumption demand in the respecified equation (5.23), and replacing flow of forced savings with stocks of the forced savings, we have the following econometric model to estimate:

$$C = DC - \frac{R1}{h1} \Delta MC$$
$$= a_0 + a_1 Z2 + a_2(YD + \varphi FSS_{-1}) + a_3(DC-SC)^e + a_4 Z2P + a_5 R1 \Delta MC + \mu_1$$
$$= a_0 + a_1 Z2 + a_2 YD + a_2 \varphi FSS_{-1} + a_3(DC-SC)^e + a_4 Z2P + a_5 R1 \Delta MC + \mu_1$$
$$= a_0 + a_1 Z2 + a_2 YD - a_2 \varphi a_5 MC_{-1} - a_3 a_5 (R1 \Delta MC)^e + a_4 Z2P + a_5 R1 \Delta MC + \mu_1$$

(5.26)

where
- DC ——— demand for consumption goods (retail sales) at constant prices in billion yuan
- C ——— actual retail sales of consumption goods at constant prices in billion yuan (**SYBC**)
- MC ——— ST-MT; household current saving deposits at constant prices in billion yuan
- ST ——— total household saving deposits at constant prices in billion yuan (**SYBC**)
- MT ——— household time deposits at constant prices in billion yuan (**SYBC**)
- ΔMC ——— $MC - (MC_{-1} P_{-1})/P$
- YD ——— WL+NLI-NC, real disposable income in billion yuan
- WL ——— real wage income in a wide sense in billion yuan (**SYBC**)
- NLI ——— real non-labour income in billion yuan (**SYBC**)
- NC ——— non-consumption expenditures at constant prices in billion yuan (**SYBC**)
- FSS ——— $-a_5 MC$, stocks of forced savings at constant prices in billion yuan
- P ——— index of retail prices; 1969=1.00 (**SYBC**)
- a_5 ——— $-1/h1$

$R1$, $h1$ ——— parameters defined as in section 5.2
$Z2$ ——— Dummy variable ($Z2=0$, for 1868-1978; $Z2=1$, for 1979-1989)
a_1, a_2, $a_3>0$; a_4, $a_5<0$ ——— structural parameters
(For the abbreviation **SYBC**, please refer to Appendix 4A).

When it comes to the empirical results, we find that the variable stocks of forced savings is a better candidate than the flow of forced savings. Since the flow of forced savings in nominal terms (financial equivalent of positive excess consumption demand) is proportional to $mc-mc_{-1}$, the disequilibrium indicator, it is easy to derive the real stocks of forced savings FSS as proportional to MC.² After closer examination, we find that using the variable FSS_{-1} instead of FS_{-1} does not violate our definition of the activated income, because the component $a_2(YD+\varphi FSS_{-1})$ in (5.26) can be expressed as

$$a_2(YD+\varphi FSS_{-1}) = a_2[YD+\varphi(FS_{-1}+FSS_{-2})]$$
$$= a_2(YD+\varphi FS_{-1}) + a_2\varphi FSS_{-2} = a_2 YE + a_2\varphi FSS_{-2} \quad (5.26a)$$

where $YE=YD+\varphi FS_{-1}$ is the activated income according to equation (5.5). While the activated forced savings (flow) φFS_{-1} may be kept in consumers' pockets and treated as extra income (see Welfe, 1989), the stocks of forced savings accumulated at the end of period $t-2$, FSS_{-2}, should be considered as having been already transformed into the form of current saving deposits. So relation in (5.26a) simply suggests that FS_{-1} affects consumption demand in a role of income, and hence part of the activated income, while FSS_{-2} influences consumption demand in a role of savings, and hence part of current savings. Although we will not make such a distinction when estimating (5.26) — still take FSS_{-1} to be one variable rather than separate it as in (5.26a), the different roles they play should be kept in mind, so that the parameter φ in (5.26) can still be used as the coefficient of activation of forced savings in calculating data on the activated income YE later.

Because the model is estimated over the period covering pre-reform and post-reform, the dummy variable Z2 is introduced to express the structural shifts occurring in the post-reform period. Referring back to Figure 5.2, we saw that, before 1979, prices remained almost unchanged at their base level of 1969 (equal to one), due to the strict controls imposed by the government. Households then did not take them into account in determining their consumption. After 1979, economic reforms gradually released the restrictions on prices, so that they grew much more rapidly than before 1979. As a result, prices began to influence household consumption decisions.

Second, based on the theoretical equation (5.19), the econometric model of normal savings is given in (5.27):

$$\Delta NS = e_0 + e_1(1-Z2)YE + e_2\Omega Z2YE + e_4 ri + e_5(DC-SC)^e + \mu_2$$
$$= e_0 + e_1(1-Z2)YE + e_2\Omega Z2YE + e_4 ri - e_5 a_5 (RI\Delta MC)^e + \mu_2 \qquad (5.27)$$

where ΔNS ———— flow of normal savings at constant prices in billion yuan
 YE ———— $YD + \varphi FS_{-1}$, activated income at constant prices in billion yuan
 FS ———— flow of forced savings at constant prices in billion yuan
 Ω ———— $1 - \exp(e_3 YEID_{-1})$
 YEID ———— index of YE; 1979=1
 ri ———— $\dfrac{(1+i)P}{PT^e_{+1}}$
 i ———— nominal interest rates on household time deposits (**ACFB**, **LIHU** and **ARCO**)
 PT ———— $P + \bar{p}$, the 'true' price
 $\bar{p}$ ———— repressed prices
 $e_1, e_2, e_4 > 0$ and $e_3, e_5 < 0$ ———— structural parameters

(For the abbreviations **ACFB**, **LIHU** and **ARCO**, please refer to Appendix 4A).

This model allows for structural changes in household saving behaviour, particularly in MPS. Prior to 1979, the income of households was at very low and stable level; housing, pension, education, medical services and so on are provided by the government. With economic uncertainty reduced and the income flow smoothed, a household's marginal propensity to save remained constant at low level. Since 1979 the results of economic reform have been a sharp increase in household income and economic uncertainty. Household farms and free and parallel markets in urban areas have emerged. The monetization of the economy has increased the demand for money. Now households income contains a large amount of possible extra money from various sources, and thus is more volatile than before. In addition, the impact on uncertainty of prospective reforms of price, housing, education and medical systems is not insignificant. Consequently, a household's motives to save have kept rising, with measured MPS increasingly larger than ever before. To incorporate this phenomenon in our model, we have made an assumption that the Chinese households behave like Keynesian consumers, with their MPS being an increasing exponential function of income (lagged one period) during the 1980s. More specifically, before 1979 MPS is e_1, while after 1979 MPS is e_2 times Ω.

Another variable which needs to be explained is ri. Here ri is the 'true real interest rate', because the nominal interest rate is divided by the 'true inflation rate' rather than official inflation rate. A problem arises as of how to measure the true price. Following Feltenstein, we define the true price as the price which would induce the observed quantity of consumption, and thus the true price is understood as the official price plus the repressed price ($PT=P+\bar{p}$). Now suppose that prices rise from the official level to the true level which results in consumption demand equalling the transacted quantity and so eliminating excess demand. In this case equation (5.26) can be manipulated as:

$$\begin{aligned}C &= a + a_2 YD - a_2\varphi a_5 MC_{-1} - a_3 a_5 (R1\Delta MC)^e + a_4(P+\bar{p}) + \mu_1\\ &= a + a_2 YD - a_2\varphi a_5 MC_{-1} - a_3 a_5 (R1\Delta MC)^e + a_4[(1-Z2)P + Z2P] + a_4\bar{p} + \mu_1\\ &= [a + a_4(1-Z2)p] + a_2 YD - a_2\varphi a_5 MC_{-1} - a_3 a_5 (R1\Delta MC)^e + a_4 Z2P + a_4\bar{p} + \mu_1\\ &= a_0 + a_1 Z2 + a_2 YD - a_2\varphi a_5 MC_{-1} - a_3 a_5 (R1\Delta MC)^e + a_4 Z2P + a_4\bar{p} + \mu_1\end{aligned}$$

(5.26b)

Comparing (5.26b) with (5.26) we find that a_4 times $\bar{p}$ equals excess demand, namely,

$$a_4\bar{p} = a_5 R1\Delta MC$$

and therefore

$$\bar{p} = \frac{a_5}{a_4} R1\Delta MC \qquad (5.28)$$

We thus decided to use this relation to calculate the repressed price $\bar{p}$ after a_4 and a_5 are estimated. The introduction of dummy variable Z2 does not alter the assumption that the observed quantity of consumption would be induced by the true price. When official price is sticky, households regard it as constant. Thus estimates of its impact on consumption are implicitly included in the intercept a_0. The estimates of impact of repressed prices, another part of true prices, on consumption demand, are implicitly given in the component, i.e., the disequilibrium indicator for excess demand.

Thirdly, by substituting (5.20) for consumption supply in (5.24), the respecified econometric model to be estimated looks like:

$$\begin{aligned}C &= SC + \frac{R2}{h2}(CT - C_{-1})\\ &= b_0 + b_1\psi CT + b_2(1-\psi)DC_{-1} + b_4 AG_{-1} + b_5 LYXY + b_6 R2(CT - C_{-1}) + \mu_3\end{aligned}$$

(5.29)

where ψ ——— $\exp(b_3 Z2t)$
SC ——— supply of consumption goods (retail sales) at constant prices
CT ——— a second-order exponential time trend in C

AG ——— index of gross output of agriculture; 1952=100 (**SYBC**)
LYXY ——— (LIID-LIIDT)/LIIDT
LIID ——— index of gross output of light industry; 1952=100 (**SYBC**)
LIIDT ——— a second-order exponential time trend in LIID
$b_1, b_2, b_4, b_5, b_6 > 0; b_3 < 0$ ——— structural parameters

(For the abbreviation **SYBC**, please refer to Appendix 4A).

Model estimates and comments on the results

We now arrive at the estimation stage of equations (5.26), (5.27) and (5.29). In equation (5.26), the income variable YD is taken as exogenous because excess supply of labour is assumed. The price variable P is thought to be responsive to the lagged excess demand, and hence is contemporaneously exogenous. The endogenous variables on the right hand side of the equation are the expected excess demand $(R1\Delta MC)^e$ and the disequilibrium indicator $R1\Delta MC$. Note that a realized and an expected value of the same variable appear. In this case, the substitution method (SM) rather than error-in-variable procedure (EVM) is to be used, for the reasons given in section 4.5. Thus concerning the treatment of expectations in the estimation procedure, the weakly rational extrapolative predictor for $(R1\Delta MC)^e$ is constructed from a regression of $R1\Delta MC$ on lagged exogenous (predetermined) variables, and is substituted back in the place of the expectation variable. Then the RE model is estimated by instrument variable method, and for the disequilibrium indicator $R1\Delta MC$ the instruments are the current and lagged exogenous variables and the predetermined variables. The estimation results are presented as follows (Estimation period: 1968-1989; yearly data):

$$C = 101.6767 + 314.3228 Z2 + 0.7975 YD + 0.6425 MC_{-1}$$
$$(5.2747) \quad (4.9402) \quad (29.4906) \quad (2.0103)$$

$$+ 1.9014 (R1\Delta MC)^e - 291.8620 Z2P - 1.7957 R1\Delta MC$$
$$(4.6687) \quad\quad (-4.7274) \quad (-3.8931)$$

$\bar{R}^2 = 0.9997$ $\quad SE = 17.4823 \quad \chi_S^2(10) = 11.9308 \quad \chi_A^2(1) = 0.13534$
$\chi_F^2(1) = 1.8236 \quad \chi_N^2(2) = 0.9867 \quad\quad \chi_H^2(1) = 0.1362$

(5.30)

where
$\bar{R}^2$ ——— the coefficient of determination corrected for degree of freedom
SE ——— the standard error of regression
χ^2_s ——— the Sargan's statistic for a general test of misspecification

χ^2_A ——— a test of residual serial correlation in LM version
χ^2_F ——— a test of functional form misspecification in LM version
χ^2_N ——— a test of non-normality of error in LM version
χ^2_H ——— a test of heteroscedasticity

of the model and instruments

Given the estimation results in (5.30), some original parameters may now be identified as:

$$\varphi = \frac{0.6425}{-a_2 a_5} = \frac{0.6425}{-0.7975*(-1.7957)} \approx 0.4486 < 1;$$

$$\eta = 1 - \varphi \approx 1 - 0.45 = 0.5513;$$

$$a_3 = -\frac{1.9014}{a_5} = \frac{-1.9014}{-1.7957} \approx 1.0589.$$

The next issue concerns the estimation of normal saving function (5.27). Before doing this, some calculations need to be done. In identity (5.7), the flow of forced savings in nominal terms, fs, is defined as financial equivalent of positive excess demand, $c - \bar{c}$. Here in real terms, it is DC-C. Thus

$$FS = DC - C = 1.7957 R1 \Delta MC$$

These results are employed to calculate data on YE, the activated income, and on ΔNS, the normal savings. Data on YE are calculated according to its definition $YE = YD + \varphi FS_{-1}$ (recall (5.27) and (5.5)):

$$YE = YD + 0.4486 FS_{-1} = YD + 0.8056 \Delta MC_{-1}$$

Identity (5.10) has also defined the following relationship: the activated income YE ($= YD + \varphi FS_{-1}$, and $YD = WL + NLI - NC$) is allocated between desired consumption expenditures DC and increases in normal savings ΔNS, that is, $YE = DC + \Delta NS$ (or $YD + \varphi FS_{-1} = C + FS + \Delta NS$). Consequently and clearly, the data on the normal savings should be calculated in this way:

$$\Delta NS = YE - DC = YE - (C + FS) = YE - C - 1.7957 R1 \Delta MC$$

Another variable, the data on which need to be computed, is the true price PT. Using relation (5.28) and the above estimates, we have

$$PT = P + \bar{p} = P + \frac{a_5}{a_4} R1 \Delta MC = P + \frac{-1.7957}{-291.8620} R1 \Delta MC = P + 6.1525 * 10^{-3} R1 \Delta MC$$

Now we are ready to undertake the estimation work for (5.27). The predictor for PT^e_{+1} is obtained in a similar manner as before, while in the regression the instruments chosen include the current exogenous variables and lagged endogenous variables. The fitted values of PT_{+1} replace the expected ones to calculate the time series of what we called the 'true real interest rates' $ri (= (1+i)P/PT^e_{+1})$, before the second step is completed. Because

(5.27) is a non-linear equation, the non-linear least squares procedure is thus applied in the second step, which leads to the following results (Estimation period: 1968-1989; yearly data):

$\Delta NS = -178.8057 + 0.0891(1-Z2)YE + 0.2089[1-\exp(-0.9031 YEID_{-1})]Z2YE$
$\quad (-2.6224)(3.3266) \qquad (26.6020) \qquad (-4.4016)$

$+124.4066 ri - 1.9145(R1\Delta MC)^e$
$(2.3172) \quad (-11.1219)$

$\bar{R}^2 = 0.9923 \qquad SE = 20.7395 \qquad \chi_A^2(1) = 0.1153$
$\chi_F^2(1) = 2.6619 \qquad \chi_N^2(2) = 0.1225 \qquad \chi_H^2(1) = 0.00199$

(5.31)

The parameter e_5 (see (5.27)) is then identified as

$$e_5 = -\frac{-1.9145}{a_5} = -\frac{-1.9145}{-1.7957} = -1.0662$$

Finally, applying the non-linear least squares procedure to the equation (5.29) yields the numerically specified model for consumption supply (Estimation period: 1968-1989; yearly data):

$C = -487.5571 + 4.6464 AG_{-1} + 473.8717 * LYXY + 0.8090 \exp(-0.0744 Z2t)CT$
$\quad (-2.8006) \quad (3.1633) \qquad (2.9229) \qquad \qquad (11.2380) \quad (-2.5393)$

$+0.8440[1-\exp(-0.0744 Z2t)]DC_{-1} + 4.1237 R2(CT-C_{-1})$
$(9.5995) \qquad (-2.5393) \qquad \qquad (6.3926)$

$\bar{R}^2 = 0.9981 \qquad SE = 46.3844 \qquad \chi_A^2(1) = 1.0965$
$\chi_F^2(1) = 0.2699 \qquad \chi_N^2(2) = 0.1189 \qquad \chi_H^2(1) = 0.0352$

(5.32)

The results from estimating these three equations appear to be remarkably good. All the estimated coefficients in the consumption demand equation (5.30) are significantly different from zero at the 5% level or better, and satisfy *a priori* signs. In magnitude, the coefficient of activation of forced savings φ (=0.4486) lies in the interval required ([0,1]), consistent with our original assumptions; the parameter of income a_2 is estimated to be 0.7975 with the highest t value (29.4906), indicating that disposable income is a major factor affecting households' consumption decisions; the estimate of a_3, the coefficient associated with expectations of excess consumption demand, is close to unity, suggesting that *excess* consumption demand may be led to just by households' expectations. The introduction of dummy variable Z2 gives rise to high t values of price variable and intercept, verifying the shifts in households' consumption behaviour brought about by economic reforms, which are particularly reflected in their negative responses to changes in the price level after 1979. Besides, the high t value, the plausible size and the right sign of a_5, the coefficient of disequilibrium indicator, justify that the increases in household current deposits have been a correct choice for disequilibrium indicators. In addition, the Sargan's statistic for misspecification of the model and instruments, and the Lagrange multiplier statistics for serial correlation, non-normality, functional form misspecification and heteroscedasticity, are all below their critical values at the level of 10%: $\chi_S^2(10)=11.9302 < \chi_{0.9}^2(10)=15.987$, $\chi_A^2(1)=0.13534 < \chi_{0.9}^2(1)=2.706$, $\chi_F^2(1)=1.8236 < \chi_{0.9}^2=2.706$, $\chi_N^2(2)=0.9867 < \chi_{0.9}^2(2)=4.605$, and $\chi_H^2(1)=0.136 < \chi_{0.9}^2(1)=2.706$. According to these diagnostic statistics, we cannot reject the hypotheses that the model, the instruments and the functional form are correctly specified, and hypotheses that the residual is serially independent, normally distributed and has a constant variance, at the 10% level of significance.

The estimated savings function (5.31) fits the data well, with all coefficients bearing the right signs, reasonable magnitudes and high t values. Since $\chi_A^2(1)=0.1153 < \chi_{0.9}^2(1)=2.706$, $\chi_F^2(1)=2.6619 < \chi_{0.9}^2(1)=2.706$, $\chi_N^2(2)=0.1225 < \chi_{0.9}^2(2)=4.605$, and $\chi_H^2(1)=0.00199 < \chi_{0.9}^2(1)=2.706$, we cannot reject, at the 10% level of significance, the hypotheses that the residual is serially independent, normally distributed and has a constant variance, and that this particularly nonlinear functional form is correctly chosen. It is interesting to compare the results using the 'true real interest rates' with those using the official real interest rates defined as $rioff=(1+i)P/P_{+1}^e$. The predictor for P_{+1}^e is generated on the same instruments as for PT_{+1}^e. Below we report the estimates:

$$\Delta NS = -202.5465 + 0.0656(1-Z2)YE + 0.2223[1-\exp(-0.6466YEID_{-1})]Z2YE$$
$$(-.9475) \quad (2.4827) \quad\quad\quad (13.1478) \quad\quad\quad (-3.9058)$$

$$+163.0557ri - 1.8244(RI\Delta MC)^e$$
$$(0.8295) \quad (-7.1295)$$

$$\bar{R}^2 = 0.9905 \quad\quad SE = 23.0708 \quad\quad \chi_A^2(1) = 0.1526$$
$$\chi_F^2(1) = 2.3402 \quad\quad \chi_N^2(2) = 1.2097 \quad\quad \chi_H^2(1) = 1.3124$$

(5.33a)

The results shown in (5.33a) are clearly worse than those in (5.31): all the corresponding t-ratios have declined; and in particular, the estimated coefficient of the interest rate variable is not significantly different from zero even at the 10% level of significance. These facts revealed model misspecification due to the inclusion of official real interest rates. Thus the 'true price' model far outperformed the official price model: households are well aware of the presence of rationing and on this basis account for interest rate changes in making their savings decisions; but the official inflation rate would be misleading as a policy target and hence bias the government's predictions and policy choices. It is also interesting to find that, if the current (YEID) rather than the lagged income variable (YEID$_{-1}$) was used in specifying the function of marginal propensity to save, the results would have been:

$\Delta NS = -223.9589 + 0.1021(1-Z2)YE + 0.2134[1-\exp(-0.8547YEID)]Z2YE$
$\quad\quad\quad (-3.1226) \quad (3.2237) \quad\quad\quad\quad (20.3249) \quad\quad\quad\quad (-3.5824)$

$+158.0087ri - 1.9973(R1\Delta MC)^e$
$(2.8426) \quad (-10.2366)$

$\bar{R}^2 = 0.9903 \quad\quad\quad SE = 23.3237 \quad\quad\quad \chi_A^2(1) = 0.0097$
$\chi_F^2(1) = 7.5871 \quad\quad \chi_N^2(2) = 1.2068 \quad\quad \chi_H^2(1) = 0.7343$

(5.33b)

Comparing (5.33b) with (5.31), one can see that, although in the former parameters and their t values do not change significantly and other diagnostic statistics are good enough, the test for functional form misspecification fails. One massage from this comparison is that, although the Chinese households' savings are determined by the current income, their *saving notions* (i.e., marginal propensity to save) are influenced by their expectations about future income, which is captured by the variable of lagged income. This result appears to be consistent with our assumptions made above.

In the consumption supply equation (5.32), the six estimated coefficients also have the expected signs and are all significant at conventional level or better. Interesting enough, we can see that, before 1979, the consumption supply displayed the strongest response to the plan variable which, after 1989, was gradually replaced by the lagged demand variable (CT and DC$_{-1}$ bear the highest t values and the largest parameters, compared to other variables with the same units), as the joint variables Z2 times t in the exponential functions are well defined statistically. Again, the high t ratio, the right sign and the plausible magnitude of the coefficient, b_6 (see equation 5.29)), confirm our correct specification of the disequilibrium indicator for the excess supply regime. Finally, four reported diagnostic statistics are all below their critical values at well above the 10% level of significance ($\chi_A^2(1)=1.0965 < \chi_{0.9}^2(1)=2.706$, $\chi_F^2(1)=0.2699 < \chi_{0.9}^2(1)=2.706$, $\chi_N^2(2)=0.1189 < \chi_{0.9}^2(2)=4.605$, and $\chi_H^2(1)=0.0352 < \chi_{0.9}^2(1)=2.706$), reflecting that we cannot reject the hypotheses of serial independence, normality and homoscedasticity of the error terms, and hypothesis of no misspecification of functional form, at this level.

So much for the technical background. One of the economically interesting results is given in Table 5.1. Here we find comparisons of various indicators of tension on the consumption goods market: the official inflation rate PI, our own index of percentage excess demand LIXD, Burkett's index of relative shortage BSH, the Portes-Winter index of percentage excess demand PWXD, and the Feltenstein-Ha virtual price rate of inflation FPI. The assumptions invoked to generate disequilibrium used in these works are quite different. As was reviewed in chapter 2, Portes and Santorum generally use the aggregative discrete switching model for generating demand and supply, assuming no disequilibrium adjustment mechanism. They also try the Burkett's method, without netting out slack. In that light, none of the resultant estimates PWXD and BSH for China's consumption markets show the excess demand regime dominating the entire period under investigation. But they have, after all, suggested an evolution of consumption disequilibrium towards positive excess demand in the post-reform period. Unfortunately, their results are available only until 1983. To have more comparisons, we decided to present FPI, the virtual price rate of inflation, calculated according to Feltenstein and Ha's suggestions that 'the annual rate of inflation of the "true" price index was approximately 8 percent higher than that of the official price index over the 10-year period' (Feltenstein and Ha 1991, p. 293). The most striking inconsistency between LIXD (our indicator) and FPI appears in 1989. In fact, it has been widely recognized and observed by the Chinese economic authorities and economists that the Chinese economy in 1989 was turned into deep slump (see Yang 1990, Xun et al 1992, Jiang 1991, and many other similar publications in various issues of *Jingji Yanjiu* (*Economic Research Journal*), 1990-1992). This economic depression had never happened since reform, and was surely the result of drastic austerity drive launched in the fourth quarter of 1988. Some economists (Guo 1992, for example) even go so far as to claim that in China the 'era of shortage' has gone for ever. In view of this, the figures for FPI for 1989 still implying a very high degree of repressed inflation (FPI>PI) is rather unrealistic at least in that year. Perhaps the underlying assumption concerning the true price remains a problem (see equation (2.40)), as it always views household savings as 'a tiger in a cage', and never permits that it might have a voluntary character, and thus release the price pressures on the consumption goods market. Our indicator LIXD shows that in the 1980s, there were three years with highest degree of market tension: 1984, 1987 and 1988, and one year with excess supply: 1989. These results are highly consistent with historical reality.

Table 5.1
Prices and excess demand

t	PI	LIXD	BSH	PWXD	FPI
1968	0.1	3.9	0.0	-1.9	n.a.
1969	-1.1	0	0.0	-2.2	n.a.
1970	-0.2	0.9	0.0	0.6	n.a.
1971	-0.7	2.5	0.7	2.0	n.a.
1972	-0.2	0.3	0.0	1.1	n.a.
1973	0.6	3.1	0.0	1.4	n.a.
1974	0.5	3.3	0.0	0.0	n.a.
1975	0.2	2.3	0.0	-0.7	n.a.
1976	0.3	0.2	2.0	2.3	n.a.
1977	2.0	1.2	0.0	-4.5	n.a.
1978	0.7	1.8	0.0	-1.8	n.a.
1979	2.0	2.6	0.0	0.8	n.a.
1980	6.0	0.1	4.5	7.2	6.5
1981	2.4	3.9	2.7	3.7	2.6
1982	1.9	2.7	4.2	5.5	2.1
1983	1.5	1.7	3.5	5.1	1.6
1984	2.8	6.1	n.a.	n.a.	3.0
1985	8.8	2.9	n.a.	n.a.	9.5
1986	6.0	1.1	n.a.	n.a.	6.5
1987	7.3	6.9	n.a.	n.a.	7.9
1988	18.5	6.4	n.a.	n.a.	20.0
1989	17.8	-13.6	n.a.	n.a.	19.2

Note: t=year. PI=percentage change of official price index. LIXD=percentage of excess demand $[100(D\hat{C}-S\hat{C})/C]$, from the model estimated in this chapter. BSH=Burkett index of relative shortage $[100(D\hat{C}-\hat{C})/\hat{C}]$, presented in Portes and Santorum (1987). PWXD=Portes and Winter percentage of excess demand $[100(D\hat{C}-S\hat{C})/C]$ presented in Portes and Santorum (1987). FPI=percentage change of true price index proposed by Feltenstein and Ha (1991). n.a.=not available

5.4 Extension of the model

The previous sections have dealt with the central part of consumption block. To complete this block for the policy simulations in chapter 6, a few more auxiliary equations need to be added. They are

$$YD = WL + NLI - NC = Y1 + Y2 + Y3 + Y4 - NC \tag{5.34}$$

$$Y1 = \alpha_0 + \alpha_1(LOS + LOP) + \alpha_2 LU + \alpha_3 Z1 + \mu_4 \tag{5.35}$$

$$Y3 = \beta_0 + \beta_1 Z2 + \beta_2(GEE + NGEE) + \beta_3 FUND + \beta_4 Z2P + \beta_5 Z1 + \mu_5 \tag{5.36}$$

$$LIID = \gamma_0 + \gamma_1 NI + \gamma_2 DC + \gamma_3 P + \gamma_4 Z2P + \mu_6 \tag{5.37}$$

$$\Delta \log(P) = \log(P) - \log(P_{-1}) = \lambda_0 + \lambda_1 DEE_{-1} + \mu_7 \tag{5.38}$$

where
$Y1$ —— total wage and salary income in both the state and non-state sectors + self-employment income of non-farmers, at constant prices (**SYBC**)
$Y2$ —— total money income of farmers at constant prices (**SYBC**)
$Y3$ —— government transfer payments advanced to households + money of governmental units for purchases of public consumption goods + other earnings of households (**SYBC**)
$Y4$ —— net credit advanced to households + money income by foreigners's purchases of domestic consumption goods, at constant prices (**SYBC**)
LU —— numbers of employees in cities and towns (**SYBC**)
$\alpha_1, \alpha_2 > 0; a_3 < 0$ —— structural parameters of (5.35)
$\beta_1, \beta_5 < 0; \beta_2, \beta_3, \beta_4 > 0$ —— structural parameters of (5.36)
$\gamma_1, \gamma_2, \gamma_3, \gamma_4 > 0$ —— structural parameters of (5.37)
$\lambda_1 > 0$ —— price adjustment parameter of (5.38)
$\alpha_0, \beta_0, \gamma_0, \lambda_0$ —— intercepts
$\mu_4, \mu_5, \mu_6, \mu_7$ —— error terms

(For the abbreviation **SYBC**, please refer to Appendix 4A). Other variables, such as YD, WL, NLI, NC, LOS, LOP, GEE, NGEE, FUND, LIID, NI, DC, P, DEE, Z1 and Z2, are defined as before (see sections 4.2 and 5.3).

Regarding equation (5.35), Y1 represents total labour income in wide sense of employees in urban areas. In fact, this category of money income accounts for a considerable proportion of working capital loans either to the state sectors or to the non-state sectors and individual businesses. It is therefore reasonable to choose (LOS+LOP) as an explanatory variable for Y1. In addition, since Y1 is not expressed in per capita terms, the number of the employees, i.e., the recipients of Y1 is thought to be another explanatory variable. In 1989, due to the economic rectification, quite a number of enterprises were closed down, and the employees were forced to stay at home without working and receiving 70% or even less of their normal pay. Thus the dummy variable Z1 is chosen to capture this unusual phenomenon.

Looking at the components of Y3, we can see that it is related mainly to government policy instruments. In other words, Y3 is viewed as a kind of 'policy income'. First, the government transfer payment advanced to households is part of government expenditures. Second, the money income of governmental institutions for purchases of public consumption goods grows as the extra-budgetary funds expand. This is why many Chinese economists attribute the expansion of public consumption to the extra-budgetary funds which they would like to see controlled. Third, households 'other earnings' are assumed to be connected with price subsidy policies, according to which households should be compensated for a number of social disutilities related mainly to inflation resulting from gradual lifting of control on prices. But the price subsidy policies were adopted mainly after 1979, as the price level was almost constant before 1979 (see Figure 5.1). The above considerations help to add three kinds of income up as Y3, and to choose government expenditures, extra-budgetary funds, price times Z2 (Z2=0 for 1968-1978; Z2=1 for 1979-1989), and Z2 as Y3's main regressors. Z1 is used in the similar way as equation (5.35).

The gross output of light industry, LIID, accounts for a part of national income, and is assumed to be positively related to NI. But actually it has grown faster than NI since 1979. The light industry consists of local state-owned and non-state-owned enterprises. Thus it is more market-dependent than upstream sectors. In the circumstance that markets are still immature, both quantity and price signals affect the producers of light industrial products which are mainly for consumption purposes. So the prices and consumption demand should be other two factors explaining why LIID has grown faster than NI. But the post-reform prices should have a stronger effect than the pre-reform ones. Due to this reason, Z2 is also introduced into equation (5.37), being associated with the price variable, and its sign is expected to be positive.

Equation (5.38) is the expression for inflation rate of retail prices. The underlying assumption is that, in the 'two-tier' price system,[3] prices of investment goods markets are subject to much stricter control than retail prices, and shortages in investment markets eventually translate into increases in retail prices. Nevertheless, we have also stated that, concurrent with investment expansion causing excess investment demand, is usually consumption funds expansion causing excess consumption demand which in turn creates favourable seller markets for the enterprises to raise their output prices. One message from this phenomenon is that the role of excess consumption demand should not be ignored in pushing up retail prices. Accordingly, inflation rate of retail prices is assumed to be determined by total excess demand in both consumption and investment markets with one year lag.

Let us now consider the estimation of these four equations. Equations (5.35), (5.36) and (5.38) are estimated by OLS, since there are no (contemporaneously) endogenous variables on the right-hand sides. Equation (5.37) is estimated by IV procedure since NI and DC are endogenous variables, although P is related to the lagged excess demand and hence contemporaneously exogenous. The results are given below:

$Y1 = 0.2047(LOS+LOP) + 0.0309LU - 140.6724Z1$
    (36.696)   (21.4231)   (-6.4447)

$\bar{R}^2 = 0.9976$ $SE = 18.2659$ $\chi_A^2(1) = 0.5146$
$\chi_F^2(1) = 0.8783$ $\chi_N^2(2) = 1.4216$ $\chi_H^2(1) = 0.2569$

(5.42)

$Y3 = -684.4488Z2 + 0.2055(GEE+NGEE) + 0.4354FUND$
    (-10.0406)   (12.8772)   (9.3057)

$+605.475Z2P - 273.5583Z1$
 (8.6526)   (-5.6667)

$\bar{R}^2 = 0.9962$ $SE = 24.8701$ $\chi_A^2(1) = 0.0512$
$\chi_F^2(1) = 0.0021$ $\chi_N^2(2) = 0.6557$ $\chi_H^2(1) = 0.0088$

(5.43)

$LIID = -992.2482 + 1.8996NI + 0.1869DC + 844.9137P + 49.8615Z2P$
      (-20.2545)   (6.916)   (3.4144)   (10.6057)   (2.0165)

$\bar{R}^2 = 0.9989$ $SE = 32.3287$ $\chi_S^2(6) = 7.3955$
$\chi_F^2(1) = 0.0153$ $\chi_A^2(1) = 0.7874$ $\chi_N^2(2) = 1.6958$ $\chi_H^2(1) = 0.0179$

(5.44)

$\Delta \log(P) = 0.01024 + 0.000302DEE_{-1}$
              (1.7353)   (12.7057)

$\bar{R}^2 = 0.9413$ $SE = 0.0135$ $\chi_A^2(1) = 0.7955$
$\chi_F^2(1) = 0.3683$ $\chi_N^2(2) = 0.3271$ $\chi_H^2(1) = 0.7079$

(5.45)

The estimation period is 1968-1989 for equations (5.42)-(5.44), but 1979-

1989 for (5.45), because Figure 5.2 clearly indicated that the price level remained constant before 1979. All the statistics reported here are defined as before. Due to the low t-ratios for intercepts α_0 and β_0 in (5.35) and (5.36) (-0.5519 and 0.052), we decided to drop them in re-estimations. It can be seen that the empirical results are also remarkably good. In the labour income equation (5.42), all t statistics past the critical value at the 1% level of significance, and all the parameters have the right signs. Working capital loans to both state and non-state sectors seem to provide major explanation of increases in labour income Y1. LM statistics show that we are unable to reject the hypotheses of serial independence, normality and homoscedasticity of the error terms, and the hypothesis of no functional form misspecification, at the 10% level. The 'policy income' equation (5.43) exhibits highly significant and positive responses to government expenditure, extra-budgetary funds and changes in price level as a result of price reform. The diagnostic tests do not allow us to reject the hypotheses that the error is serially uncorrelated, and its distribution is normal and homoscedastic, and the functional form is correctly chosen. The four estimated coefficients of the equation (5.44) have the expected (positive) signs, and three are significant at the 1% level and one at the 5% level, implying that the output of light industry can be well explained by national income, consumption demand and price level (with shifts in the parameter after 1979, though small). Since this equation is estimated by IV method, the Sargan's test is presented along with other four LM statistics. They suggest that the following hypotheses cannot be rejected at the 10% level or above: the model and the instruments are correctly specified; the error terms are serial independent; and the error distribution is normal and homoscedastic; and there is no functional form misspecification. The high t ratio in the inflation rate equation (5.45) reveals the fact that the retail price level, in the post reform period, was no longer completely rigid, and responded positively and to a large extent to the domestic market situation but with one year lag. The diagnostic tests also indicate no model misspecification in terms of serial correlation, incorrect functional form, non-normality and heteroscedasticity, at the 10% level or above. To sum up, our initial hypotheses about equations (5.35) through to (5.38) are confirmed by the statistical data, and as such we decided to use these estimates in model simulations for policy analysis.

5.5 Conclusions

Based on the above empirical results, a few points may now be made in conclusions. First, by adopting the disequilibrium indicator approach with a modified budget constraint and utility function, excess demand and hence forced savings are determined as a result of the estimation of consumption demand. This in turn helps to distinguish voluntary (especially normal) savings from gross savings, and to obtain true prices, true real interest rates and activated income for the estimation of normal savings.

Second, consumption goods supply is found to be increasingly less responsive to plan signals, but more to demand signals in the post-reform period. This indicates the effect of far-reaching market-oriented reform on the down stream sectors. However, as the income grows more quickly than productivity, and as prices have not yet been fully liberalized, supply still could not match demand. There is one exception in 1989, when government decided to rectify the overheated economy by strictly tightening budgetary expenditures and money supply, and even through administrative orders stoping on-going investment projects. As a result, the consumption market turned from shortage into slack.

Third, in the study made of the savings behaviour of Chinese households by Qian (1988), an abrupt shift in propensity to save was assumed. This assumption would result in a MPS (marginal propensity to save) at the beginning of reforms equalling that after ten years of reforms, despite income in 1989 more than twice that in 1979. Unlike his study, this chapter has shown a gradual rise in propensity to save, which seems more plausible. The MPS cannot, however, increase without limit. The empirical results have indicated that the ceiling on the MPS, in terms of normal savings, is around 0.21 (see equation (5.31)). This ceiling is a property of the exponential function, and as such we have chosen that particular function to use.

Finally, allowing for a distinction between forced and voluntary savings, and nesting these two extreme hypotheses, one may say yes to the question posited at the end of section 5.1. One of our findings is that the existence of both behavioral change and repressed inflation contributed to the rapidly rising personal money balances in the 1980s, because the increase in total savings contain three elements: the increase in forced savings, in normal savings, and the neutralized fraction of previous period's forced savings, namely

$$\Delta S = \Delta FS + \Delta VS = (\Delta FS + \eta FS_{-1}) + \Delta NS$$

This identity clearly says that the increase in forced savings, as a result of market disequilibrium, will directly raise total savings, while a higher propensity to save, as a result of sharp rises in household income, degree of economic uncertainty and monetization, will increase total savings indirectly through adding to normal savings. Accordingly it is not appropriate to rule out either possibility in both model specification and estimation. Table 5.2 gives a picture about the relative roles of these two 'competing' factors. Column 3 sets out the figures on the part of savings which result entirely

Table 5.2
Changes in MPS and components in gross savings

t	ΔMPS	ΔMPS*YE	ΔFS+ηFS$_{-1}$	ΔNS	ΔS
1979	0.02207	35.59	27.81	84.21	112.02
1980	0.03507	66.80	-15.06	199.25	184.19
1981	0.04787	96.84	72.63	93.87	166.50
1982	0.05247	114.79	21.31	149.35	170.66
1983	0.05840	141.77	11.82	218.32	230.14
1984	0.06611	197.13	137.45	293.87	431.32
1985	0.08915	314.55	19.42	396.95	416.37
1986	0.09080	354.46	-2.18	562.96	560.78
1987	0.09628	415.39	232.66	449.64	682.30
1988	0.10110	477.68	138.08	569.80	707.88
1989	0.10493	466.32	-112.14	822.93	710.79

Note: *t=year. MPS=marginal propensity to save. ΔMPS=differences between the pre-reform MPS and the post-reform MPS, calculated by $e_2\Omega$-e_1 (see equation (5.27)). YE=activated income. FS=flow of forced savings. ΔFS=FS-FS$_{-1}$. ΔNS=flow of normal savings. ΔS=increase in total savings. All the figures concerning savings are in billion yuan at the price level of 1969* from changes in MPS. We can see that it has kept rising steadily during the last decade. The fourth Column presents the figures on the part of savings which attribute to market disequilibrium. Obviously the effect of market non-clearing is much more erratic on household savings. Sometimes the *ex ante* normal savings could be larger than the *ex post* gross savings, indicating that the household original saving desires are subject to adjustments according to market situation in the current and previous years. This is consistent with our discussions on the modification of the classical budget constraint. Thus one must conjecture that, in the 1980s, the household behaviour shift was an overwhelming factor which encouraged higher savings, while the repressed inflation only played a subordinate role.

Notes

1. Charemza and Gronicki (1988) proposed a utility function from which the future-constrained consumption demand function could be obtained in its linear form.
2. According to the relation in the equation (5.21), we have:

$$mc_t = mc_{t-1} + h1fs_t = mc_{t-2} + h1fs_{t-1} + h1fs_t$$
$$= \cdots = mc_0 + h1fs_1 + h1fs_2 + \cdots + h1fs_{t-1} + h1fs_t$$

If $mc_0=0$ is assumed, the following equation shows that fss_t is proportional to mc_t:

$$mc_t = h1fs_1 + h1fs_2 + \cdots + h1fs_{t-1} + h1fs_t$$
$$= h1\sum_{i=1}^{t} fs_i = h1fss_t$$

Dividing both sides by prices, and letting FSS_t denote fss_t/p_t, and MC_t denote mc_t/p_t, it is then seen that

$$FSS_t = \frac{1}{h1} MC_t = -a_5 MC_t$$

3. The 'two-tier' price system means the existence at the same time of two prices for commodities, one being the list price set by the state and the other being the fluctuating market price decided by market forces or agreed on by the parties engaged in a transaction. The part of output or inputs that changes hand under state plan is allocated, purchased, sold, or distributed at state-set prices. Any amounts that are in excess of figures set in the state plan are marketed or purchased at market prices.

6 Ex-post policy experiments

6.1 Introduction

In this chapter, the impact of various policy shocks on the economy is considered, using the estimates of the parameters obtained in chapters 4 and 5, and through some standard simulation exercises. Dynamic multipliers, allowing for all contemporaneous and lagged feedbacks and representing the system's response to individual interventions, are used to examine the sensitivity of the endogenous variables to changes in particular exogenous policy variables. For the purpose of this empirical investigation, the simulation model is presented below in its full notation. The model contains four blocks, namely, consumption, investment, production and price:

(1) Consumption

$$DC = 101.6767 + 314.3228Z2 + 0.7975YD + 0.6425MC_{-1}$$
$$+ 1.0589(DC - SC)^e - 291.862Z2P \qquad (6.1)$$

$$SC = -487.5571 + 4.6464AG_{-1} + 473.8717LYXY$$
$$+ 0.809\exp(-0.0744Z2t)CT + 0.844[1 - \exp(-0.0744Z2t)]DC_{-1} \qquad (6.2)$$

$$C = \min \{ DC, SC \} \qquad (6.3)$$

$$YD = Y1 + Y2 + Y3 + Y4 - NC \qquad (6.4)$$

$$Y1 = 0.2047(LOS + LOP) + 0.0309LU - 140.6724Z1 \qquad (6.5)$$

$$Y3 = -684.4488Z2 + 0.2055(GEE + NGEE) + 0.4354FUND \\ + 605.475P - 273.5583Z1 \tag{6.6}$$

$$LIID = -992.2482 + 1.8996NI + 0.1869DC \\ + (844.9137 + 49.8615Z2)P \tag{6.7}$$

$$MC = \frac{MC_{-1}P_{-1}}{P} + \frac{1}{1.7957}(DC - SC) \tag{6.8}$$

(2) Investment

$$DI = -323.177 + 0.2310DC + 1.176DIL + 0.8381DIP + 0.5563GEE \tag{6.9}$$

$$DIL = -256.6033 + 0.5628FUND + 0.4522UNE + 0.3959(DI - SI)^e \\ -250.0157Z1 \tag{6.10}$$

$$DIP = -204.8875 + 0.5256RNRTP + 268.348P_{+1}^e - 0.2421INV_{-1} \\ -1268.8RI \tag{6.11}$$

$$SI = -113.2164 + 2.9959\Delta NI + 0.2719(LOS_{-1} + LOF_{-1}) \\ + 0.5437GEE + 0.5397IMP \tag{6.12}$$

$$IMP = -581.384 + 0.6057NI_{-1} + 0.2097DEE_{-1} + 1021.8OPE \\ -128.9237\Delta EXC \tag{6.13}$$

$$FUND = -152.9204 + 0.1915(LOS + LOF) + 6.5004REB \\ -90.8896Z3 \tag{6.14}$$

$$RTSP = -517.7217 + 0.1978(LOS + LOP) + 0.2820DC_{-1} \\ + 614.6028RPS - 339.4357Z1 \tag{6.15}$$

$$RNRTP = RTSP - WLP - TP \tag{6.16}$$

$$INV = 3.4136\Delta NI_{-1} + 0.2969NI - 0.4362\Delta DEE \tag{6.17}$$

(3) Production

$$\log(NI) = -13.1892 + (1.5989 - 0.2967Z2)\log(\overline{L}) \\ + 0.5118Z2\log(\overline{K}) + (0.3656 - 0.2181Z2)\log(\overline{GEE}) \tag{6.18}$$

$$K = K_{-1} + \Delta K \tag{6.19}$$

$$\Delta K = 0.26R + 0.26R_{-1} + 0.20R_{-2} + 0.12R_{-3} + 0.09R_{-4} + 0.07R_{-5} \qquad (6.20)$$

$$R = I - DPR \qquad (6.21)$$

$$I = \min\{DI, SI\} \qquad (6.22)$$

(4) Price

$$DEE = DI - SI + DC - SC \qquad (6.23)$$

$$\log(P) = \log(P_{-1}) + 0.000302 DEE_{-1} + 0.01024, \quad \text{if } DEE_{-1} \geq 0 \qquad (6.24)$$

To derive the effects of various policy shocks, a base run of the model is first constructed, using its historical path over the estimation period 1979-1988. A new solution run is then generated by perturbing an appropriate policy variable by a given amount. During the simulation experiments, all the estimated residuals were held at their base-run values. In this manner, the simulation can be run without having the residuals influence the differential effect on endogenous variables. Technically, the methods of obtaining the simulated time paths for those expectation variables ($(DC-SC)^e$, $(DI-SI)^e$ and P^e_{+1}) come from Charemza and Gronicki (1988): they are simply results of conditional forecasting from the corresponding dynamic regression equations which were used in the estimation of the model in the previous chapters. The deviation of the new solution run from the base run represents the response of the economy to changes in policy variables. It is the main purpose of this chapter to analyze these policy effects.

In principle, the simulations performed in this study are not immune to the Lucas critique, according to which a policy change sufficiently atypical to amount to a change in 'policy regime' could well induce behavioural responses by private sector agents that would shift the parameters of the model's equations. However, many researchers (e.g. Sheffrin 1983, Mishkin 1979, Sims 1980) have pointed out that, as long as policy actions are exercises within a stable framework, parameters of econometric models may remain constant in the face of policy actions. In this study, the scope of policy evaluation is restricted to the range of policy variation observed during the model's estimation period, so the Lucas critique may not be especially relevant. This point also applies to the issue of linearity. To the extent that the model can be regarded as approximately linear, the results can be interpreted as ready reckoners. Thus, the effect of a 10 percent decrease in government expenditure on non-economic construction (to be explained in Note 2 of this chapter) can be roughly calculated by changing the sign of the simulation results describing the impact of a similar increase; or the results of a 10% increase in domestic credit can be approximately estimated by doubling the effects shown in the 5% case. This is, however, legitimate only in the neighbourhood in which the linear approximation holds; and the size of the neighbourhood should mainly cover the set of politically acceptable policy changes. For example, it is technically feasible, as far as the model is concerned, to generalize the results from, say, an increase in saving interest rates by 1.1 times to a complete equivalence of loan interest rates (about 2-3 times the former) in the black financial markets. But this generalization is inappropriate, as it goes beyond the range of politically acceptable policy changes in the 1980s: the simulations might then be regarded as introducing a new policy regime in which interest rates are endogenously determined in financial markets. Financial markets did not and could not emerge in China in the 1980s when even product markets were subject to frequent administrative interferences.

In the following sections, six standard policy simulations are discussed. Attention is focused on major macroeconomic indicators, particularly consumption demand and supply, excess consumption demand, investment demand and supply, excess investment demand, the price level and real output. The six simulations are:

(ia) A permanent increase of 5 percent in domestic credit (DOCR)[1] from the base values (i.e., DOCRS=1.05DOCR).

(ib) A one-year increase of 214 billion yuan (in real terms) of domestic credit for 1980 (i.e., $DOCRS_{1980} = DOCR_{1980} + 214$).

(iia) A permanent increase in government expenditure on economic construction (GEE) of 10 percentage points from its values in the base solution (i.e., GEES = 1.1GEE).

(iib) A one-year increase of 214 billion yuan (in real terms) in government expenditures on economic construction for 1980 (i.e., $GEES_{1980} = GEE_{1980} + 214$).

(iii) A permanent 10 percent increase in nominal interest rate NRI from its base values (i.e., NRIS% = 1.1NRI%).

(iv) A permanent 10 percent cut in the government expenditures on non-economic construction NGEE from its base value (i.e., NGEES = 0.9NGEE).

The first four shocks (ia, ib, iia, and iib) are assumed to be expansionary policies The shocks have been chosen to facilitate a comparison of the relative effects of monetary and fiscal instruments when the government is attempting to stimulate the economy. Policies (iii) and (iv) are, on the other hand, contractionary, and have been selected to illustrate the impact of government attempts at reducing aggregate demand and cooling down the already overheated economy.

6.2   Simulation results

An increase in domestic credit (DOCR)

In simulation (ia), the historical base of the policy variables are used in 1979. From 1980 onwards, domestic credit is then set at 5 percent above its historical values. Figure 6.1 depicts the time path of the major macroeconomic variables concerned following the credit expansion.

The first result of an exogenous increase in the credit is an increase in consumption demand, the magnitude of which is 1.43% in 1980, and reaches peak at 10.68% in 1988. The increase in consumption demand is due to increases in the two components of household money income, both wage income Y1 and 'policy income' Y3. In fact, the wage income accounts for a considerable proportion of working capital loans, and hence grows as the latter expands. The 'policy income' consists, among other things, of price-related income, which reflects one of state's short-run economic reform policies. According to the policy, households should be compensated for social disutilities arising mainly from inflation due to price reform. Hence, in the case of credit expansion, the overall household money income rises by more than the amount necessary to offset the down-ward pressure of inflation on consumption demand. This is one of the reasons why consumption demand goes up persistently and accelerates, in spite of persistent price rises.

Both local governments' and the non-state sector's investment demand increases gradually, and steadily, in response to this permanent credit expansion. For local governments, the increases in their investment demand range from 3.88% (1980) to 11.79% (1988), while for the non-state sectors, the figures are 7.00% (1980) and 32.68% (1988) correspondingly. The credit expansion influences local government investment demand in two ways. First, it directly raises the level of extra-budgetary funds FUND which, since the launch of reform, have become a major pecuniary source of local government investment. Secondly, it aggravates the degree of shortage expected by local governments in investment market $(DI-SI)^e$, which in turn further increases their demand for investment goods. The effect on non-state sectors' investment demand is even greater. The reason is that the credit expansion works by affecting two positive and one negative determinants of the demand: sales income, expectations of next-year's price level and real interest rates. Finally, aggregate investment demand rises as well, as a result of the assumption built into the system, that it depends positively on consumption demand, local government investment demand and non-state sectors' investment demand (see chapters 3 and 4).

Let us now turn our attention to the supply side of the economy. The rise in domestic credit stimulates investment supply with a one year lag. Since investment supply grows along with investment demand, realized investment which is equal to the minimum of the demand and supply, also increases. This, through distributed lags function of effective increases in the capital stock (see equation (6.20)), gradually uplifts the total output of the economy (real national income in this study). Consumption supply responds to the credit expansion in a more complicated way, being influenced by both lagged consumption demand DC_{-1} and light industry output LIID. As credit expands, households' consumption demand keeps rising; as for light industry output, it expands in response to the increases in consumption demand, national income and the price level resulting from the credit swelling. All the above factors ultimately lead to an increase in consumption supply. Since both consumption demand and supply increase, realized consumption grows as well.

Note that, in the case of credit expansion, the growth of supply is less than that of demand. Consequently, expansionary monetary policy can not eliminate or mitigate excess demand, but rather worsens disequilibria in both consumption markets and investment markets (see DCE and DIE in Figure 6.1). The worsening shortage then translates into severer inflation with the deviation of price level from its base run being 1.69% in 1981 and reaching 50.27% by the end of this experiment. The average inflation rate per year with this credit expansion would be 11.27%.

In the simulation of a temporary monetary policy shock (ib), Figure 6.2 illustrates that the one-year expansion of credit acts as a kind of 'primer' on the economy, since the policy multiplier for prices keeps rising through the simulation period from 0.018% in 1981 to 0.14% in 1988. But the policy multiplier for the output of the economy also rises from 0.12% to 1.49% over 1981-1988, indicating that money supply does have some positive impacts on output.

An increase in government expenditure on economic construction (GEE)

Let us first conduct experiment (iia), in which a 10% increase in government expenditure on economic construction (hereafter referred to as the government construction expenditure or spending) above its historical values is imposed from 1980 through 1988. The simulation results are reported in Figure 6.3. Government construction expenditure accounts for the largest fraction of total government expenditure, and reached 51% in 1988.[2] It should be made clear that the government construction expenditure is not identical to government investment expenditure in fixed assets, for the following reasons. First, government construction expenditure contains expenditure on both fixed assets investment and working capital investment. Second, expenditure on fixed assets investment is, by the definition, a kind of financial appropriation. This implies that some of the expenditure would not be embodied in fixed assets, unlike government investment outlay which is unfortunately unknown due to lack of such data. Although the government construction expenditure distinguishes from government investment in fixed assets, it still plays a very important role in affecting the economy, especially investment demand (of fixed assets examined in this study).

Unlike the previous experiment, an increase in GEE produces lower estimates for the policy impacts on consumption demand and supply, with consumption demand being raised by only 0.63% in the first year and by 2.40% in the last year, and consumption supply being raised by 0.19% and 1.85% in these two years respectively. Moreover, calculating the ratio of ΔDCE to ΔGEE and that of ΔDCE to ΔDOCR, we find that increasing government construction expenditure leads to less excess consumption demand than does increasing the money supply (see Table 6.1). This implies that government construction expenditure has a greater impact on consumption supply, than do increases in the supply of money. However, the impact of government construction expenditure on consumption supply is limited, because it is directly and mainly aimed at the investment goods sector or upstream sector. Also, as has been analyzed in chapter 3, under the multi-sovereignty mechanism, the central government can no longer assure that its accumulation funds will be exclusively spent on investment. Some of them will become consumption funds one way or the other. In addition, an increase in government construction expenditure will lead to an increase in employment, individuals' income and hence consumption funds. Given these two channels, it is not surprising to observe that consumption demand still exceeds consumption supply.

The investment demand of the non-state sectors indicates a more rapid expansion than local government investment demand, as in the case of credit expansion. The reasons for this are somewhat similar to those given in the previous simulation.

Aggregate investment demand illustrates a smaller upward move at the beginning but a larger one by the end, with its percentage increase going from 4.01% to 6.28% over time. Aggregate investment supply rises by 4.87% and 4.33% in the first two years, but then the rate of increase remains approximately at between 2.76-3.41%. Thus, the intensive investment of the central government in the investment goods sector does immediately stimulate more supply than demand. Consequently, excess investment demand falls in the first year, although this reduction does not persist. First, considering supply, the bigger initial increase in aggregate investment supply is mainly due to a sudden jump in $(NI-NI_{-1})$ resulting from the increase in government construction expenditure. However, output growth will return to relatively constant speed, despite a permanent increase in government construction expenditure, and so will aggregate investment supply. On the other hand, aggregate investment demand depends on government construction expenditure, consumption demand and the investment demand of downstream sectors. In the theoretical studies of investment demand (see chapter 3), it was stated that the central government policy stance towards capital accumulation is one of the major factors influencing the magnitude of aggregate investment demand, and could cause severer disequilibrium (shortage) in the investment goods markets. In the econometric modelling of the investment block (see chapter 4), government construction expenditure was used as a proxy for that policy stance. If the central government's policy stance is to achieve a higher rate of capital accumulation (reflected by higher value of GEE), and at the same time it does not retrieve the 'sovereignty' from subunits, then the greater competition among economic agents (central government, local governments and individuals etc.) for resources will stimulate friction amongst capital accumulation and consumption, and between investments in the upstream and downstream sectors. As consumption demand and local governments' investment demand continue rising in response to the increase in government construction expenditure, aggregate investment demand will soon outweigh aggregate investment supply. This is a necessary result of non-cooperative strategic behaviour of economic agents in the public-ownership economy (refer to chapter 3 for more details). Therefore, in this empirical investigation based on policy simulations, it is shown that a permanent increase in government construction expenditure will, in the subsequent duration of a few years, result in more excess investment demand than a permanent expansion of domestic credit (see RI2 and RI1 in Table 6.1).

However, at the aggregate level and in long run, expansionary monetary policies still cause more *total* excess demand than expansionary fiscal policies (comparing R1 with R2 and RI1 with RI2 in Table 6.1). The reason for this is because the increase in government construction expenditure demonstrates a greater impact on total output. To illustrate this, compare the results of one-year fiscal and monetary policy shocks (iib and ib). Figure 6.2 shows that the policy multiplier of government construction expenditure for output is raised by 7.22% in 1981 and by 2.65% in 1988.

Table 6.1
Policy multipliers for excess demands

t	RC1	RC2	RI1	RI2	R1	R2
1980	0.198	0.103	0.288	-0.101	0.486	0.002
1981	0.262	0.141	0.198	0.343	0.460	0.484
1982	0.294	0.131	0.251	0.513	0.545	0.644
1983	0.331	0.114	0.355	0.489	0.686	0.603
1984	0.347	0.128	0.433	0.524	0.780	0.652
1985	0.377	0.145	0.542	0.630	0.919	0.775
1986	0.389	0.161	0.669	0.633	1.058	0.794
1987	0.437	0.198	0.829	0.846	1.266	1.044
1988	0.545	0.277	1.373	1.212	1.918	1.489
a.s.	0.353	0.155	0.549	0.565	0.902	0.721

Note: $t=year$. $RC1=\Delta DCE/\Delta DOCR$. $RC2=\Delta DCE/\Delta GEE$. $RI1=\Delta DIE/\Delta DOCR$. $RI2=\Delta DIE/\Delta GEE$. $R1=RC1+RI1$. $R2=RC2+RI2$. $\Delta DOCR$ and ΔGEE are permanent increases in domestic credit of 5% and in government construction expenditure of 10%, respectively. a.s.=average sum

The corresponding figures for the output multiplier of monetary policy were 0.12% and 1.49% respectively. As for prices, the fiscal policy shock signifies lower multipliers than the monetary policy in all but one year of the simulation period. The assumptions underlying the results are described briefly below. As a result of economic reform, the investment decision-making powers of lower administrative levels and state-owned enterprises have been considerably enlarged. Nevertheless, both lower level governments and enterprises make investment first of all for welfare purposes. At the same time, they are biased towards projects which make easy profits in a short span of time, and lack enthusiasm for long-term projects of a technologically innovational nature, or of improving the infrastructure of economy. This shift of investment toward nonproductive, and short time-horizon, projects has led to severe imbalances in industrial structure and bottlenecks in the economy. The high level governments, particularly the central government, therefore have to retain the responsibility for mitigating the imbalances or bottlenecks by undertaking intensive investment in the projects of technological transformation and infrastructure construction. This is done mainly by the expenditure on economic construction. The expansion of domestic credit, on the other hand, provides more extra-budgetary investment funds which aggravate the structural distortion of industries, and hence slows down the growth of output. However, one must be very careful about the role of government construction expenditure as a sort of 'blasting fuse': its gains would be at costs of severer investment market tension for a certain period, unless the central government re-centralizes the decision-making power to assist its economic policies. This actually provides evidence in support of the demand-determined hypothesis of shortage, in that, due to the fundamental contradictions of a POE and multi-sovereignty mechanism (see chapter 3), increasing supply will at same time leads to even higher demand. For fiscal policy this is particularly reflected in investment markets, while for monetary policy, the case seems to occur mainly in consumption markets.

An increase in nominal interest rates (NRI)

The interest rate enters the model explicitly through the investment demand function of the non-state sector and implicitly through affecting the expectation formation of economic agents. The interest rate takes on its historical values in 1979, but then from 1980 to 1988 it is increased by 10% times its historical values, that is, NRIS%=1.1NRI%. NRI represents, as before, the historic time series for the nominal interest rates, and NRIS is then used in place of NRI in the simulation model.

Figure 6.4 sets out the simulation results. In observing them, we would first look at the investment behaviour of the non-state sectors. Since a direct downward pull is exerted, a drastic fall of non-state sectors' investment demand can be observed, which is estimated at -8.59% in the first year of this policy shock. Afterwards, the investment demand fluctuates within the range -5.17% and -8.8%. This is probably because increases in nominal interest rates reduce the inflation rate, which in turn further increases real interest rates, and thus reinforces the negative impacts of increases in nominal interest rates on the demand variable. Note, however, that the multiplier effects generated by an increase in nominal interest rates on the investment demand of the non-state sectors seem to be quite large. However, we still think that they are plausible and acceptable for the following reasons. First, as we commented in section 4.5, due to data limitation, the interest rate of household time deposits rather than that of loans in the black financial markets was used in estimation. As the state banks even cannot satisfy the state sector's 'insatiable demand' for funds, they become highly limited capital sources for the non-state sectors, and the loan interest rate in black financial markets (outside the state banking system) is therefore much higher than (usually 2-3 times) the time deposit interest rate. This implies that a small rise in the time deposit interest rate will lead to a large increase in the loan interest rate in black financial markets, and thus generates a large (negative) multiplier effect on the non-state sector's investment demand. Second, in the absence of complete price system, prices in investment markets are under strict control. A fall in investment demand due to increases in the interest rate does not cause a reduction in investment goods prices. If, on the other hand, investment goods prices are free enough so as to affect negatively the non-state sectors' investment decisions, their declines should increase the non-state sectors' investment demand, and hence offset the negative effect of an increase in the interest rate. A lack of flexibility of investment goods prices is another reason for a large multiplier effect of an increase in the interest rate observed here.

The local government investment demand also declines because of their lower expectations of excess investment demand, but to a much lesser degree. In fact, the interest rate increases have by themselves a positive impact on investment expectations, as local governments would expect more voluntary savings by households, and hence more bank loans available for their investment. Therefore, in the first two years of the experiment, slight increases of 0.55% and 0.26% in local government investment demand is observed. On the other hand, the sharp reductions in the non-state sectors' investment demand soon eliminates that positive impact, reducing eventually local governments' expectations about investment shortages. In a word, due to the soft budget constraint, the state-owned sector is more sensitive to quantity signals but less so to price signals, than the non-state sector is. The present experiment also displays a negative effect of higher interest rates on consumption demand. The drops in consumption demand is estimated at from -0.61% to -2.31% over the simulation period. It is not surprising to see that consumption demand declines steadily, though not considerably. The reason is due to the assumption that the interest rate acts on consumers' behaviour indirectly by changing their expectations about repressed inflation (or equally excess demand) in consumption markets. The transmission mechanism is as follows. The Chinese households could save income only in the forms of cash and saving deposits, since there were no bond markets.[3] As illustrated in chapter 5, gross savings consist of forced and voluntary (normal) savings, the latter being dependent on the 'true real interest rate'. Raising nominal interest rates will increase the opportunity costs of money holdings, and therefore result in households tending to save more and consume less voluntarily. Meanwhile, more savings imply more funds available for local governments to invest in downstream sectors.[4] Hence the supply of consumption goods may increase, which should slow down the falls in consumption supply. The above two factors combined will reduce the degree of shortage in consumption markets. If household hold rational expectations of the future values of the 'true inflation rate', they will include the changes in interest rates, exogenously determined by the government as one of its policy instruments, in their information set. Households will then further increase their voluntary savings because of expected increases in the true real interest rates (or decrease in the expected values of the true inflation rate in the next period). As a result, consumption demand and excess consumption demand should be further reduced, and so are the households' expectations of excess consumption demand. In a word, the strong channel of interest rate policy, mainly via assets, is probably the reason for affecting households' expectations and their consumption decisions.

As all the determinants of the aggregate investment demand discussed above contract in response to the interest rate increases, it drops as well by the percentage points shown in Figure 6.4.

Turning now to the supply side, we can observe that the responses of supply variables, especially of investment supply, tend to be more sluggish than demand variables. However, the consumption supply response is not as sluggish as investment supply. Actually the production of consumption goods is more market-dependent, and therefore adjusts slightly faster to the change in consumption demand. Investment supply, however, is by and large subject to the control of the central government. Thus, the indirect macroeconomic policy tools, such as interest rates, may have a negligible impact on investment supply, and so on output. Given the decrease of excess investment demand as well as that of excess consumption demand, aggregate excess demand declines, pulling down the price level steadily.

A cut in government expenditure on non-economic construction (NGEE)

Government expenditure on non-economic construction (referred to as the government non-construction expenditure hereafter) can be more or less regarded as government consumption expenditure. Figure 6.5 shows the results of the experiment in which NGEE is cut by 10% (i.e., NGEES=0.9NGEE) over the period from 1980 to 1988. The deflationary impact of this cut is immediately imposed on consumption demand, and is reinforced by the decline in forced savings. The government non-construction expenditure enters the model through the 'policy income' equation (see equation (6.6)). Referring back to the section 5.4, we can see that the 'policy income' Y3 has two major categories: government transfer payments advanced to households, and the money holdings of governmental units used for purchases of public consumption goods. Therefore, it has a strong relation with government expenditure, of witch the government non-construction expenditure is another main part. Also the variable of consumption expenditure C chosen in the model (see the minimum condition (6.3)) includes that of governmental units as well. Thus, a decrease in the government non-construction expenditure pulls down the consumption demand of both households and governmental units directly through reducing 'policy income'. Furthermore, the stimulus to consumption demand of lowering the price level is counteracted by a decline in the price-related income. As a consequence, consumption demand falls between -0.51% and -2.64%, and following this, consumption supply deviates downward from its historical path, though by less than consumption demand.

Through the expectation mechanism, the effect of this reduction is transmitted from the consumption market to the investment market. The reduction in the government non-construction expenditure, by decreasing both sales income and the expected level of future prices, has a fairly strong negative effect on the investment demand of the non-state sectors. The decreases in private investment demand, then lowers the degree of shortage in investment markets expected by local governments, exerting a small downward pressure on their investment demand. Over time, a fall is entailed in aggregate investment demand and supply. The resulting reduction in realized investment decreases slightly the level of fixed assets and hence the level of output. Overall, aggregate supply responds to the cut of government non-construction expenditure more sluggishly than aggregate demand, and this provides a deflationary effect, which translates into lower prices.

6.3 Summary and conclusions

Having conducted simulations under six alternative policy scenarios, a few key policy implications of the model are highlighted.

The first implication of the model relates closely to the interesting debate between Chinese economists on whether the general shortages in the Chinese economy are demand-determined or supply-determined. The demand-determined hypothesis of shortages argues that, however high the level of aggregate supply might be, and regardless of the degree to which the economic efficiency could possibly be improved, aggregate demand will always increase at a faster speed, thus generating a general shortage and/or inflation. In this view, the fundamental cause of shortages lies in the demand augmentation mechanism, and has nothing to do with the level of aggregate supply. The ultimate remedy for shortage relies on prolonged economic reform eliminating those defects of the system causing demand augmentation. However, in the short run it is possible for the government to adopt certain macroeconomic policies and administrative means to suppress aggregate demand and mitigate shortages.[5] The supply-determined hypothesis of shortages, on the hand, takes aggregate demand as given or certain, and expounds that excess demand results from production inefficiencies and hence insufficient supply. It is suggested that to eliminate or reduce the degree of shortage, countermeasures should be focused on improving economic efficiency and on stimulating supply responses.[6] In fact, it is not that one or other of these two hypotheses are wrong; both embrace some truth. In other words, the existing economic system is characterized by both the demand augmentation mechanism and production inefficiencies. Both theories rightly recognize that the ultimate way to overcome these institutional drawbacks is to push forward economic reforms. Nevertheless, in terms of the short-run policy implications these two hypotheses are quite different. In the short run, demand is more volatile than supply. Those factors determining supply, such as institutional, technological and resource-allocation conditions cannot be quickly changed. On the other hand, factors such as interest conflicts and resource contentions, directly and at any time change the magnitude of demand. Accordingly one may ask advocates of supply-determined hypothesis: Can an already overheated economy with substantial excess demand be cooled down in the short run by improving efficiencies or stimulating more supply, if those underlying conditions are given and hard to change? History has said 'no'. Then is the government really at the end of its tether when facing the problem of drastic macroeconomic imbalances before economic reform is successfully completed? Again the answer is 'no'. The second question is equivalent to asking what the roles of economic policies are in generating problems of shortage, which is implied by the demand-determined hypothesis but actually ignored by the supply-determined hypothesis. Thus, the former does implicitly remind the government to carefully use economic and administrative instruments because demand may easily be expanded, while the latter could possibly encourage the government to misuse inflationary policies since stimulating supply can reduce shortage. Our results of simulations clearly support the demand-determined hypothesis of shortage.[7] In terms of policy effects the model is basically demand-inclined, for all policy shocks. Both expansionary and contractionary policies seem to have a greater impact on demand variables than on supply variables. It is argued that, *under the existing system*, any policies aimed originally at increasing supply to reduce excess demand will end up with the opposite results: severer shortages and/or a higher price level. This empirical conclusion well fits into the theoretical framework developed in chapter 3, which analyzed the non-cooperative behaviour of economic agents and its consequences under the existing system.

Second, the simulation results tell us that, in the 1980s, the role of monetary policy gained increasing importance and effectiveness in the national economy. This contrasts sharply with the pre-reform period in which there was no independent monetary policy as money supply was simply passive and subordinate to the central plans. Since 1979, the authority to invest has been delegated to lower levels, and concurrent with the delegation have been the historical change of banks becoming a principal funds supplier for local investment activities and the subordinateness of local banks to local governments (to a certain degree). Banks have provided economic agents with 'financial' instruments, and enabled them to play non-cooperative games in the distribution of national income and the allocation of investment resources. As a result, there has emerged a causality between wage, investment and credit expansions. Therefore, it is inevitable that expansionary monetary policy has assumed more and more responsibilities for the overall demand swelling. Comparing experiment (i) with (ii), it seems that the once dominant position of fiscal policy has been being gradually taken over by monetary policy, in terms of demand management. Additionally, in simulations (ib) and (iib), it is shown that the inflationary impact of expansionary monetary policy is larger and its output effect is smaller than that of fiscal policy, a Keynesian-type result. But one thing should be kept in mind that expansionary fiscal policy, especially the government construction expenditure, could create graver tension in the investment resource allocation under the multi-sovereignty mechanism. The above conclusions may have far-reaching implications for the design of stabilization and growth programs.

Third, the role of interest rates is also a controversial issue in China. Some economists attribute the overall demand expansion to the presence of too low interest rates. Others, however, reject this claim, and attach no significance to the role of interest rates. Our results show that, as far as consumption is concerned, the interest rate effect is small, but its effect on investment is quite significant. Although the investment demand of the state-owned sector is interest-inelastic, the non-state sectors' investment demand is rather susceptible to the changes in interest rates, and the latter has accounted for an increasingly sizable proportion of total investment demand. The ratio was 24% in 1980, and 39% in 1989. Consequently, the claim that high interest rates discourage investment is not utterly groundless. A further tool which plays an important role in dealing with the augmentation of consumption demand is the reduction of government non-construction expenditure. Nevertheless, its implementation usually encounters more and more resistance in various disguised forms from top to bottom, because this instrument is of an administrative nature.

The final implication of the model is that, in an incomplete market system with price deformation (i.e., prices in factor markets are subject to control, while in others they are more flexible), the behaviour of non-state sectors is also atypical, as they over-respond to the regulations of macro-economic policies. For example, in all experiments performed here, the percentage increases (decreases) in non-state sectors' investment demand are larger than those in local governments' investment demand. Unlike the private-owned firms in typical market economies, the non-state sectors in the Chinese economy do enjoy a seller market of their products due to persistent and pervasive shortages and low prices in factor markets. When this favourable macroeconomic environment is reinforced by government expansionary policies, the motives of profit-maximization will drive non-state sectors to expand production and hence increase investment demand rapidly. This suggests that, before establishment of an effective system of macro-economic regulation, its sound micro-foundations, i.e., market-dependent firms as well as a complete and mature market (price) system, are indispensable. The former ensures that firms *will* be responsive to price signals, while the latter ensures that prices are *not misleading* as a policy target of regulation and as an indicator of macroeconomic performance. Only through further market-oriented reforms, can this objective be achieved.

Notes

1. DOCR = working capital loans to the state sectors LOS + fixed assets loans to the state sectors LOF + loans to the non-state sectors LOP.
2. According to the Statistical Yearbook Of China, the government expenditure (excluding extra-budgetary expenditure) is classified into six categories: (1) expenditure on economic construction; (2) expenditure on social culture and education; (3) expenditure on national defence; (4) administrative expenditure; (5) expenditure on public debt and (6) other expenditure. Thus government expenditure on non-economic construction=(2)+(3)+(4)+(5)+(6).
3. It is worth noting that in China in 1977 (before economic reforms), currency was 50% of the money stock (defined as M_2, currency plus saving deposits). Only after 1979 did saving deposits increase considerably, reaching 73.5% of the money stock by 1989.
4. Recall our theoretical hypothesis for local government investment behaviour in chapter 3: the interest elasticity of investment demand is low, due to the soft budget constraint.
5. For more details of the demand-determined theories of shortage, please see Fan G. et al (1990), Fan G. (1992), and Zhang S. (1993).
6. The supply-determined theories of shortage are mainly developed in Hu R. (1987 and 1991) and Ma Q. (1989).
7. Here we are talking about the short-run policy effects. In chapter 7, we will consider the impacts of further economic reform on the behaviour of the Chinese economy, incorporating in our reform package some truth suggested by both demand- and supply-determined hypotheses, i.e., eliminating demand augmentation mechanism and increasing supply responses. But this is an issue of long run.

Appendix 6A - Simulation results

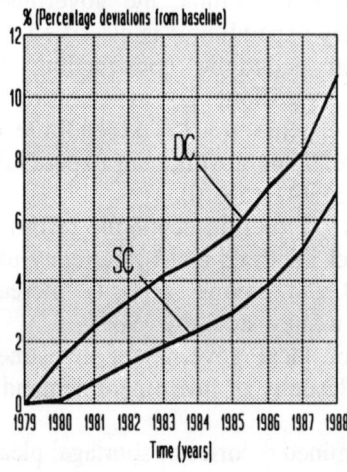

DC=Real consumption demand
SC=Real consumption supply

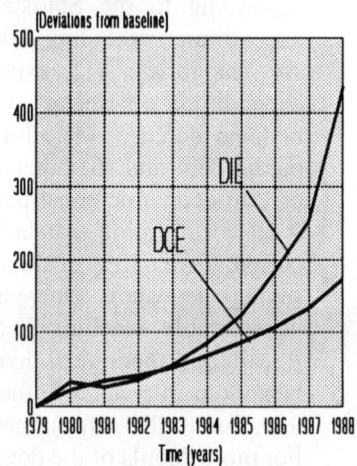

DCE=Real excess consumption demand
DIE=Real excess investment demand

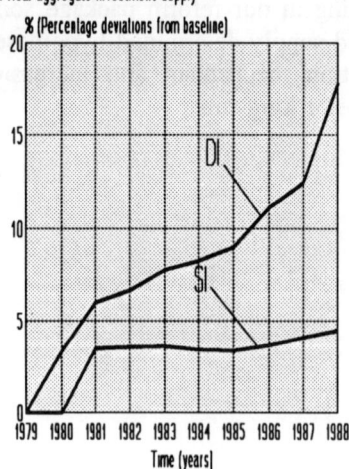

DI=Real aggregate investment demand
SI=Real aggregate investment supply

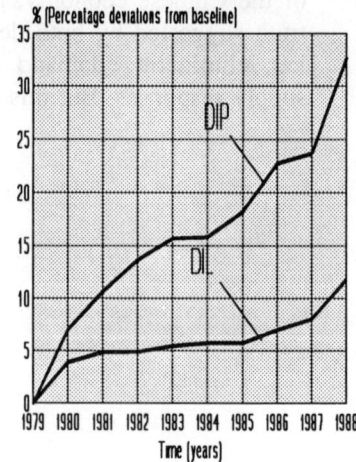

DIP=Real non-state sectors' investment demand
DIL=Real local governments' investment demand

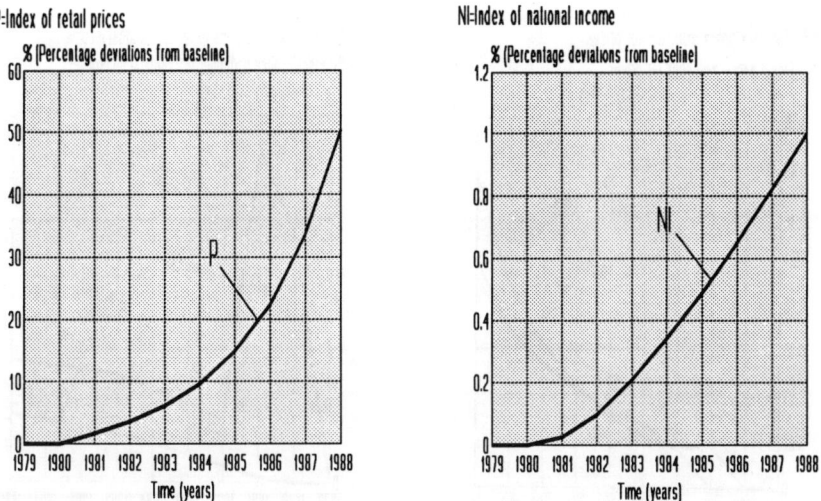

Figure 6.1 A permanent 5% increase in domestic credit

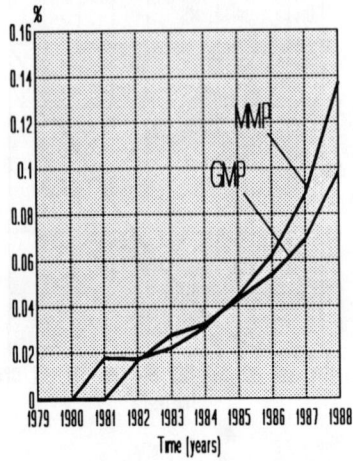 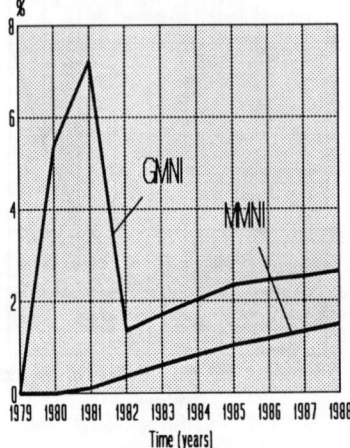

Figure 6.2. A temporary increase in domestic credit of 214 billion yuan; and a temporary increase in government construction spending of 214 billion yuan

DC=Real consumption demand
SC=Real consumption supply

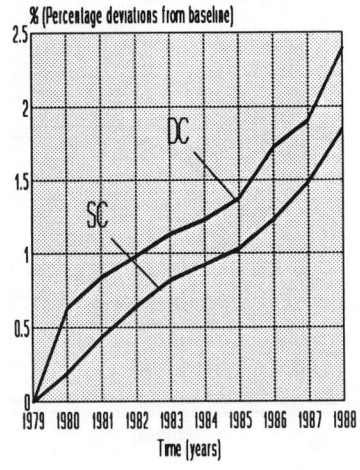

DCE=Real excess consumption demand
DIE=Real excess investment demand

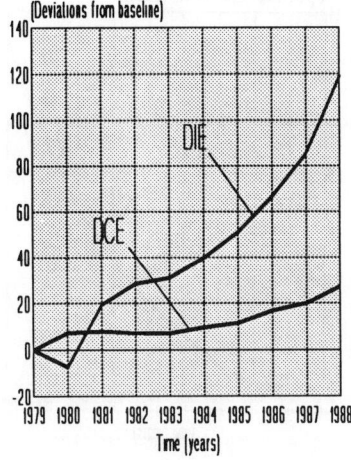

DI=Real aggregate investment demand
SI=Real aggregate investment supply

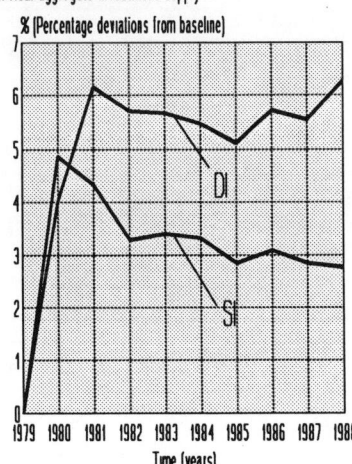

DIP=Real non-state sectors' investment demand
DIL=Real local governments' investment demand

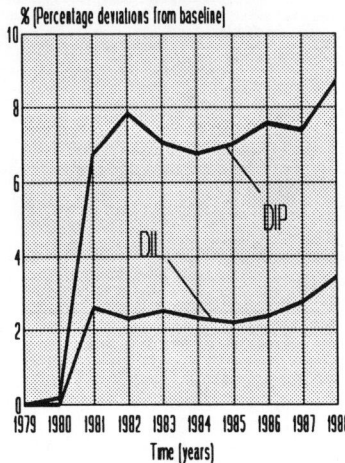

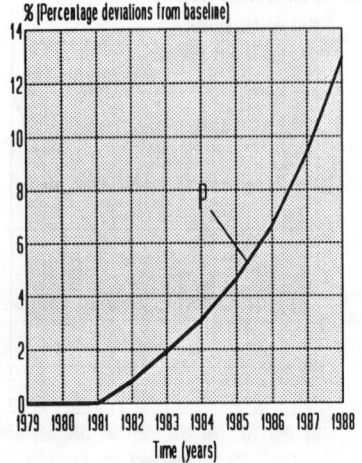 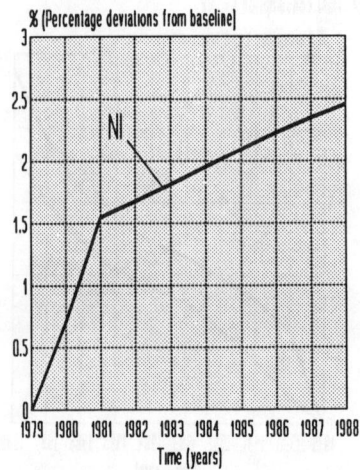

Figure 6.3 A permanent 10% increase in government construction spending

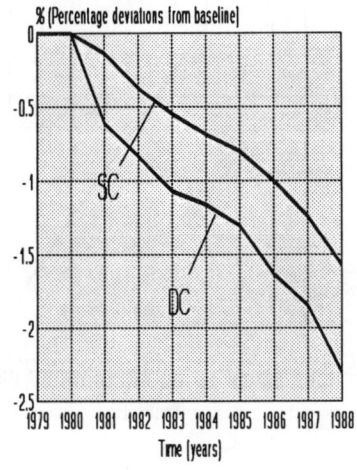

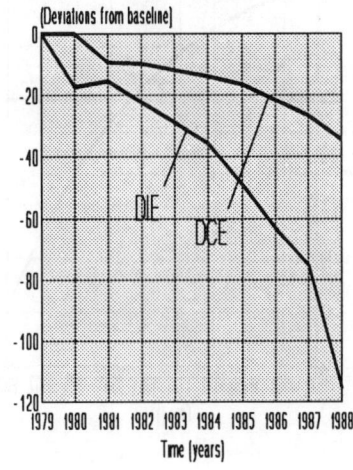

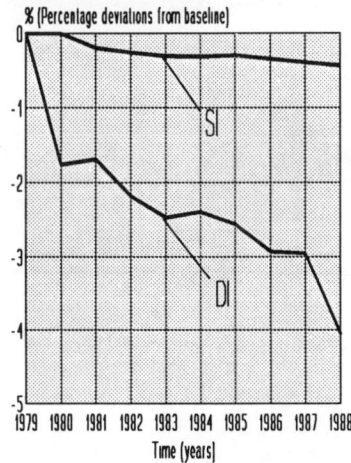

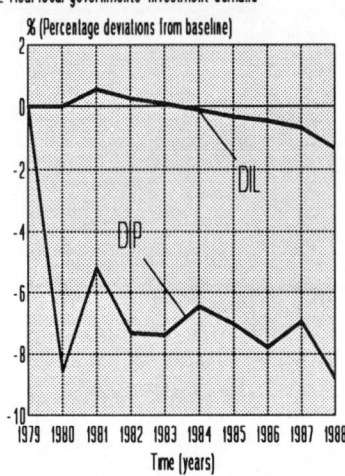

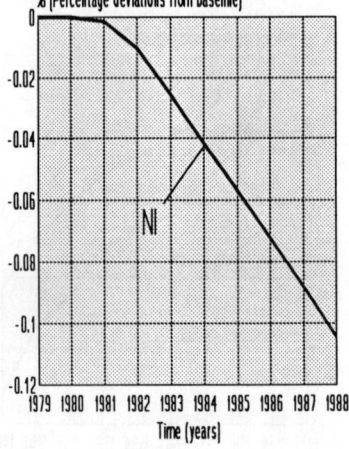

Figure 6.4 A permanent increase in nominal interest rates by 1.1 times

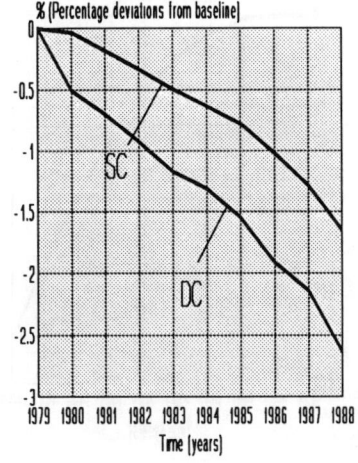

DC=Real consumption demand
SC=Real consumption supply

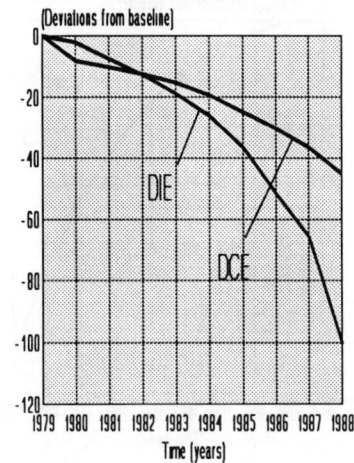

DCE=Real excess consumption demand
DIE=Real excess investment demand

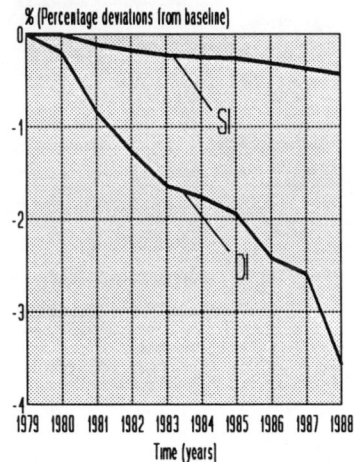

DI=Real aggregate investment demand
SI=Real aggregate investment supply

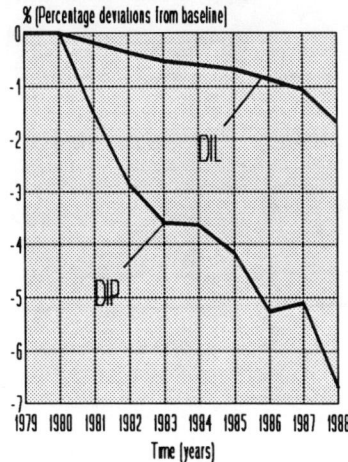

DIP=Real non-state sectors' investment demand
DIL=Real local governments' investment demand

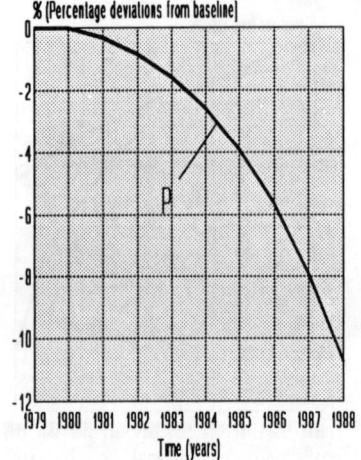 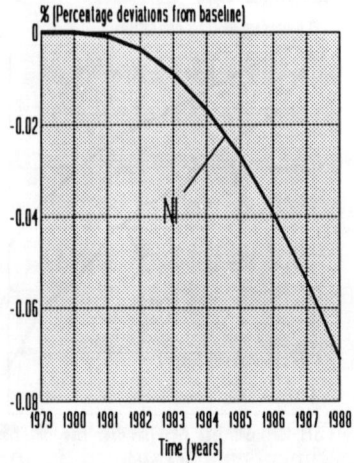

Figure 6.5 A permanent 10% cut in government non-construction spending

7 Searching for a policy package of further Market-Oriented Reforms

7.1 Introduction

Chapter 6 has considered the results of a number of *ex post* simulation experiments and examined the impacts of various policy shocks which could have been applied to the Chinese economy in the 1980s. All of these experiments have provided us with the commonly observed results that monetary and fiscal policies have a fairly limited power in *equilibrating* consumption and investment markets, and yet maintaining harmonic growth, in long run. From the perspective of comparative statics, a set of expansionary policies could stimulate more supply to reduce the gap currently formed between aggregate demand and supply. From the perspective of dynamics and particularly regarding the socialist economy with the public-ownership economy (POE) as a major sector, however, aggregate demand could normally expand at a faster speed than aggregate supply, irrespective of how large the aggregate supply magnitude is and how high its growth speed is. On the other hand, even if the growth rate of aggregate supply is low or even negative, this will not necessarily prevent aggregate demand from being restrained or even from declining more quickly than aggregate supply, in certain circumstances. These are consistent with the main ideas of demand-side determination theory, proposed in Fan G et al (1990) and further developed and elaborated in chapter 3 of this book. According to this theoretical framework, the POE itself inevitably and continuously generates the contradictions between the individual's strong desire to consume ('income illusion') and government's strong desire to invest (enthusiasm of high accumulation); the contradictions between the government's strong desire for high growth rate and actual possibilities of growth; conflicts of interests on investment between subunits and monetary competition between subunits for scarce resources due to the indefiniteness of the source of income (general definition of soft budget constraint). All of these are represented by non-cooperation between economic agents in the economy. Meanwhile, the supply-side determination theory also contributes to the explanations of general shortages in the supply respect: the inefficiencies of allocation, organization and production unavoidably give rise to low supply responses. If we seek the reasons for general shortages from the Chinese economic system, both of them contain some insights. In other words, as long as there exist such fundamental contradictions and institutional defects, there will be a lack of co-ordination between demand and supply determinations which is characterized by supply lagging behind demand.

Different systems yield different social forms of demand determination embodied in different behavioral patterns of economic agents, which in turn cause different economic problems. It seems to be logically clear from the above considerations that the ultimate way of moving the economy towards equilibrium, or at least towards the typical 'best' disequilibrium regime with moderately repressed inflation, lies in successful market-oriented reforms to eliminate those particular conditions of the system which causes persistent excess demand. Removing the mechanism of demand augmentation is, however, only one side of the issue. If we want an economy with low (repressed) inflation but harmonic growth, efforts must also be made to enhance efficiencies so as to increase the supply responses. Consequently in this chapter, we focus our attention on the reform experiments: searching for a policy package of reforms, and conducting some simulations on the amended model which captures the features of the policy package. These efforts are made to see what the response of the 'new' economy would be to the changes in policy variables, if, for example, the POE sector was reduced and prices were completely free to clear markets. To avoid confusion, it should be made clear that the policy package here does not refer to such macroeconomic devices as monetary, fiscal policies etc. It rather refers to a set of measures or steps which are taken to change the structure of economy and the behaviour of economic agents, and which cannot take effect at a stroke.

The reform experiments are undertaken mainly by reducing the role of POE sector and introducing more market allocation mechanisms into the model. Consequently, those variables representing quantity or plan signals are replaced by the price variables, in the belief that economic agents would respond to price signals if they were more market-dependent and subject to a tougher budget constraint. Obviously the model generated by introducing a further reform package is a representation, not of the real world which existed in the past and exists now in China, but rather of a counterfactual world which would and could appear in the future if the policy package was implemented and proved effective. Therefore, historical data cannot be used to estimate the parameters of the system, as the counterfactual theoretical relationships are not fitted to them and cannot be tested statistically at present. Since there do not seem to be any clear-cut rules to follow, and precedents to go by, those non-existing, yet indispensable, simulation parameters are obtained on a 'what if' basis (see section 7.4 for more details).

7.2 The amended model structure corresponding to the policy package of further reforms

The contents of policy package

A policy package should be based on China's present reality and dovetail with those already adopted in the current reforms. This implies that it should not go too far beyond the present initial conditions of China. The above considerations thus recognise the following policy contents:

(1) Firmly push forward the reform of public ownership, either allowing those small and medium-size enterprises (especially in the downstream industries) to be sold, leased and contracted to individuals or collectives, or by transforming them into enterprises of stock-ownership.

(2) Abandon completely the administrative interference of local governments in the enterprise's affairs and day-to-day business activities.

(3) Reduce the role of direct controls on, and of mandatory plans for, the state-owned upstream industries, expanding the market's influences in maintaining the balance between consumption and accumulation and the balance in industrial structure.

(4) Merge the 'two-tier' price system into a unitary (market) price system i.e., let prices be determined solely by the supply and demand situation of markets.

(5) Abolish the policy of price subsidy to households connected with price reforms.

Clearly, these policy measures are closely connected with each other.

The first — reforming the public ownership — is the prerequisite for the other policy measures to take effect. Without reforming the traditional public ownership, the aforementioned contradictions and conflicts cannot be resolved, and the softness of budget constraints would presumably prevent the enterprises from participating further in the market competitions and from responding quickly and properly to price signals. These facts have been well recognised in China. Nevertheless, the question of how to reform public ownership still remains knotty and controversial, since it is not only a economic issue but also related to political and ideological problems. The government has rejected the proposal of large-scale privatization, in fear that this would lead to massive unemployment, poverty, class polarization, and what's more the collapse of socialist system. As a result, the sales to individuals and collectives of state-owned enterprises are only limited to small and some medium-sized firms and yet, the efforts have been called for to explore the new realized forms of property organization in public ownership. This is aimed at clarifying the vague relationships of the property rights, and hardening budget constraints on enterprises, while preserving the essence of public ownership. So far, a variety of proposals for reforming public ownership have been put forward, such as a contract responsibility system, a lease system and a stock-ownership system etc. It is beyond the scope of our studies here, however, to discuss in greater detail the merits/shortcomings of these alternative proposals, or even to make fresh and relevant suggestions. Our assumption is merely that, under the new institutional arrangement, the management of state-owned enterprises would be rationalized with an eye to profit-maximization (rather than per-capita-income-maximization) and with the mechanisms of self-development, self-adjustment and self-checking, so as to form a sound micro-foundation for effective macroeconomic regulation.

For a successful reformation of public ownership, the complete separation of enterprise's operations from local government's function is both necessary and possible. Economic reforms have so far involved two important aspects: streamlining administrative departments and delegating power to lower levels. This is intended to cancel the system of centralized management, and has contributed to the invigoration of the economy. However, as the administratively subordinated relationship between the state-owned enterprises (including financial instiitons) and local governments' economic departments still dominates, the enterprises have not yet enjoyed full autonomy in operation. Consequently their decision-making processes and business activities are, to some extent if not completely, subject to frequent interferences from higher level management organizations. In comparison with enterprises, local governments are less subject to the restriction of economic efficiency, a drawback shared by the central government. Their activities are hardly influenced by changes in prices, the cost of raw and semi-finished materials, or interest rates. To fulfil their purpose, they can use their political might to go beyond the law of the market. These innate characteristics of local governments' behaviour have been clearly observed in a bizarre phenomenon, i.e., monetary competition, where local governments compete with each other by increasing the money supply (granting more loans) to themselves (the enterprises and other units in the local) to extend their purchasing power and to accommodate their production and investment plans. The institutional conditions for this kind of competition are the multi-sovereignty economic management system and the subordinations of money suppliers to money demanders (see chapter 3). Local governments are directly involved not only in economic management but also in the specific economic activities, and thus become one of the supervisors of the local banks in the region. The local banks must obey the orders of granting more loans from their bosses which are responsible for the localities' economic development and performance. This peculiar behaviour, if allowed to go unchanged, may lead local governments to ignore the market economy and continuously to aggravate macroeconomic imbalances and cause big inflationary pressure. To eliminate this irrational behaviour, those underlying institutional conditions must be changed so that the administrative links between enterprises including banks and local governments can be cut off, and the full autonomy in operation can be returned to enterprises. The economic functions of local governments are then turned into indirect management through industrial policies, tax and subsidy policies, and laws and regulations.

The upstream industries consist mainly of large-sized enterprises and the infrastructure of the national economy such as agriculture, heavy industry, transportation, and postal and telecommunication services. They are regarded as vital factors determining the extent of bottle necks and hence conditioning the growth of output as a whole. Thus keeping them under the control of the central government, given that state ownership is unchanged, has certain attractions. It would assure the availability of large sum of funds whenever needed for their production and investment, so as to alleviate promptly the contradictions in the industrial structure, since no one else but the central government can afford, or is enthusiastic, to invest in such a long-term project which does not make easy and quick returns. It would retain the central government's commitment to considering the general picture of the country as a whole, balancing aggregate demand and supply, and to long-term policies of coordinated development. But there are disadvantages too, particularly regarding the traditional techniques of economic management. First, mainly because of an incompleteness of information about economic data (including the information about other agents' behaviour), the central government's desire to accumulate cannot conform to the true 'optimal ratio' of investment to consumption. This leads to errors of investment plans and fluctuations in planned investment as the central government advances by 'trial and error'. Second, the central government evaluates the economic variables such as the rate of growth, consumption, or capital accumulation by its special preference scale which involves political and ideological considerations. Therefore, the economic decisions made with the government's participation in the decision-making process, must diverge from the economically optimal point, and these distortions cannot be 'corrected' by trial and error, since errors from government preferences are not perceived as errors. On the basis of the above analysis, the reasonable options seem to be as follows: the further reduction of mandatory plans of production, of raw materials supply and of product marketing; giving the enterprises in the upstream industries greater freedom of operation and more dependence on markets. The mandatory plans should only centre on the management of large-scale investment projects, while the focal point of the investment management is the management of funds resources.

The two-tier price system emerged as state mandatory planning gradually receded in production, supply, marketing, and other major operations of enterprises. In such a context, for every additional unit of output above the plan, which is sold at the market price, the enterprise obtains extra revenue, whereas every unit of input saved means one unit less to be purchased on markets, at the market price. Hence more cost-reduction for the enterprise. The enterprise, therefore, in making decisions regarding its own production and investment, should boost output or economise on inputs at market prices instead of state-set prices. This implies that market prices have assumed a decisive role in the incremental output and input decisions of the enterprise, and that through this marginal role they have become signals and levers which help to readjust short-term supply and demand. However, the role of the two-tier system is limited in regulating long-term supply and demand and the allocation of resources, and is ineffective in straightening out the twisted relative price system. In regulating long-run supply and demand, total cost and revenue play a greater role than marginal cost and revenue. Market prices relate only to the enterprise's marginal output; total revenue and total profit are mainly affected by state prices as well. Unless there is a considerable reduction of mandatory planning for enterprises, a state-set price will continue to dominate the determination of the long term economic behaviour of enterprises. Apart from this, there is another impediment. In the implementation of two tier system, the control on the prices of the upstream sector's products, such as investment goods, raw materials, energy, electricity, and transportation services, is more strict than on those of the downstream sector, and the proportion of the products independently marketed by the enterprises in the upstream sectors is much smaller than in the downstream sectors. Theoretically and logically, when readjusting the price system, the prices of upstream-sector's products should be raised first and by the largest percentage, because the upstream sectors bear the full pressure of structural shortage. But in reality, one would be surprised to see the opposite facts: it is usually the prices of the downstream sector's products that are first increased and by the largest percentage. On the other hand, when rectifying markets, the prices of the upstream sector's products would be the first target of attack.[1] In a word, two-tier system in the context of the POE makes the relative prices of upstream sector's products even lower, and hence the industrial structure deteriorates further. The necessary solution for these problems lies in the complete lifting of price controls. Arbitrary price readjustments would only lead to the preservation of the two-tier system. The assertion of 'readjusting prices to market prices' is in itself not scientific at all. Market prices are dynamic and volatile. As soon as a batch of prices are arbitrarily set in light of the market prices which happen to be formed at a certain time, they will start to deviate from actual market prices formed at present. Moreover, the market prices in the two-tier system are not yet real and true market prices. Without real market prices, there would be no standards whatsoever to go by in the readjustment of prices 'to market prices'.

The abolition of the price subsidy policy is necessary, first for making price a real binding force on the consumption demand, and secondly for reducing the government's financial deficit. According to this policy, households should be compensated for a number of social disutilities connected mainly with inflation due to price reforms. Actually real incomes of households continue to rise by even more than the amount necessary to offset the downward pressure of price rises on consumption demand. Thus in reduced form, consumption demand is a positive function of prices. This is the reason why consumption demand goes up continuously and accelerates, in spite of persistent inflation.

The counterfactual model and the list of variables

To see what consequences these policy measures would bring to the economy through simulation experiments, an amended model is needed. As was stated before, this model represents the resultant economy generated by our policy measures, and hence has a different structure from its old counterpart in the previous chapters. This new model is therefore given below in its full notation.

The Structure of Model 2

(1) Consumption block

$$DC = 428.6399 + 0.79YD + 0.7546MC_{-1} + 200\dot{\Pi}^e_{+1} - 320PC \tag{7.1}$$

$$SC = -486.8572 + 4.6404AG_{-1} + 0.3691LIID + 1245PC \tag{7.2}$$

$$C = \min\{DC, SC\} \tag{7.3}$$

$$YD = Y1 + Y2 + Y3_1 + Y3_2 + Y4 - NC \tag{7.4}$$

$$Y1 = 27 + 0.2047(LOS + LOP) + 0.0309LU \tag{7.5}$$

$$Y2 = -624.246 + 8.1369AG_{-1} + 1.075LOA \tag{7.6}$$

$$Y3_1 = -420 + 0.9705NI + 0.1674NGEE + 0.1429GEE_{-1} \tag{7.7}$$

$$Y3_2 = -77 + 0.0925FUND + 0.4318NGEE \tag{7.8}$$

$$MC = 21 + 0.0939YD - 1342.1NRI + 0.2999MC_{-1} \tag{7.9}$$

$$LIID = -994.0422 + 2.2826NI + 1228PC \tag{7.10}$$

$$FUND = -152.9204 + 0.1915(LOS + LOF) + 6.5004REB \tag{7.11}$$

(2) Investment block

$$DI = DIU + DID \tag{7.12}$$

$$SI = -337.3376 + 4.271(NI - NI_{-1}) + 0.3938IMP + 1150PK \tag{7.13}$$

$$I = \min\{DI, SI\} \tag{7.14}$$

$$DIU = -234 - 0.1734DID + 0.4567GEE + 0.4405NI - 800(PK - PK_{-1}) \tag{7.15}$$

$$DID = 245 + 0.5256NSZE + 268.348PC^e_{+1} - 0.2420INV_{-1} - 500PK - 1268.8ri \tag{7.16}$$

$$IMP = -22.9932 + 0.6124NI_{-1} + 800(PK - PK_{-1}) - 128.7994\Delta EXC \tag{7.17}$$

$$NSZE = 97 + 0.4593(LOS + LOP) + 942.0088(PC - PC_{-1}) \tag{7.18}$$

$$INV = 3.4136\Delta NI_{-1} + 0.297NI - 0.4362\Delta DEE \tag{7.19}$$

$$DEE = DI - SI + DC - SC \tag{7.20}$$

$$ri = NRI - \dot{\Pi}^e_{+1} \tag{7.21}$$

(3) Production block

$$\log(NI) = -13.1892 + 1.3022\log(\overline{L}) + 0.5118\log(\overline{K}) + 0.1476\log(\overline{GEE}) \tag{7.22}$$

$$K = K_{-1} + \Delta K \tag{7.23}$$

$$\Delta K = 0.26R + 0.26R_{-1} + 0.20R_{-2} + 0.12R_{-3} + 0.09R_{-4} + 0.07R_{-5} \quad (7.24)$$

$$R = I - DPR \quad (7.25)$$

(4) Price block

$$\log(PC) = \log(PC_{-1}) + 0.0006(DC - SC) \quad (7.26)$$

$$\log(PK) = \log(PK_{-1}) + 0.0006(DI - SI) \quad (7.27)$$

List of Variables

(1) Endogenous variables

DC	Demand for consumption goods (retail sales) at constant prices
SC	Supply of consumption goods (retail sales) at constant prices
C	Actual retail sales of consumption goods at constant prices
YD	Total disposable money income of households at constant prices
Y1	Total wage and salary income in both state sectors and non-state sectors + self-employment income of non-farmers, at constant prices
Y2	Total money income of farmers at constant prices
$Y3_1$	Other earnings of households at constant prices
$Y3_2$	Government transfer payment advanced to households + Money of governmental units for purchases of public consumption goods, at constant prices
FUND	Extra-budgetary funds in the economy at constant prices
MC	Current deposits of households at constant prices
LIID	Index of gross output of light industry
DI	Aggregate investment demand in the economy (investment demand of upstream sectors + investment demand of downstream sectors) at constant prices
SI	Aggregate investment supply in the economy at constant prices
I	Total actual investment in the economy at constant prices
DIU	Investment demand of state-owned upstream sectors at constant prices
DID	Investment demand of downstream sectors at constant prices
IMP	Total imports at constant prices
NSZE	Total retail sales minus Y1, as a proxy for net returns of downstream sectors, at constant prices
ri	real interest rates
PC	Aggregate price index of consumption goods
PK	Aggregate price index of investment goods
$\mathring{\Pi}^e_{t+1}$	Expectations of inflation rate at time t for time t+1

NI	Index of national income
ΔNI	$NI-NI_{-1}$
K	Fixed assets at constant prices; $\bar{K}=(K+K_{-1})/2$
ΔK	Effective increase in fixed assets at constant prices
R	Accumulation of fixed assets at constant prices
INV	Change in inventory stocks (accumulation of circulating assets) at constant prices
DEE	Total excess demand in domestic markets at constant prices
ΔDEE	$DEE-DEE_{-1}$

(2) Exogenous variables

GEE	Government expenditures on economic construction at constant prices; $\overline{GEE}=(GEE+GEE_{-1})/2$
NGEE	Government expenditures on non economic construction (total government expenditures minus expenditures on economic construction), at constant prices
NRI	Nominal interest rates
EXC	Exchange rate, yuan/dollar
ΔEXC	$EXC-EXC_{-1}$
REB	Indicator of the degree to which the economic decision-making power is delegated to local governments, proxied by the ratio of extra-budgetary funds to budgetary funds
LOS	Working capital loans to state sectors at constant prices
LOF	Fixed assets loans to state sectors at constant prices
LOP	Loans to non-state sectors at constant prices
LOA	Loans to farmers at constant prices
LU	Number of employees in cities and towns
AG	Index of gross output of agriculture
Y4	Net credit advanced to households + money of foreigners for purchase of consumption goods, at constant prices
NC	Tax payment of households to the state + purchase of means of production by farms + other expenditures than consumption, tax and purchase of means of production, at constant prices
L	Number of employees in the whole country; $\bar{L}=(L+L_{-1})/2$
DPR	Depreciation of total fixed assets at constant prices

The comparisons between the counterfactual and the historical models

Comparing the counterfactual model (hereafter referred to as Model 2 consisting of equations listed above) and its historical counterpart (hereafter referred to as Model 1 consisting of equations in section 6.1), we find that major structural changes have been made in the investment block. As a result of our policy measures, local governments' investment demand DIL and non-state sector's investment demand DIP disappear in Model 2. They merge into a single variable DID which now represents the investment demand of those economic agents becoming completely market-dependent. This implies that in the new regime, the role of DIL is reduced to zero, and it is replaced by the extension of the role of DIP. Therefore, the specification of DID is the same as that of DIP in Model 1 with only exemption that the price of investment goods PK is added as a new explanatory variable (see euqation (7.16)). The introduction of PK into the DID equation in Model 2 is due to the complete lifting of controls on investment goods prices which used to be subject to more strict controls than retail prices in the 1980s.

The net returns of non-state sectors was expressed in Model 1 (RNRTP) as retail sales of non-state sectors RTSP minus wage and salary income in non-state sectors and self-employment income of non-farm WLP minus tax on non-state sectors TP (see equation (6.16)), while RTSP was assumed to be a function of loans to both state and non-state sectors (LOS+LOP), lagged consumption demand DC_{-1} and the degree to which the non-state sector develops RPS (see equation (6.15)). Analogously, the net returns of the whole downstream sector NSZE in Model 2 should be obtained by total retail sales minus wage and salary income in state-owned downstream sectors and non-state sectors minus tax on these two sectors. However, the data required on some variables were unavailable. To avoid this problem, we simply decided to express NSZE, rather than total retail sales, as a function of total loans to state and non-state sectors LOS+LOP and increases in the consumption goods prices $PC-PC_{-1}$ (equation (7.18)), assuming that the data on NSZE is generated in this way. Thus the variable DC_{-1} in Model 1 (equation (6.15)) was replaced by $PC-PC_{-1}$. RPS, the indicator of the degree to which non-state sectors develop, disappears in Model 2 (equation (7.18)) as it no longer plays a role of gradually institutional changes.

In Model 1, the investment demand of state-owned upstream sectors DIU (as an indicator of the investment behaviour of the central government) was implicitly reflected in the aggregate investment demand function. In Model 2 this is explicitly given (see equation (7.15)). According to the policy measures, the role of the central government is greatly reduced in determining the ratio of accumulation to consumption; the conflicts between the central government and individuals in the distribution of national income are settled as a result of successful reforms of public ownership; and market influences are considerably expanded on these sectors. Consequently, we assume that DIU is no longer responsive to consumption demand, but rather responds to price signals in the investment goods market, and national income newly added, as an indicator for resource availability. On the other hand, the central government still retains, to some extent, responsibility for maintaining balances in industrial structure and mitigating bottle necks. As a result, DIU would still be a positive function of GEE, though to a lesser degree than in Model 1 (note that the parameter associated with this variable has been set to be smaller than its counterpart in Model 1). The sign of the downstream sectors' investment demand DID has been equated with that of DIP in Model 1, because, if in Model 1 we subtract DIL and DIP from DI to get DIU (recall that DI=DIU+DIL+DIP), the parameter of DIP would be 0.8381-1=-0.1619. This might imply that, in the old regime, the central government is already prepared to make a concession to the non-state sectors but not to the state-owned downstream sectors, probably because the former is bound by market forces while the latter is always driven by the 'investment hunger'. This assumption is kept in the place of DIP now replaced by DID.

The investment goods are mainly the output of upstream sectors. Under the assumption of a new regime, the budget constraints of upstream sectors are much tighter, and thus it is price signals instead of the availability of funds that are introduced into the investment supply function. Meanwhile, the impact of economic growth would increase if production efficiencies were improved, and the role of imports would decrease if the economy imported more consumption goods than before.[2] Speaking of import demand (equation (7.17)), the changes in Model 2 are the regressor $PK-PK_{-1}$ being a substitute for DEE_{-1} in Model 1, and the elimination of OPE, the indicator of the degree of openness of the economy. We are again assuming that it no longer plays the role of gradual institutional change. Other variables and their parameters remain almost unchanged in the import equation.

Here we turn our attention to the change in the consumption block. Consider first the demand side. The position of expected excess demand is taken over by the expectations of the future inflation rate in consumption markets, as individuals stop playing non-cooperative games with the central government in the distribution of national income (recall equations (3.33), (3.34) and (5.9) for the reasons for formation of individuals' expectations). In Model 1, Y3 is treated as the 'policy income', and households' other earnings $Y3_1$ was one of the two parts of Y3, because $Y3_1$ consists, by and large, of the reform-related (i.e., price-related) income which reflects one of the state's short-run economic reform policies. In the new economy, $Y3_1$ should be incorporated into households' *labour* income. For this reason, Y3 is then partitioned into two parts: $Y3_1$ and $Y3_2$, the latter now being treated alone as the 'policy income'. It is assumed that $Y3_1$, now in the form of labour income, would expand as the economy grows, and that increases in current NGEE and lagged GEE would too lead to increases in $Y3_1$. But the variable PC vanishes from the function of $Y3_1$ as any subsidies related to price reforms would end with the successful completion of the reform. As for $Y3_2$, the new 'policy income', we keep the two explanatory variables in the equation of old 'policy income' Y3, namely FUND the extra-budgetary funds and NGEE the government non-construction expenditure. Recall that, in section 5.4, we stated the reasons of introducing FUND and NGEE in the equation of Y3. In $Y3_2$, one of the two components (i.e., government transfer payment advanced to households) should still be part of NGEE. The other component (i.e., the money of governmental units for purchases of public consumption goods), which used to be strongly related to the extra-budgetary funds, is now supposed to have more links with NGEE but less links with FUND, if this component is gradually brought into line with budgetary plans. Thus the role (parameter) of FUND has been considerably reduced in the equation of $Y3_2$ in Model 2. Current saving deposits MC (stocks, not flows), no longer the result of forced savings accumulated over time, now become positively affected by households' disposable income YD and its lagged stocks MC_{-1}, but negatively affected by interest rates on time deposits NRI.

With regard to consumption supply (see (7.2)), both the variables CT and DC_{-1} are dropped in Model 2, the former having been a proxy for consumption plans, the latter having acted as a market signal in the absence of a complete price system. During the 1980s, the role of planning had already been curtailed and supplanted, to some extent, by the role of market mechanisms (see the consumption supply equation (6.2) in Model 1). Again, if our policy measures were successfully implemented, consumption supply would respond to price signals rather than to plan and quantity signals. At the same time, the output of light industry replaces its fluctuations in the consumption supply function, assuming that the centrally planned targets for the production of light industry no longer exist, and hence the deviations of output of light industry from the targets no longer influence consumption supply. Only the output level of light industry itself now affects the supply level of consumption goods. The variable DC representing quantity signals is dropped as well in the function of light industry output LIID (see (7.10)), for the same reasons as given above.

The policy measure (4) led to significant changes in the price block. In the two-tier price system, retail prices were the least sticky, and the shortages in both consumption and investment markets eventually (with one year lag) translated, to some extent if not fully, into the increases in retail prices. So it is not surprising to find that there is only one price adjustment equation in Model 1. When prices in both consumption and investment markets are completely free of any influences except those of market forces, they may adjust instantaneously to equate demand and supply. Thus in Model

2 we have a simple version of two standard Walrasian price adjustment equations respectively for consumption and investment markets. Finally, the function of extrabudgetary funds, the production block and inventory stocks are assumed to remain intact in the new regime (see (7.11), (7.22)-(7.25) and (7.19)).

7.3 The simulation results

To reach an empirical judgement on which economy — an economy within the old institutional arrangement (Model 1) or an economy within the new institutional arrangement resulting from the policy measures (Model 2) — would be better in equilibrating domestic markets, lowering inflation yet maintaining harmonic growth, the same standard simulations as in chapter 6 are conducted, but the simulation period covers 14 years. Since Model 2 is calibrated to the single year's data of 1980, it is used as the baseline for simulations. The reasons for choosing data observed in 1980 as the 'control solution' are given in section 7.4. In fact both Model 1 and 2 include non-linearities. This implies that differing impacts of identical policy scenarios in Models 1 and 2 might result from both different model structures and different base-run values. To ensure that differences in base-run values do not influence the comparisons between the simulation results, or in other words, to see if the resulting economy is in itself doing better, we decided to simulate Model 1 on the same control solution (i.e., the 1980's data set) as well, and report the results again along with those of Model 2 to facilitate comparisons. By doing this, any differences observed between policy impacts on the behaviour of Model 1 and Model 2 are merely the results of different model structures, and hence provide precisely a picture of how much improvement our package of further reforms would make to the performance of the economy.

Figures 7.1 through 7.6 set out the results of the six simulations of both Model 1 and Model 2: (1) a permanent increase of 5% in domestic credit; (2) a permanent increase of 10% in the government expenditure on economic construction (or government construction spending for short); (3) a permanent increase in the nominal interest rate by 1.1 times; (4) a permanent reduction of 10% in the government expenditure on non-economic construction (or the government non-construction spending for short); (5) a temporary increase of 219 billion yuan (in 1980 prices) in domestic credit; (6) a temporary increase of 219 billion yuan (in 1980 prices) in the government construction spending. All the above permanent policy shocks begin in year 2 and end in year 14, while those temporary policy shocks are imposed only in year 2.

Investment behaviour

The most striking result observed is that, in all the experiments of permanently expansionary policies, the investment markets suffer only a short period of high excess demand which wears off as time goes by. The credit expansion, for example, creates an immediate increase in excess investment demand (DIE) of only some 12.64 billion yuan (in real terms). This increase then rapidly declines until it becomes 0.0092 billion yuan six years latter, and continues to approach to zero thereafter (see Figure 7.1, (Model 2)). The bubble (inflationary side effects) in the investment markets, due to credit expansions, is dramatically reduced in Model 2, compared with the results of Model 1 in Figure 7.1, where the corresponding figure is 32.97 billion yuan in the first year of the policy shock, and then keeps rising acceleratedly throughout the simulation period. The experiments of expansionary fiscal policy (a permanent increase in government construction spending) also demonstrate roughly the same pattern for the increases in excess investment demand, with the increases jumping immediately to a peak of 6.83 billion yuan, and then declining gradually towards zero (see DIE in Figure 7.2 (Model 2)). These results are in contrast to those obtained in the simulation of Model 1 (see DIE in Figure 7.2 (Model 1)) where excess investment demand grew continuously in response to the expansionary fiscal policy. Contractionary policies (a permanent increase in the nominal interest rate, and a permanent reduction in the government non-construction spending) provide the qualitatively similar pictures of the behaviour of investment markets to those generated by the expansionary policies, though with negative signs: in Model 2 investment supply declines as does investment demand, and therefore investment markets gradually return from slack to equilibrium in 7-8 years (see DIE in Figures 7.3 and 7.4, (Model 2)), while the old economy (Model 1) sees a continuous fall in investment demand but a somewhat reluctant decrease in investment supply. Hence the slack in investment markets gets worse and worse (see DIE in Figures 7.3 and 7.4, (Model 1)).

The behaviour of investment demand in the downstream sector (DID) also deserves a mention. DID used to be divided into two types: the local governments' demand DIL and the non-state sector's demand DIP. With the removal of the local governments' role from enterprises' investment activities, and with the complete lifting of controls on the entire price system, these two investment demands now become one which is much more strongly influenced by the market situation. Thus, unlike Model 1, Model 2 produces a small and stable rise (or decrease) in DID which levels off at between 4.74% (year 5) and 4.12% (year 14) (Figure 7.1, (Model 2)), -1.57% (year 8) and -1.84% (year 14) (Figure 7.2, (Model 2)), -6.45% (year 6) and -6.06%

(year 14) (Figure 7.3, (Model 2)) and between -1.33% (year 5) and -1.24% (year 14) (Figure 7.4, (Model 2)), after a bubble of a few years duration. This is because the positive (negative) impacts of expansionary (contractionary) policies are offset by the negative (positive) effects of price changes. It is interesting to notice that, in the case of a permanent increase in government construction spending, the investment demand of downstream sectors, DID, falls from the fourth year of the policy shock (Figure 7.2, (Model 2)), in contrast with Figure 7.2 (Model 1) where DID rises steadily and accelerates. We have explained in the previous chapters (chapters 3 and 6) that, in the old institutional arrangements with the fundamental contradictions of the POE, the multi-sovereignty mechanism, non-price (market) adjustments, the effective right of local governments to supply money, and so on, the central government's high accumulation intention via increases in construction expenditure will inevitably cause a chain of conflicts for the limited investment resources in the economy. There are no constraints what so ever on the expansion of economic agent's investment demands in Model 1, until the central government finds it necessary to launch a new austerity campaign to prevent the economy from deteriorating further. This kind of vicious circle, mainly resulting from the competition for resources, is now broken by our reform package. When the central government decides to invest intensively in the upstream sectors (i.e., increase its construction expenditure), the prices of investment goods will rise. This in turn suppresses investment demand of downstream sectors, because they are now subject to harder budget constraints, and because prices of investment goods are now completely free. In a word, by eliminating the mechanism of interest conflicts and by fostering the mechanism of market clearing, the economy is able to re-allocate resources without causing massive demand expansions.

The responses of the investment market to one-period shocks in credit and the government's construction expenditure come to our notice as well. The excess investment demand sees a pulse in Figure 7.5 (Model 2), and several pulses in Figure 7.6 (Model 2). The pulse-like movements also appear in aggregate investment demand and supply, and in the downstream sector's investment demand, but all damp down to circa zero sooner or later after the policy shocks are removed (see Figures 7.5 and 7.6, (Model 2)). In the simulations of Model 1, however, the expansionary impacts of the same temporary policy shocks on (excess) investment demand persisted right through to the end of experiments (see Figures 7.5 and 7.6, (Model 1)).

Consumption behaviour

Similar behaviour to that of investment markets is observed in the consumption markets. Excess consumption demand shows a rise to its maximum of 8.57 and 3.38 billion yuan corresponding to experiments (1) and (2) respectively, and then a gradual drop down to its equilibrium paths (see Figures 7.1 and 7.2, (Model 2)). Symmetrically, in the experiments of contractionary policy shocks, excess consumption demand also returns to a state of equilibrium after a fall to its minimum -3.34 and -11.54 billion yuan in Figures 7.3 (Model 2) and 7.4 (Model 2) respectively. In other words, no policy perturbation (whether expansionary or contractionary) fails to create an almost-zero excess demand for consumption markets in long run. So, the improvement is obvious, if comparing the results here with those of Model 1 where the (excess) consumption demand rises (or declines) persistently (see DCE and DC in Figures 7.1 through 7.4, (Model 1)). The small and slow responses of consumption demand to policy shocks in the new regime may principally result from two factors. One is the abolition of price subsidy policies, and the other is the shift of household current savings (as opposed to time saving deposits) from being involuntary to being voluntary (see chapter 5). The first makes consumption demand respond actually inversely to the price changes, while the second eliminates the role of forced savings as an accelerator.

In observing the results of a one-period shock, we find that consumption behaviour is pretty much like investment behaviour. Consumption demand directly responds to the disturbance of credit with a sudden rise of 2.11% in the first year of the shock, and then returns back to slight increases of around 0.06% in a few years after the disturbance is removed (Figure 7.5 (Model 2)). It takes two years for consumption demand to reach a peak rise of 1.99% and then level off at 0.12%-0.14% (Figure 7.6 (Mode 2)), in response to the temporary shock of government construction expenditure GEE, because of the one-period lag of GEE built into the system (see equation (7.7)). Through the price adjustment mechanism, consumption supply tries to follow the movements of consumption demand: Figure 7.5 (Model 2) shows that SC rises by 1.13% along with a 2.11% increase in DC in the year of credit expansion, but declines lagging behind DC in the subsequent a few years. The similar picture can be seen in Figure 7.6 (Model 2) as well, regarding the movements of consumption supply. Thus both Figures 7.5 and 7.6 (Model 2) again demonstrates a pulse-like wave motion in excess consumption demand, but eventually excess consumption demand settles down to its original path prior to the policy shocks. This implies that Model 2, in contrast to Model 1, does prevent a one-period policy shock from acting as a kind of 'pump-priming' on the system.

Price behaviour

Excess demand (supply) in consumption and investment markets pushes up (pulls down) the prices of consumption and investment goods, but eventually the prices stop rising (falling) and flatten out at a certain level as the corresponding markets are cleared. These results are observed in all the experiments conducted for permanent policy shocks here (see Figures 7.1 through 7.4, (Model 2)), but there are some differences between policy effects on the prices. The credit expansion, the increases in the government construction spending and the increases in the nominal interest rate have stronger impacts on the prices of investment goods PK than on the prices of consumption goods PC. The decreases in government non-construction expenditure, on the other hand, reduce PC more than in PK. This is not surprising, probably because the first three policy instruments mainly or directly act on investment markets, while the last one acts on consumption markets.

Another obvious result is that the increases (decreases) in investment goods prices PK and consumption goods prices PC are not as substantial as the price increases (decreases) in Model 1 (see Figures 7.1 through 7.4, (Model 2) and (Model 1), for price behaviour). Also we can see the differences in inflation profile of PK and PC: the former rises (falls) more rapidly than the latter, in the first three experiments. These suggest that the introduction of an investment goods price equation in Model 2 does remove, from retail prices, the pressure of disequilibrium in investment markets. Without this, the resource allocation would be misguided. The reasons can be seen as follows. Endnote 3 of chapter 4 explained that retail prices can be approximately regarded as the prices of consumption goods. If the shortages in the investment markets are translated into the increases in retail prices, this will lead investment funds to consumption goods sectors rather than to investment goods sectors. An obvious example we have already seen is the investment demand of non-state sectors which respond to expansionary policies more sensitively than the investment demand of state-owned sectors (see chapter 6). The non-state sectors are more market-guided than the state sectors, and as such the shortages in investment markets further increase the investment demand of non-state sectors by increasing retail prices (but not increasing investment goods prices!), the future expectations of which positively affect the non-state sectors' investment demand (see equation (6.11)). As a result, investment resources tend to flow into consumption goods sectors (because non-state sectors are mainly in consumption goods sectors or downstream sectors), which in turn further exacerbates the structural shortage and the situation of investment markets. The experiment (2) in Model 2 with the behaviour of DID has already indicated that, this problem can only be resolved in the new regime with the integrated price adjustment system.

Much of the short-run behaviour can be observed by looking at one-period shock experiments (Figure 7.7). In terms of time-paths, there are differences between Model 1 and Model 2. The former presents a continuous rise in prices, while the latter illustrates a pagoda-like time path for prices. In terms of relative policy effects on prices between monetary and fiscal expansions, Model 2 is similar to Model 1, in that the inflationary effects of monetary expansion are larger in consumption goods markets (prices), compared to those of fiscal expansion, while the inflationary effects of fiscal expansion are larger in investment goods markets (prices), than those of monetary expansion. Finally, in terms of relative policy effects on output, Model 2 is essentially the same as Model 1, because fiscal policy is again better than monetary policy in maintaining output. So, the reform package will not affect the stability of certain macroeconomic policies.

7.4 Model calibration and robustness of simulation results

Model calibration

Our policy package of further reforms would result in counterfactual economic relations which are not fitted to the historical time series data. To obtain a fully specified numerical model of the new economy, we have to resort to the calibration procedure most commonly used in applied general equilibrium analysis. This procedure is outlined in Shoven and Whalley (1984). Typically, calibration involves only one year's data, or a single observation represented as an average over a number of years. The economy under consideration is assumed to be in equilibrium, a so called 'bench-mark' equilibrium. An important feature of the calibration procedure is that, once it is complete, it should be possible to reproduce the bench-mark equilibrium data set as an equilibrium solution of the model. Because of the reliance on a single observation, the bench-mark data typically do not identify a unique set of values for the parameters in a model. Particular values for the relevant elasticities are usually specified on the basis of other research, and these serve to identify uniquely the other parameters of the model along with the equilibrium observation.

The above basic features of the calibration procedure are applied in the study here, but with some modifications according to the particulars of the problems being dealt with. The single data point to which Model 2 is calibrated is from an observation of 1980. Our previous studies indicated that the Chinese economy in 1980 had the least estimates of aggregate excess demand in domestic markets in the 1980s,[3] which was 0.9% in aggregate demand. This was due to China's first economic retrenchment programme in the 1980s, and the programme was successful and effective, which led to the best macroeconomic environment in the 1980s, as many Chinese economists indicated latter. Thus this year's data is chosen to represent a situation closest to equilibrium in this decade. Since the literature is sparse on some parameter values in our model here, the calibration has to be undertaken on the mixed basis of our previous results, theory, experience, observation and common sense etc. Specifically, for the parameters which are almost unlikely to be affected by the policy package, their values in Model 1 are somewhat intact in Model 2. For instance, the marginal propensity to consume (MPC) in Model 1 was 0.7975, and we simply put 0.79 in Model 2. As to those variables which should be eliminated by further reforms, they are removed from Model 2. This is equivalent to imposing a zero parameter value. Now come the problems of the variables which start to play important roles in the new regime. Some of their parameters can be uniquely identified by already chosen parameters or be determined by changing intercepts to get required values. Where there is a newly introduced behavioral equation with several parameters to be determined at the same time, we decided first to run a regression, on the argument that it would at least provide us with a rough idea for a sensible range for those parameter values. Then based on the results of regression, we adjust these parameter values to assure that both sides of the equation are absolutely equal to each other. All the parameters obtained by this kind of deterministic calibration will serve as the 'best guess' values for a sensitivity analysis later on. Finally a replication check is done to make sure that the model will exactly reproduce the base year (1980) data set or the bench-mark equilibrium data set.

Sensitivity analysis

Before the success of the policy package of further reforms can be claimed, one key issue with the model needs to be addressed: How robust are the simulation results to alternative parameter values? Because the calibration procedure was used to select parameter values, meaningful statistical tests of any model specification are usually not possible. Policy conclusions drawn from the model results are often left with a sense of discomfort that any given results could disappear, or even change qualitatively, if alternative parameter values were chosen.

One response to the robustness issue has been to perform a sensitivity analysis. The kind of sensitivity analysis conducted in this report is somewhat informal. Formal sensitivity analysis usually applies a weighting procedure, in which the normalized joint probabilities for each simulation provide the weights used when reporting the results of the simulations (Harrison and Kimbell, 1985). In this study, however, the covariance matrix for Model 2 is not known, and presumably cannot be guessed at. Thus we decided not to do the probability weighted sensitivity tests, but just to give a sketch of the likely range of possible results, in the hope that the range is small and hence the results not sensitive to the precise numerical assumptions made in the process of model calibration.

Wigle (1986) outlined three possible approaches to sensitivity analysis: Limited Robustness, Conditional Systematic Sensitivity Analysis (CSSA) and Unconditional Systematic Sensitivity Analysis (USSA). Our approach seems to fall into the second one CSSA: it involves a series of solutions of the model in which each parameter is perturbed a certain number of times from its value used in the central-case specification, holding all of the other parameter values at their central-case specifications. The approach of USSA, on the other hand, involves a series solutions of the model with each parameter being perturbed conditional on the other parameters also being perturbed. Obviously the number of solutions required to calculate a full USSA is prohibitively high, and that is why CSSA is preferred here. We consider three (sometimes four) alternative values for each parameter, including the 'best guess' ones which reflect our own best guesses for the new model structure resulting from the package of reforms pursued in this chapter. The policy experiments are similar to those conducted before, for the sake of comparison, but in most cases we chose a permanent 10% increase in domestic credit (DOCR=LOS+LOP+LOF). If a parameter to be perturbed is explicitly attached to the policy variables, such as government construction expenditure (GEE) or nominal interest rates (NRI) etc., in a behavioral equation, then a permanent 10% increase in GEE or a permanent 2 percentage points increase in NRI etc. will be performed correspondingly. In all cases reported below, the initial solution values of the model for the given policy change are obtained with all parameters set equal to their 'best guess' values. Given these solution values as reference paths for the sensitivity analysis simulations involving a perturbed parameter, we are able to investigate the robustness of model results by comparing the new paths against the reference ones.

A systematic sensitivity analysis, even of the kind CSSA, across all the parameters in the model is a huge undertaking, though it produces a great deal of information. To keep things manageable, however, we do not report every single result. Only the most important results of excess consumption and investment demand, for some key parameters resulting from our policy package, are reported here, since the policy package is mainly aimed at generating a better economy which would automatically move towards a new equilibrium in consumption and investment markets, after policy shocks.

Figures 7.8 through 7.22 (in Appendix 7B) set out the impacts on excess consumption and investment demand, of the given policy changes under three or four alternative values for each parameter in question. A perturbation of a parameter is made by multiplying a multiplicative factor σ and the parameter under consideration (Brandsma, Hughes Hallett and Swank 1987, Hughes Hallett 1987). Thus if σ = 1, the parameter multiplied by that value of σ represent the so called 'best guess' parameter value specified in the process of model calibration, and it also identifies the 'bench-mark' results (referring to the results obtained when best guess parameter values are used) in Figures 7.8-7.22. Tables 7.1 and 7.2 (in Appendix 7C) summarises the sensitivity elasticities of these two disequilibrium indicators with respect to the parameters considered. Column 1 of the table indicates which equation the parameter is in and with which variable it is associated. For example, the 'consumption demand-expected inflation rate parameter' refers to the parameter attached to the variable, the expected inflation rate, in the consumption demand equation. The 'consumption price adjustment parameter' means the parameter related to the excess consumption demand in the equation of consumption goods prices, and so forth. Column 2 of the table is straightforward, and does not need any further explanation. Columns 3 and 4 give the measures of sensitivity elasticity which are calculated using the following formula:

$$SE = \frac{\partial \log(TGVA)}{\partial \log(PRMT)} = \frac{(\Delta TGVA)\%}{(\Delta PRMT)\%} \tag{7.28}$$

where SE is sensitivity elasticity, TGVA represents a target variable (excess consumption or investment demand in particular here), and PRMT stands for the parameter subject to perturbations. The percentage changes in a target variable are obtained directly from single year simulation results, mostly in the first year of policy shocks, but sometimes in the second year and even in the third year. This depends on the lags of the variables concerned in Model 2. For percentage changes in a parameter, its best guess value is used as point of comparison.

Discussion of the robustness of the results

A number of interesting points are illustrated by the simulations. First, a general feature across the whole model is apparent: the results of every plausibly alternative numerical assumption are qualitatively identical to, though somewhat quantitatively larger/smaller than, the bench-mark results. In the experiment using a 10% permanent increase in domestic credit (DOCR), for example, all simulations demonstrate a similar pattern of movement in both excess consumption and investment demand: consumption and investment markets suffer only a short-period disequilibrium which wears off sooner or later, although the degree of disequilibrium differs. The same results are also observed in the other three kinds of experiments. This is the most important information, as it tells us that the nature of the bench-mark results is not crucially dependent on the particular parameter values we have chosen.

Second, the simulations indicate the importance and significance of the role of price adjustment mechanism in clearing markets. The consumption and investment equilibrium gains (or decreases in the degree of disequilibrium) from price liberalization can be clearly observed. They are all increasing in increases in demand-price or supply-price elasticities (see Figures 7.9, 7.10, and 7.17). To pinpoint where the sensitivities are, let us have a look at Tables 7.1 and 7.2 (in Appendix 7C). Row 3 in Table 7.1 shows that, if the consumption demand-price parameter reduces to 0.01 times or increases to 10 times its best guess value, the sensitivity elasticities of excess consumption demand are -0.1034 or -0.0508. On the other hand, row 4 in Table 7.1 gives the corresponding figures for variations in the consumption supply-price parameter of -0.5722 ($\sigma=0.01$) and -0.0851 ($\sigma=10$) respectively, which are bigger than their counterparts in row 3. Again Table 7.2 signifies that when the price or inflation-related parameters in the equations of investment demand and supply are subject to a given error, the disturbances of excess investment demand are large, in terms of the supply-price parameter (see rows 2, 5 and 6 in column 4). Consequently, the equilibrium gains are more sensitive to the errors in the supply-price elasticities than to those in the demand-price elasticities. The fact that the sensitivity is in the supply-price elasticities does suggest that, after the mechanism of demand augmentation is eliminated (so that demand begins to be more responsive to the price signals), the improvement of production efficiencies, and hence of the behaviour of supply, should be put in high priority.

More obviously perhaps, the equilibrium gains also increase as the parameters in the price-adjustment equations increase (see Figures 7.21 and 7.22 in Appendix 7B). These parameters reflect, to a certain degree, how flexible prices are. If, to take an extreme example, prices are completely sticky, that is, the parameters are set equal to zero ($\sigma=0$), then a different picture will appear with the deviations of excess consumption and investment demand remaining at very high level (around 44 billion yuan in Figure 7.21 and 54 billion yuan in Figure 7.22 respectively, in real terms) by the end of simulation period. On the other hand, for sufficiently high price-adjustment parameters, the degree of disequilibrium approaches zero and becomes relatively insensitive to the assumptions about the flexibility of prices. Table 7.1 shows that, as the consumption price adjustment parameter increases from

0.1 times its best guess value to 10 times that value, the sensitivity elasticities of excess consumption and investment demand declines in absolute terms from 1.1417 to 0.0928 and from 0.179 to 0.0145 respectively. An increase in the investment price adjustment parameter also reduces these two elasticities (see Table 7.2). Note from Tables 7.1 and 7.2 that, when the price adjustment parameters are below certain values, the absolute values of these two sensitivity elasticities become even larger than 1. This suggests that the free market pricing policies would not only become more robust (i.e., smaller disturbances for a given error) than their sticky counterparts, but they would be relatively *more* robust the *larger* the *increase* made in the parameters. That extreme example ($\sigma=0$) is, of course, contrary to our policy package of further reforms which includes a complete lifting of control over prices. Nevertheless, it does serve to highlight the point that the failure of price reforms would lead to the failure of the whole economic reform.

Third, comparing column 3 with 4 in Tables 7.1 and 7.2, the absolute sensitivity elasticities of excess consumption demand are larger than those of excess investment demand in Table 7.1, but the former are smaller than the latter in Table 7.2. The upshot of all this is that particular assumptions concerning consumption relationships at other points are somewhat irrelevant to the investment disequilibrium, and vice versa. That is to say, the excess-investment (consumption)-demand outcome of the simulation is almost insensitive no matter what other assumptions are made concerning the potential for elasticities in the consumption (investment) block. This is because the quantity signals from consumption markets no longer have a significant impact on investment demand, and excess investment demand no longer needs to translate into an increase in prices in consumption markets. If the mutually-strengthened influences between consumption and investment disequilibria in Model 1 were assumed here, there would be higher sensitivity of one market situation to the changes in the other market's relationships. So our policy package would ensure a more stable economy than without it.

The fourth point to note is that altering the upstream-downstream investment demand parameter, and even changing its sign, does not matter much in long run, but it does in short run (see Figure 7.15). In Model 2, the investment demand of the upstream sectors is inversely related to that of the downstream sectors, in contrast to Model 1. The underlying assumptions were already stated before: the central government is ready to make a concession to downstream sectors (now consisting of private firms), no longer fearing that an expansion of investment in downstream sectors will result in severe bottlenecks and hence structural shortages. Instead the market mechanism would actually help to appropriately adjust the industrial structure. Now this underlying assumption by the central government can be supported here by sensitivity analysis. Whether the upstream sectors respond positively (when σ becomes negative) or negatively (when σ becomes positive) to the downstream sectors' investment demand, the investment goods markets will return to equilibrium in the same length of time. This is clearly a result of the market regulation mechanism. Figure 7.15 takes σ=5 and σ=-5 as two extreme cases and shows that three trajectories meet and begin to approach together to zero in three years after policy shocks. But the difference between these three numerical assumptions is also obvious: the short-period shortage in investment markets gets worse if σ declines from positive to negative values (i.e., the parameter increases from negative to positive values). Now that the market mechanism can do something about this in long run, and since raising the parameter makes things even worse in short run, why should the central government bother?

In summary, the CSSA exercises have actually shown that the simulation results are robust enough, although we did not report all of them. They are not changed *qualitatively* by varying parameter values within plausible ranges, despite somewhat different numbers. In other words, we have identified no parameters whose reasonably alternative values would make our conclusions essentially different from those based on their 'best guess' values in Model 2. But the model outcomes seem more sensitive to the errors of price adjustment parameters than to the misspecifications of other parameters, particularly in the cases where the price adjustment parameters have low values. This indicates that the price reform is a crucially important determinant of the success of our policy package.

7.5 Conclusions

In this chapter we have pursued a policy package for further reforms. It is aimed at removing those fundamental drawbacks of the economic system which have caused both demand augmentation and production inefficiencies leading to pervasive and persistent shortage in the economy in the 1980s. This is done by adopting a model-based approach, i.e., by creating and simulating a new model which represents the economic world resulting from the policy package. The new model is formed by applying a model calibration procedure: some of the parameters in the old model are set to zero, some are increased in their size, and some are even created, on a 'what if' basis, in accordance with the policy package. In doing so, we believe that the policy package would lead to a dramatic change in the existing economic structure, if it was implemented effectively.

Our studies have demonstrated that the measures contained in the policy package would clearly improve the behaviour of the economy. The degree of demand augmentation would be considerably reduced, and the supply would quickly catch up the pace of demand. There are a few main points we would like to stress below as conclusions.

1. The most direct role in equilibrating demand and supply is surely played by price adjustment mechanism. It suppresses demand for consumption and investment goods on one hand, and stimulates supply of consumption and investment goods on the other. It also provides a good guide for the allocation of resources between the consumption and investment sectors. According to the results of the sensitivity analysis, the crucial mechanisms in the economy (or the success of the reform) lie in the flexibility of prices, as far as the equilibrium gains are concerned. The quicker prices adjust to clear markets, the less the economy will suffer from disequilibria. Thus, one can see how important the successful price reforms are to the whole economic reform.

2. The prerequisites for an effective price mechanism, however, should not be ignored. The reform of public ownership and the removal of local government's role make the entire downstream sector's investment demand responsive to price signals. The upstream sector's investment demand is no longer effected by consumption demand, which used to be an unusual accelerator for the expansion of investment demand in Model 1, and is also pulled down by price increases, mainly because the central government reduces its influences on the sector. Moreover, the mechanism of demand augmentation, as a result of the no-cooperative games in which players competing with each other for resources, is considerably weakened. This is because the institutional conditions of 'games' are undermined by the reform of public sectors and by the removal of local governments' role in interfering directly in the economy. The former resolves the problem of interest conflicts, while the latter leads to a deregulation of the banks and a decontrol of the credit granting system; and both measures are commonly aimed at subjecting economic agents to hard budget constraints, so as to shift their responses towards price rather than quantity signals. Without these reforms of ownership and management systems, even if prices are completely free to reflect market situation, they still cannot play a role in equilibrating demand and supply and in reallocating optimally resources between sectors.

3. These policy measures do not merely change the behaviour of demand, but change the behaviour of supply (especially investment supply) as well. The results of the sensitivity analysis reveal that, in reducing the degree of disequilibrium, the supply responses (positive) to the price changes would contribute more than the demand responses (negative) to the price changes. So, supply management policies, mainly involving readjustment of economic (industrial) structure, improvement of organizational efficiencies and innovation of technology, should gain significant importance.

In a word, the liberalization of the price system and the restructuring of ownership and macroeconomic management system are cores of further market-oriented reforms. As we have seen in this chapter, such a reform programme would lead to an economy which creates growth at much lower cost in terms of inflation and/or disequilibrium than the existing economy.

Notes

1. Economists always blame the fixed price system or the distorted relation between relative prices, but very few of them have ever raised the following questions: Why cannot frequent price adjustments correct, but sometimes even worsen, the distortion between relative prices? Why just would not the central planner adjust what should first be adjusted? Is the central planner as irrational as that? Fan G. et al (1990) argue that this behaviour of the central planner is actually rational for the following reasons: the effects of the rise in the prices of upstream-sector's products would be far-reaching on the costs of other products, and hence on the interests of every enterprise, subunit, and locality concerned in the POE. Accordingly, before doing that the central planner has to 're-negotiate' and 'bargain' with them one by one about the rate of the profit retained to that turned over, about the rate of budgetary revenue shared between local governments and between local and central governments, etc. The bargain of this sort has proved really tough and time-consuming. Meanwhile, the central planner would encounter stronger resistance and opposition in trying to raise the prices of the upstream sector's products than in trying to raise the prices of the downstream sector's products. In a word, the irrational consequences brought about by the 'rational' behaviour of the central planner has its in-depth roots in the basic contradictions of the POE, and what should be blamed is the innate logic in the economic process itself.
2. According to Almanac of China's Foreign Trade (1990), before 1979 investment goods accounted for more than 80% of total imports; in 1980s the figures were still around 70%.
3. The following figures are the estimates of aggregate excess demand in domestic markets in percentages of quantity transacted: 3.66% (1979); 0.94% (1980); 3.20% (1981); 2.22% (1982); 1.87% (1983); 5.72% (1984); 3.02% (1985); 2.21% (1986); 7.37% (1987); 7.26% (1988); -12.5% (1989).

Appendix 7A - Policy simulations of Model 2 and Model 1

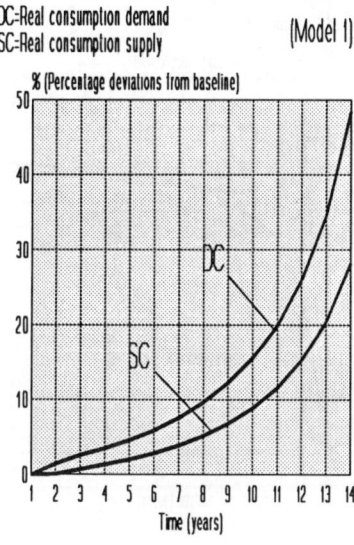

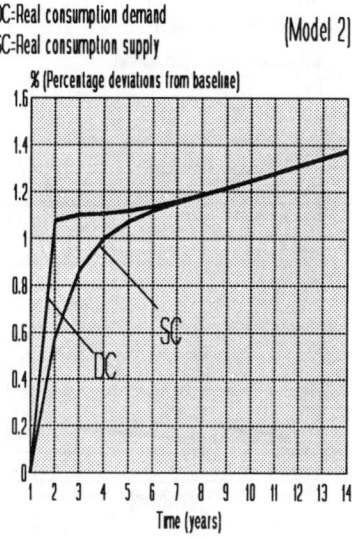

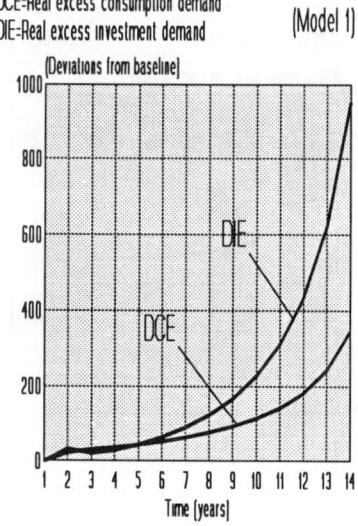

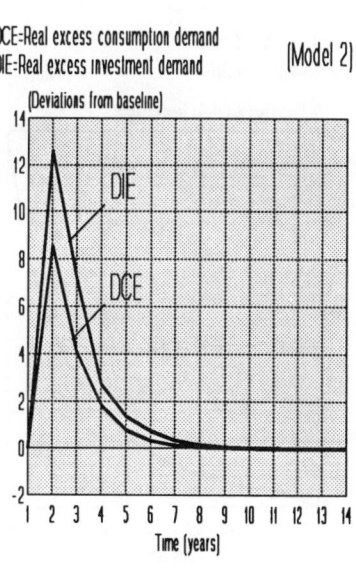

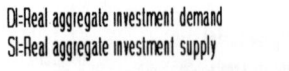
DI=Real aggregate investment demand
SI=Real aggregate investment supply (Model 1)

DI=Real aggregate investment demand
SI=Real aggregate investment supply (Model 2)

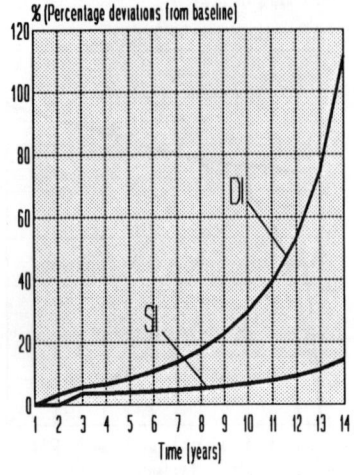

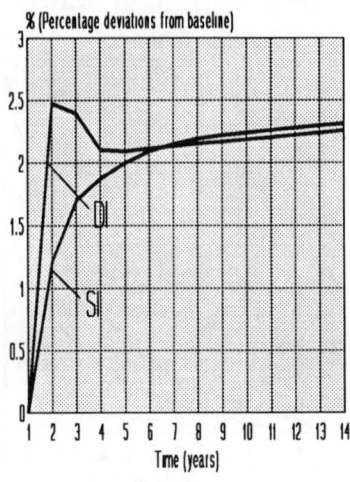

DID=Real investment demand
of downstream sectors (Model 1)

DID=Real investment demand
of downstream sectors (Model 2)

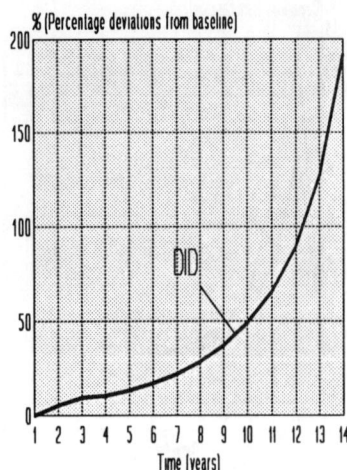

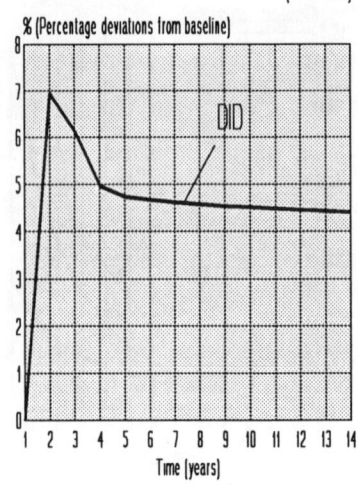

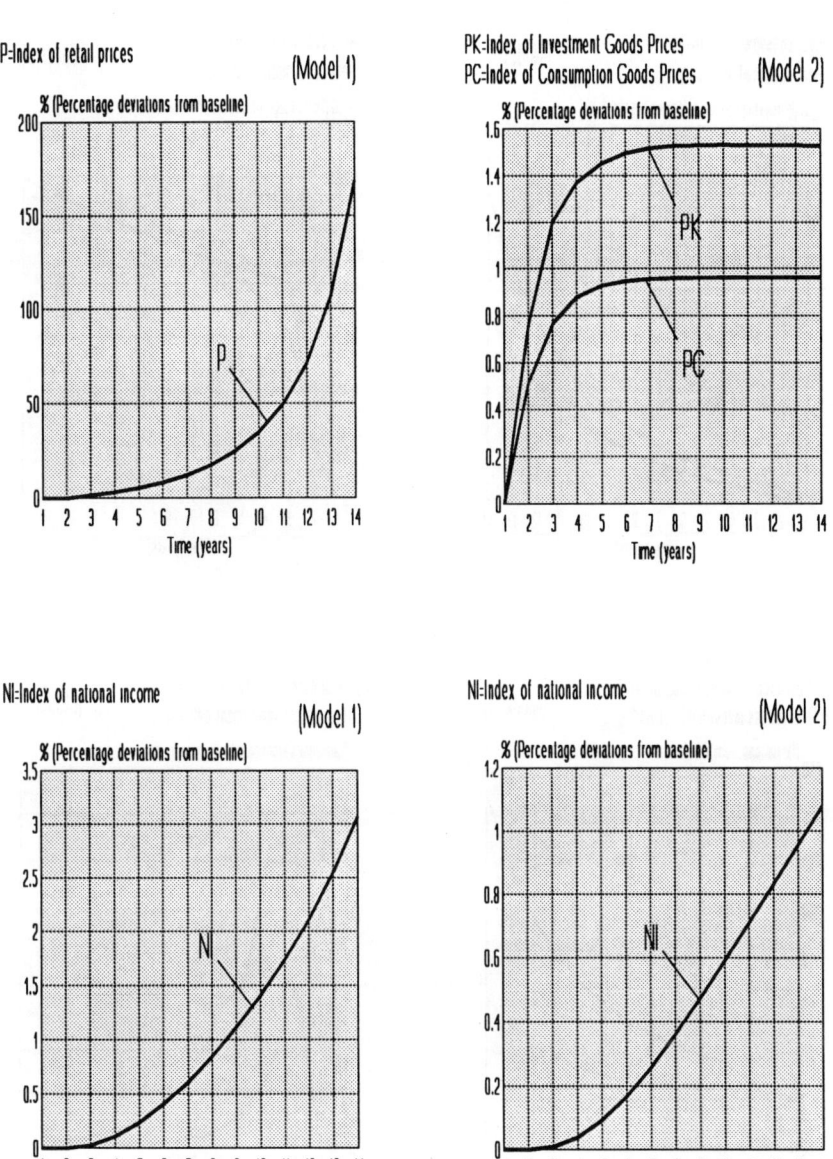

Figure 7.1 A permanent 5% increase in domestic credit

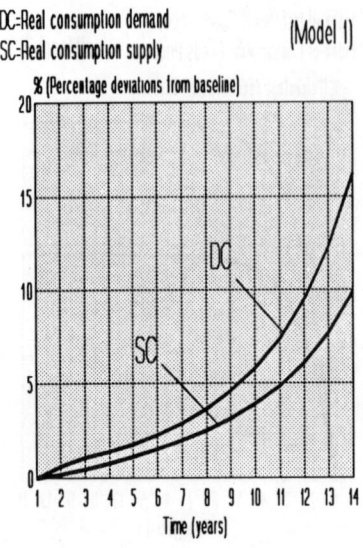

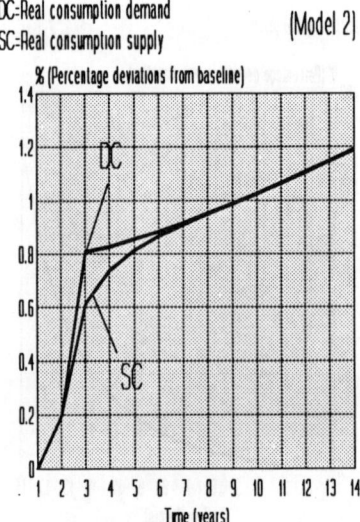

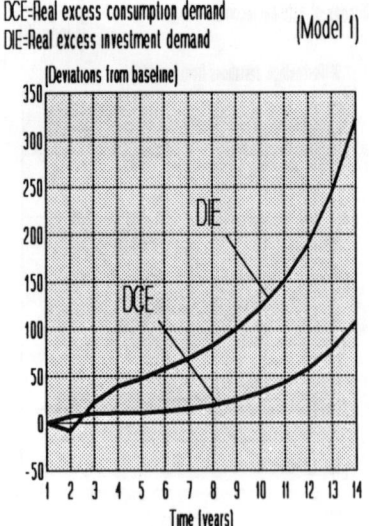

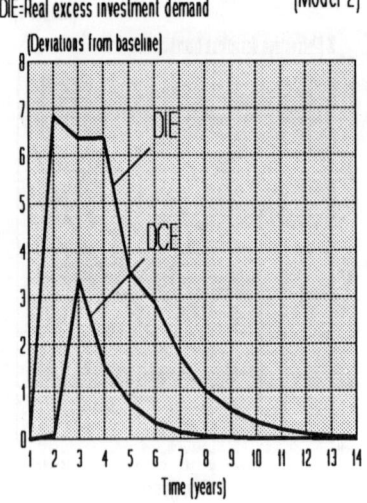

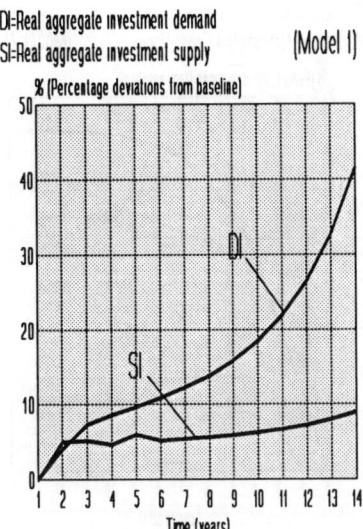
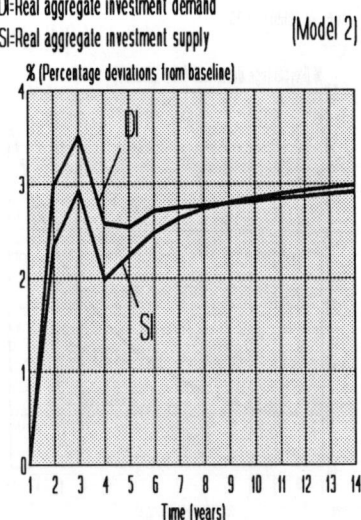
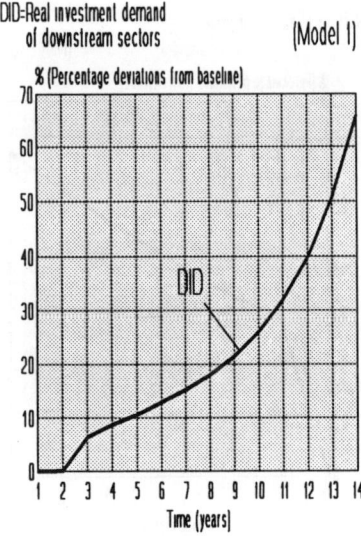
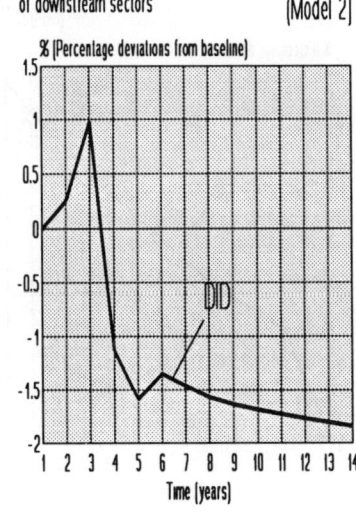

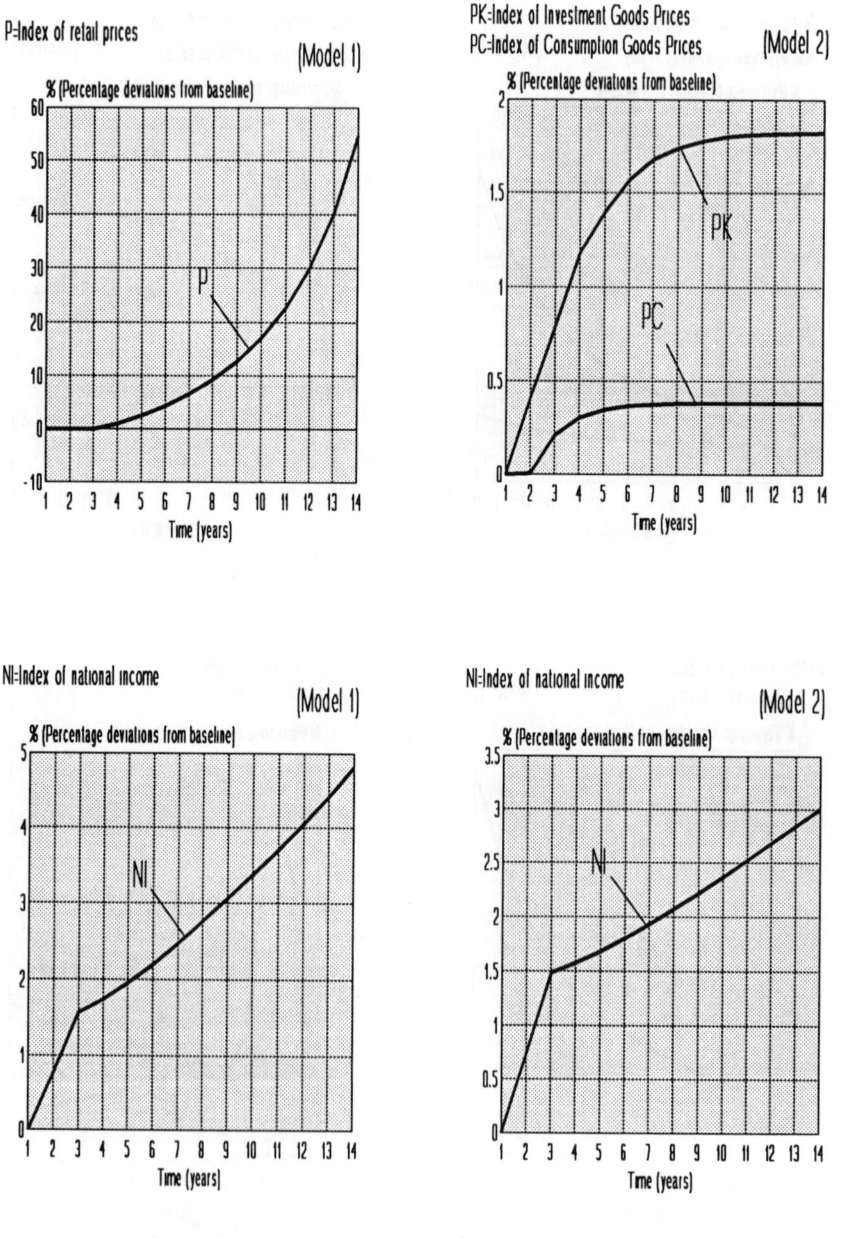

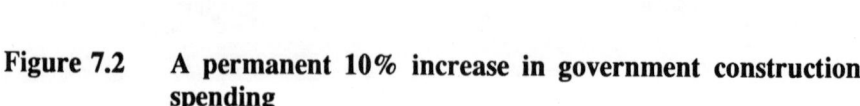

Figure 7.2   A permanent 10% increase in government construction spending

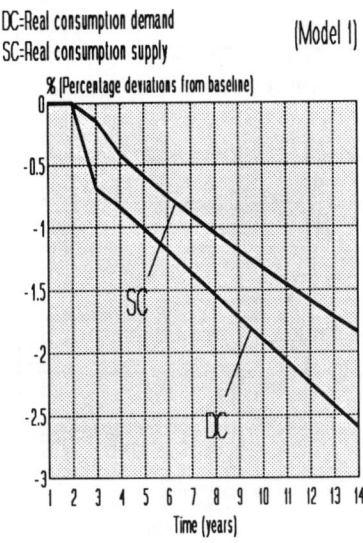

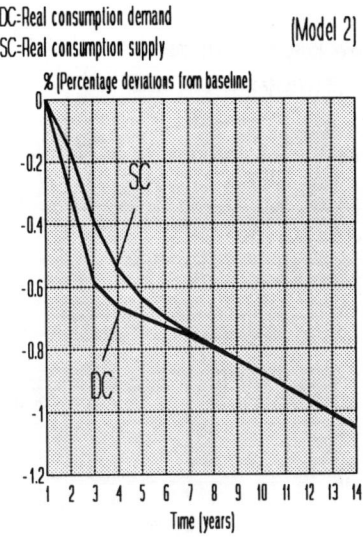

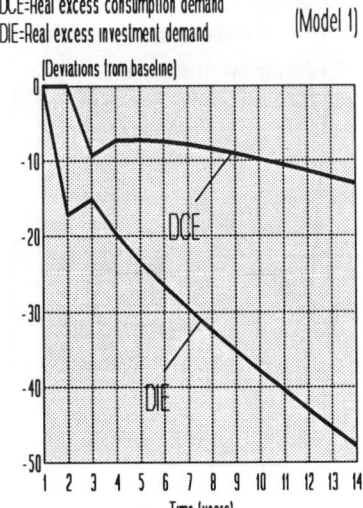

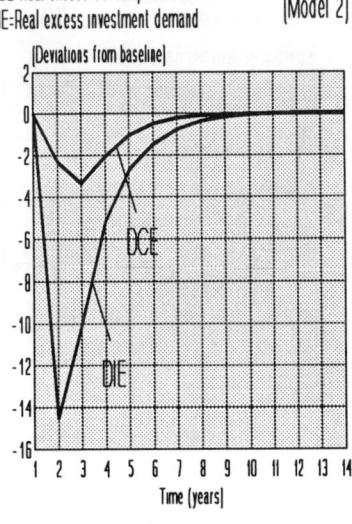

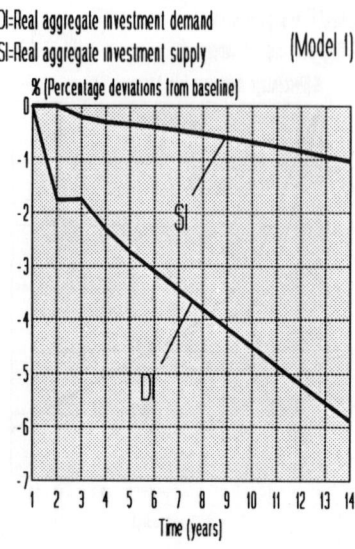
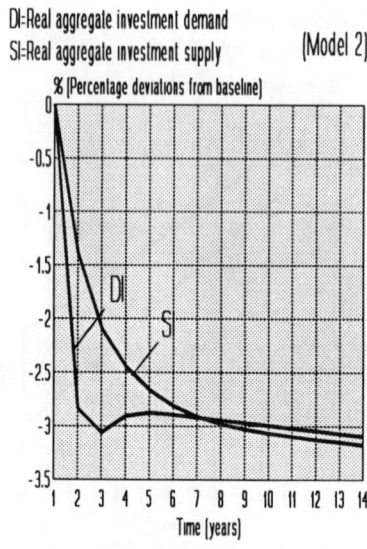
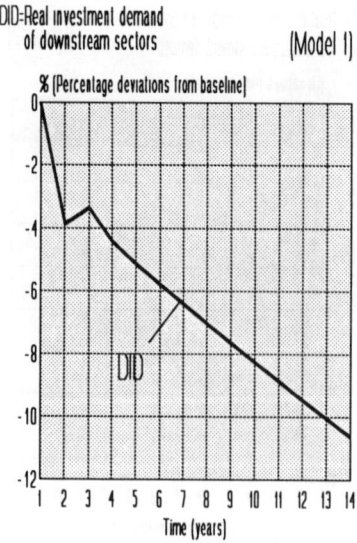
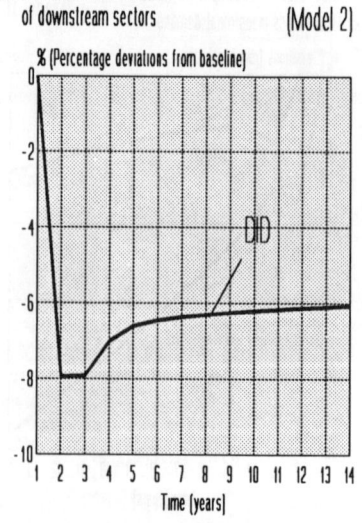

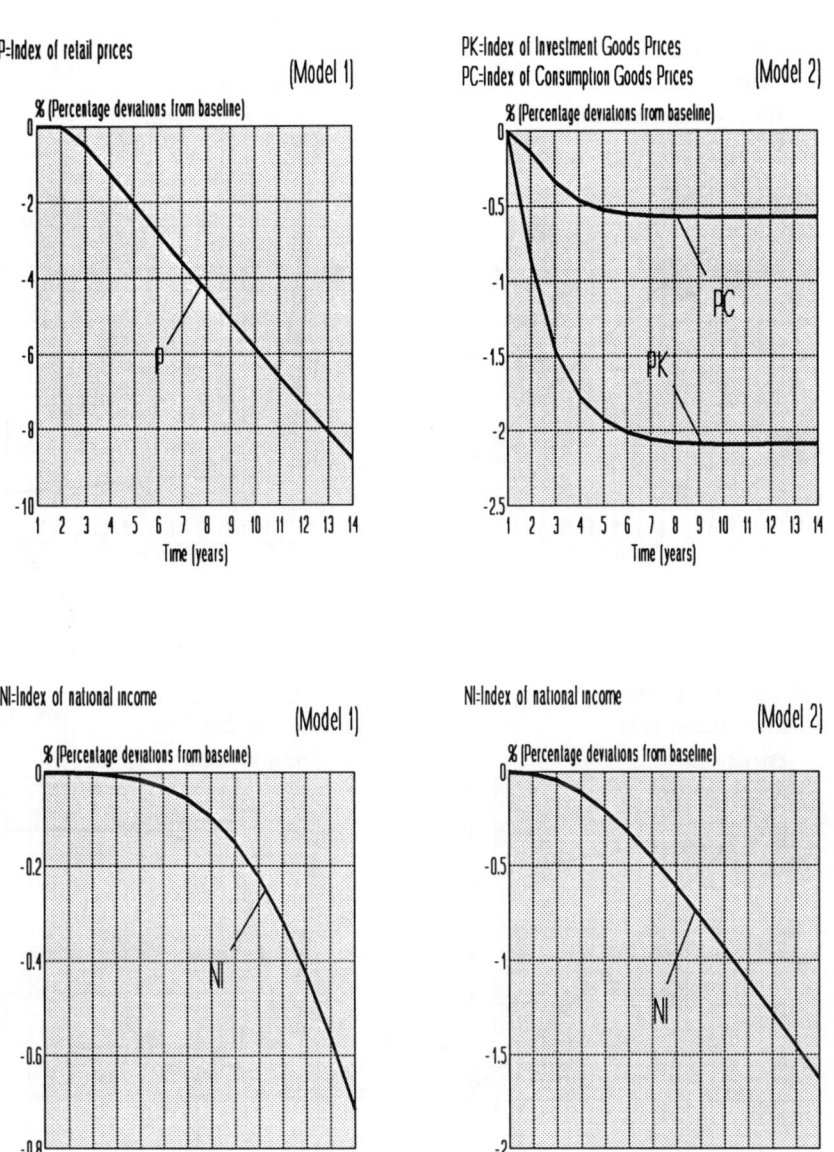

Figure 7.3 A permanent increase in nominal interest rates by 1.1 times

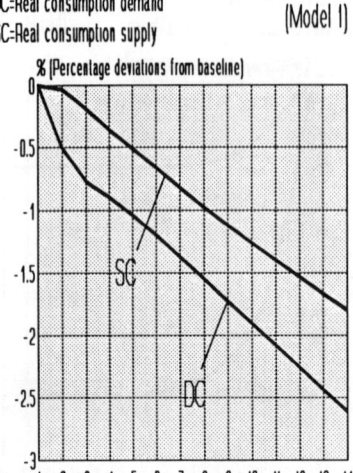

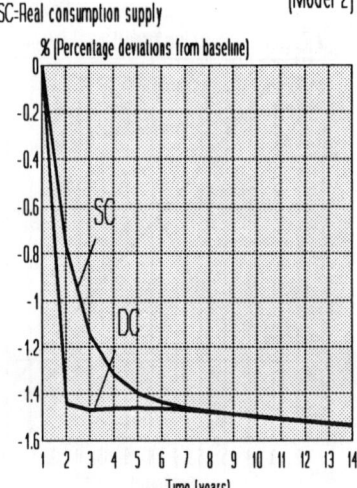

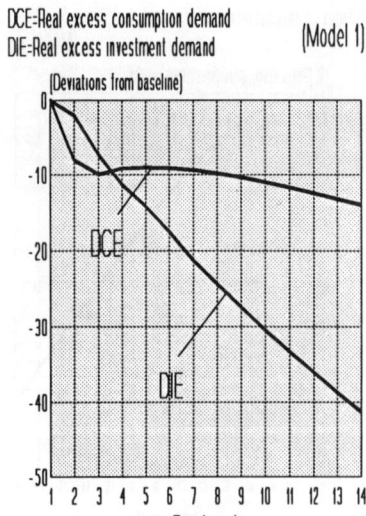

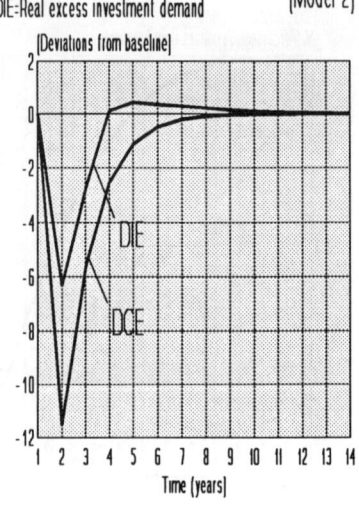

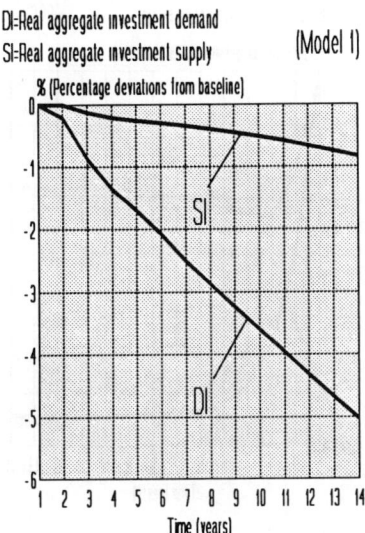

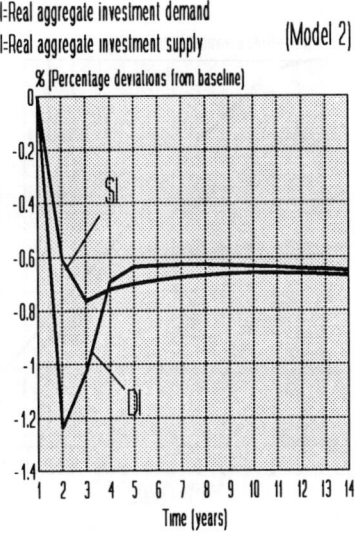

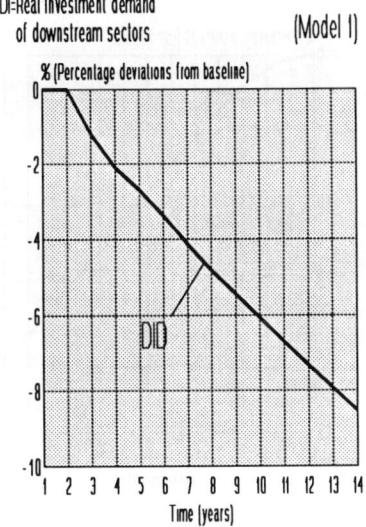

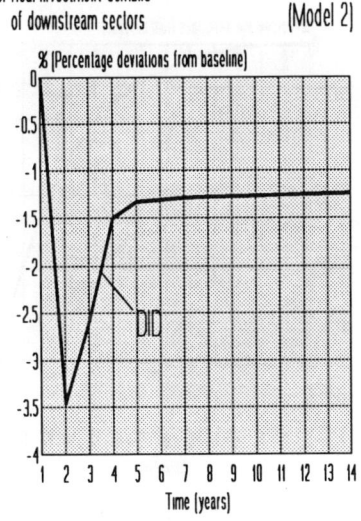

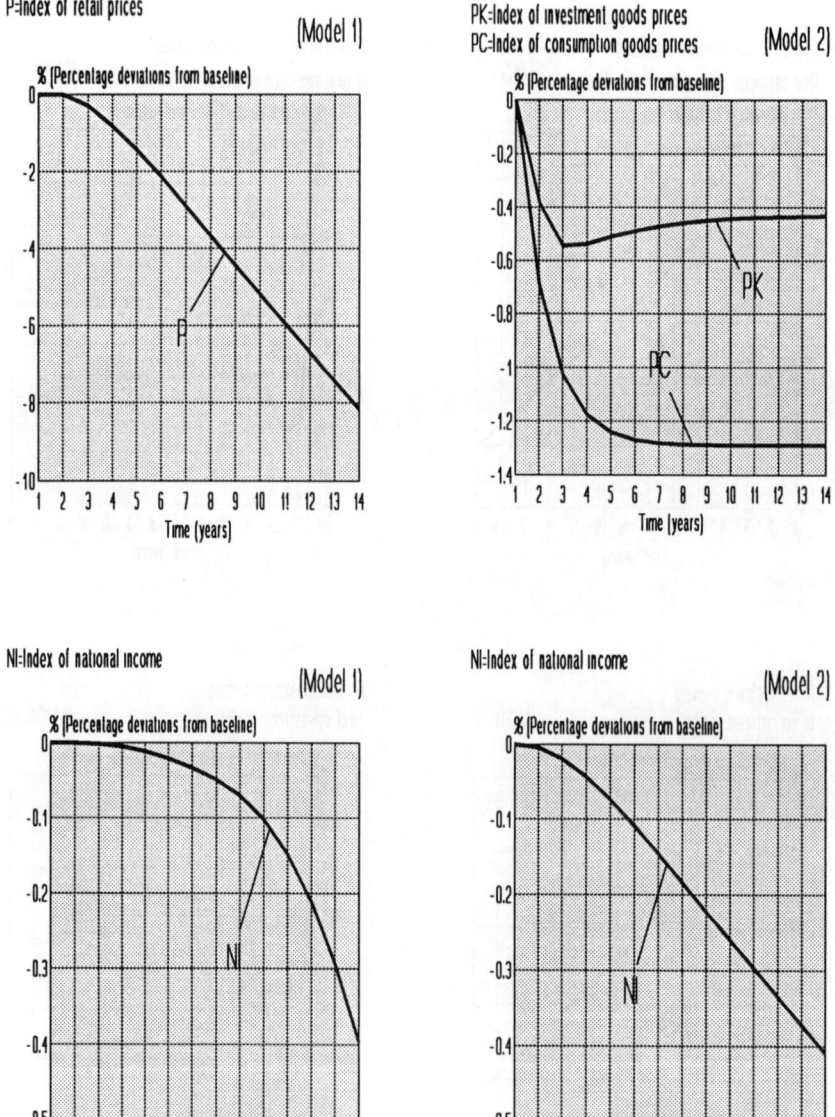

Figure 7.4   A permanent 10% cut in government non-construction spending

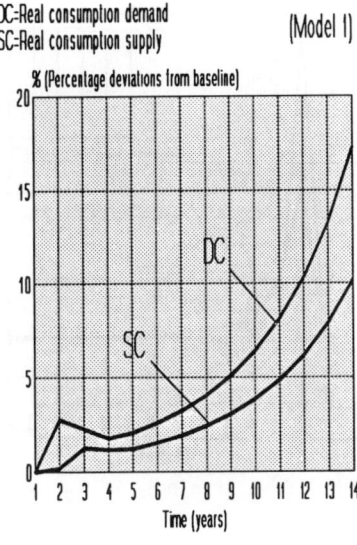

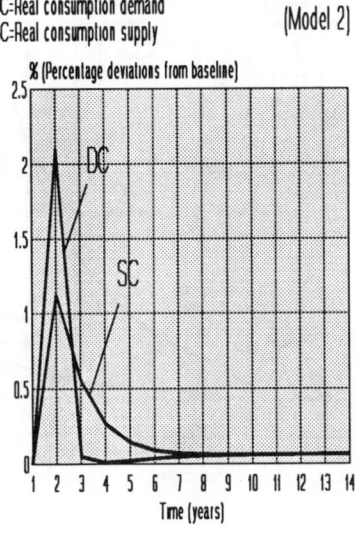

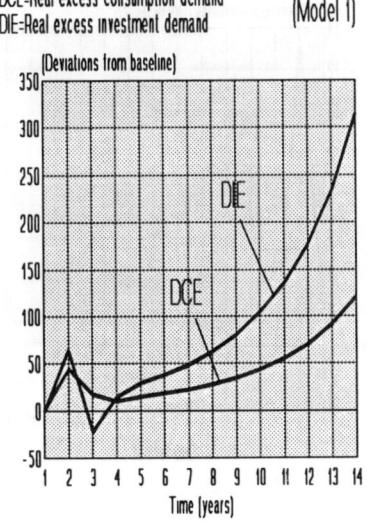

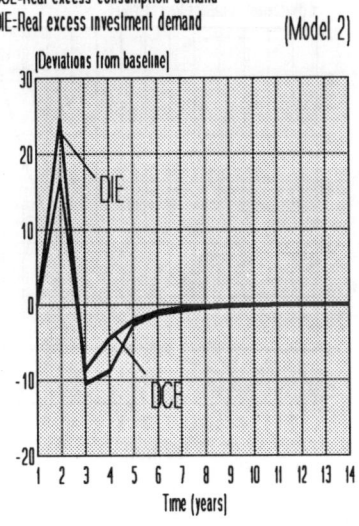

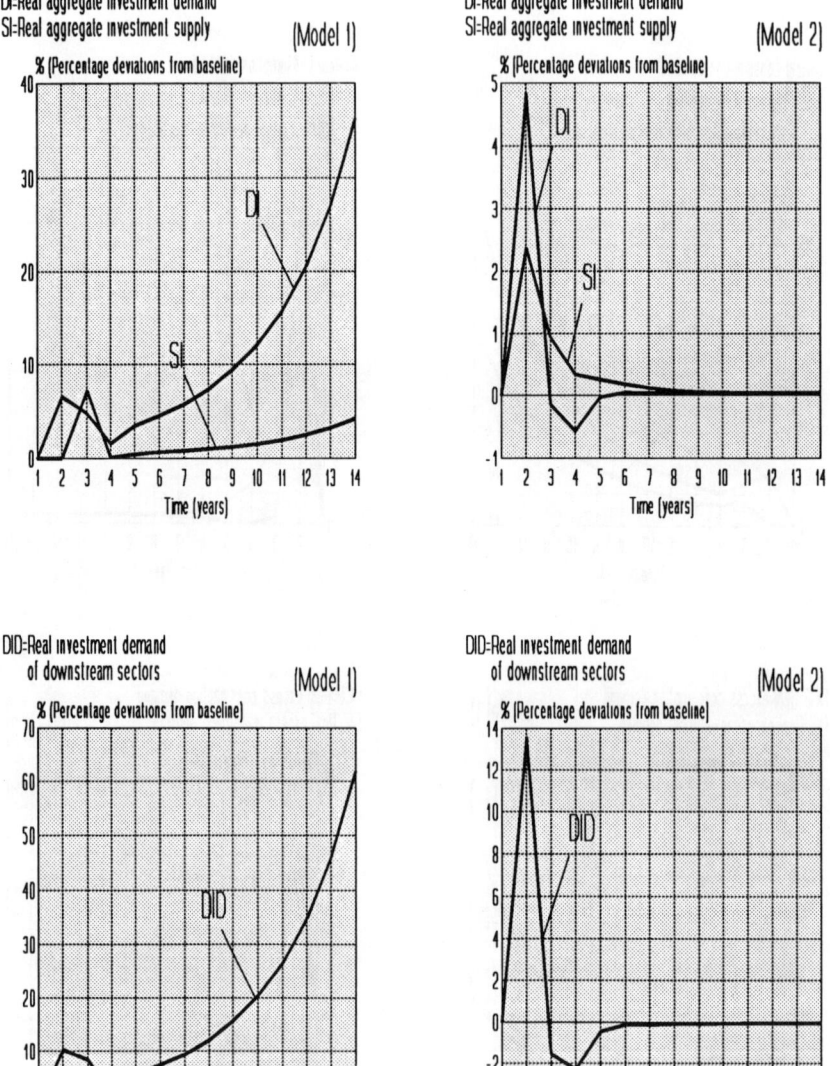

Figure 7.5   A temporary increase in domestic credit of 219 billion yuan

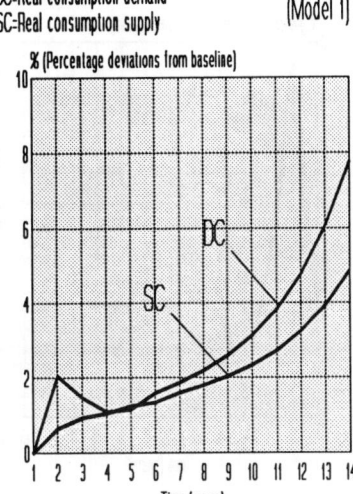
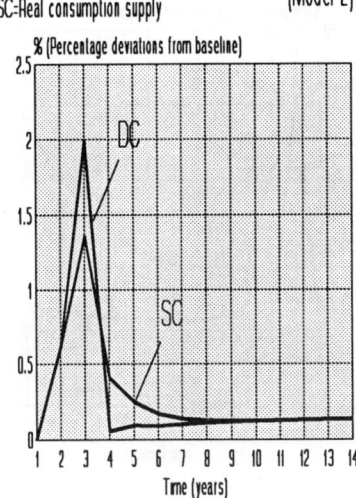
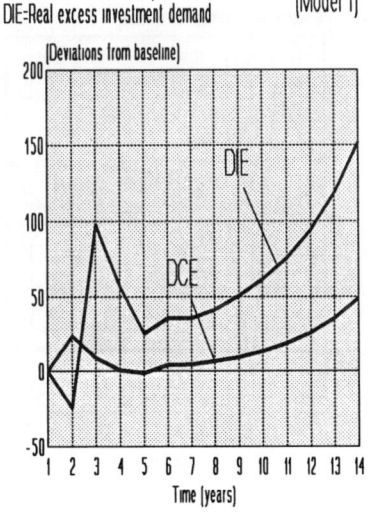
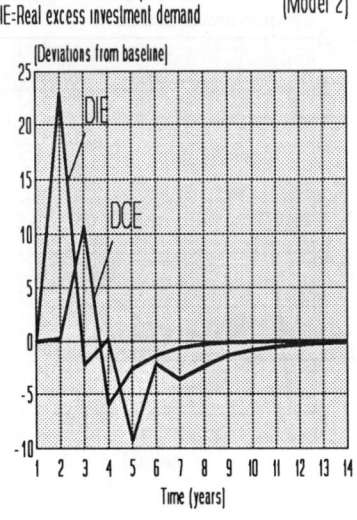

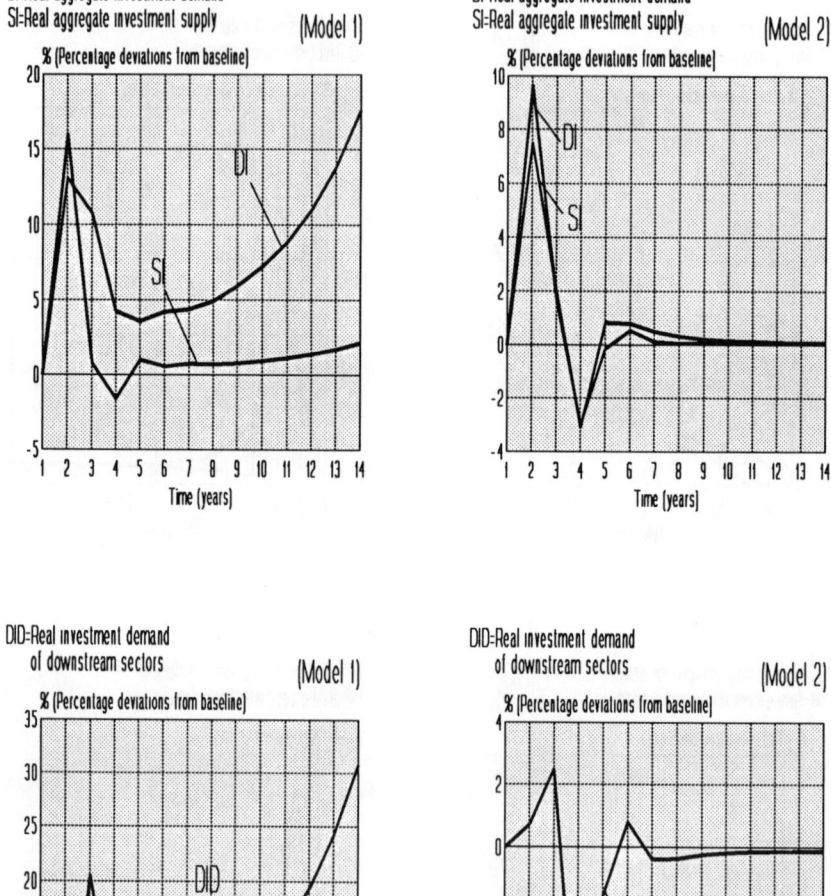

Figure 7.6 A temporary increase in government construction spending of 219 billion yuan

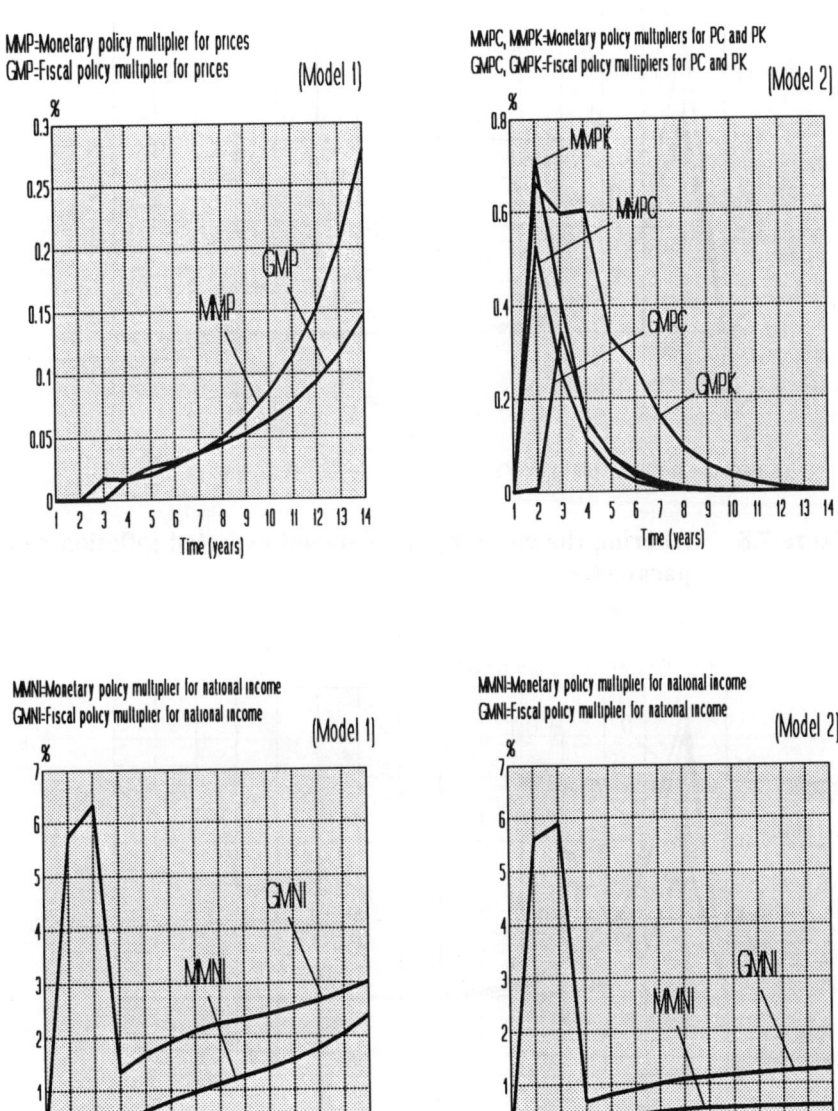

Figure 7.7   Monetary and Fiscal Policy Multipliers

Appendix 7B - Simulations of Model 2 with parameter perturbations

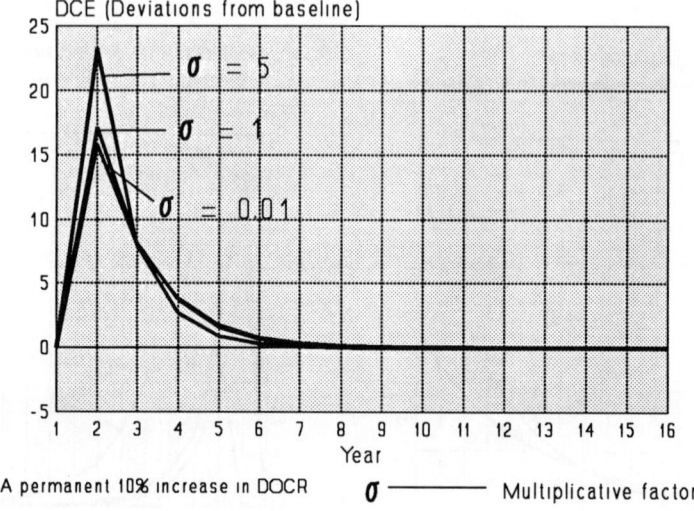

Figure 7.8 Altering the consumption demand-expected inflation rate parameter

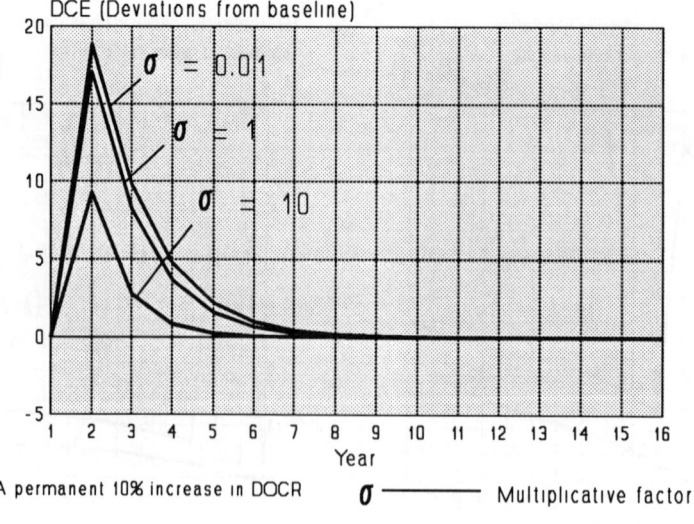

Figure 7.9 Altering the consumption demand-price parameter

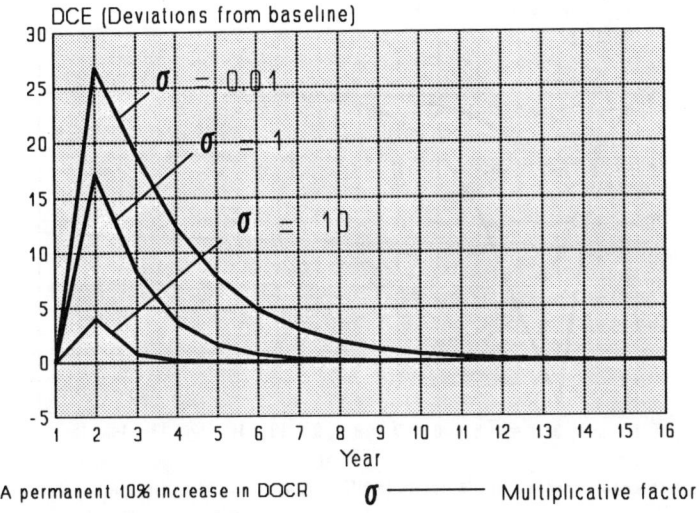

Figure 7.10 Altering the consumption supply-price parameter

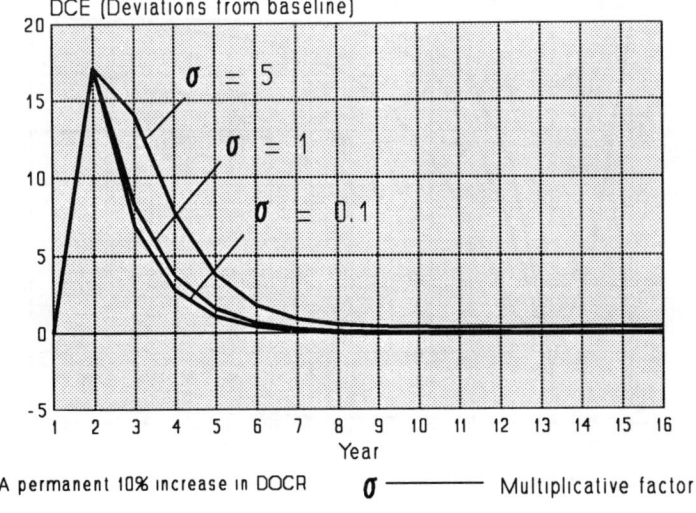

Figure 7.11 Altering the current savings-disposable income parameter

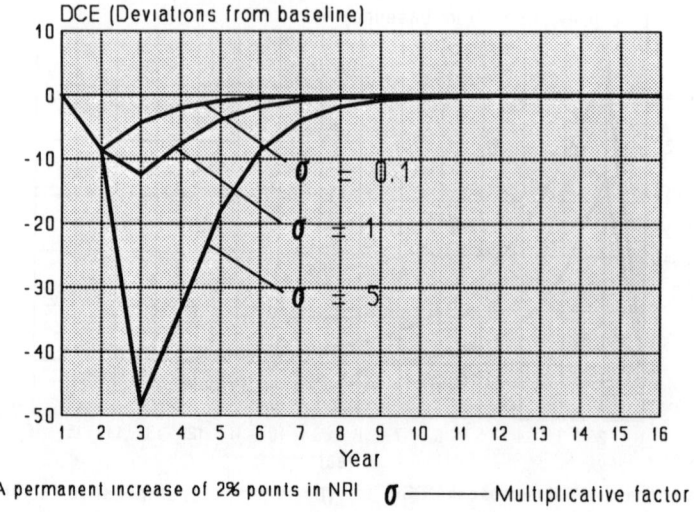

Figure 7.12 Altering the current savings-interest rate parameter

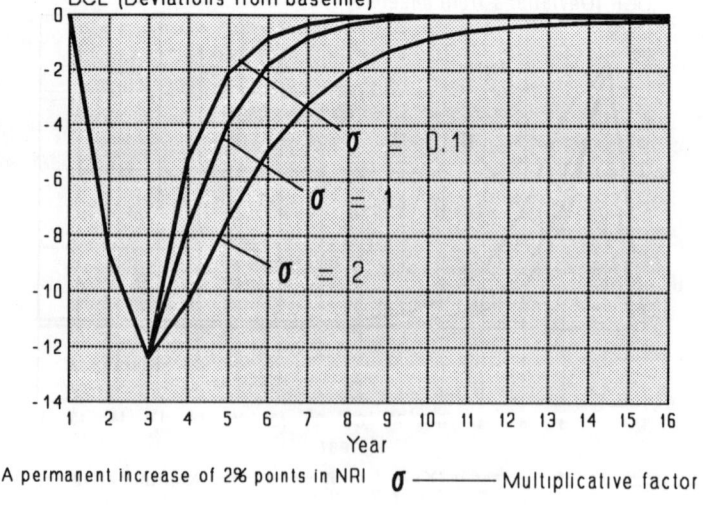

Figure 7.13 Altering the current savings-its lagged stocks parameter

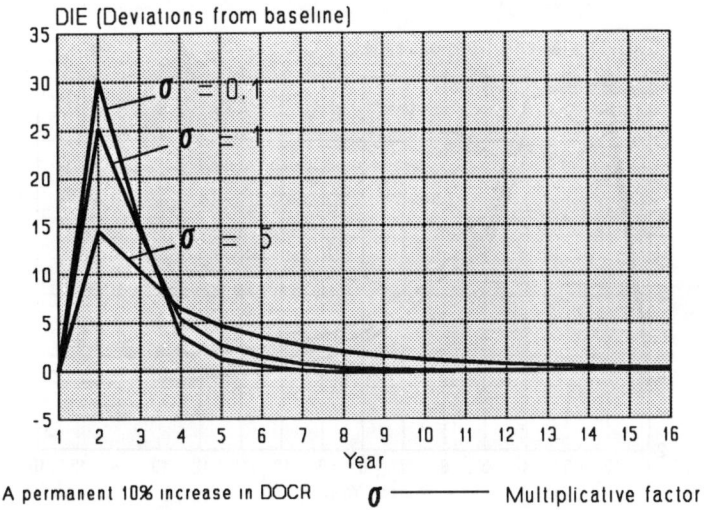

Figure 7.14 Altering the upstream investment demand-inflation rate parameter

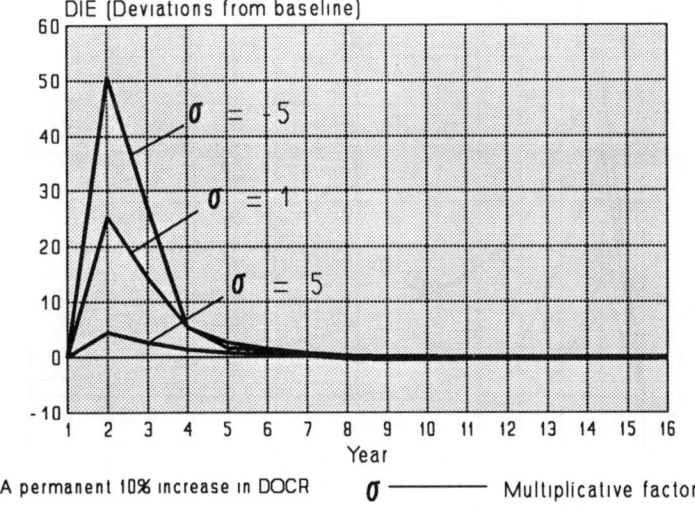

Figure 7.15 Altering the upstream-downstream investment demand parameter

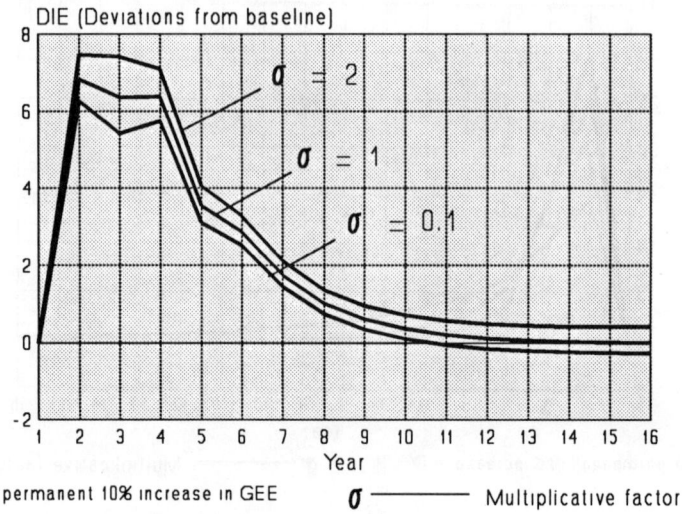

Figure 7.16 Altering the upstream investment demand-national income parameter

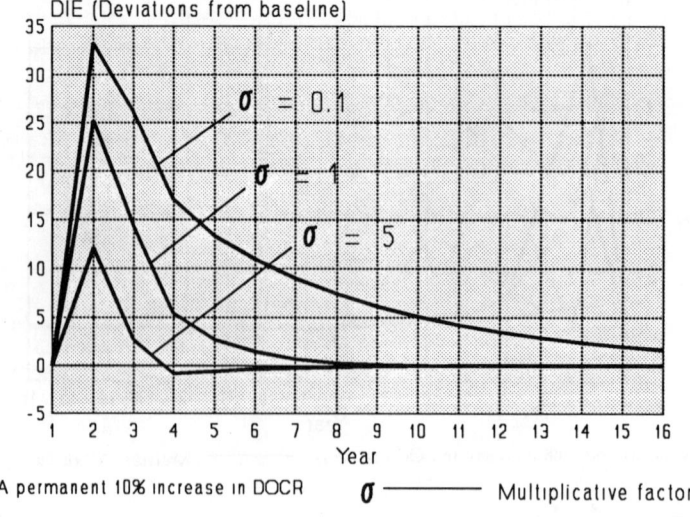

Figure 7.17 Altering the aggregate investment supply-price parameter

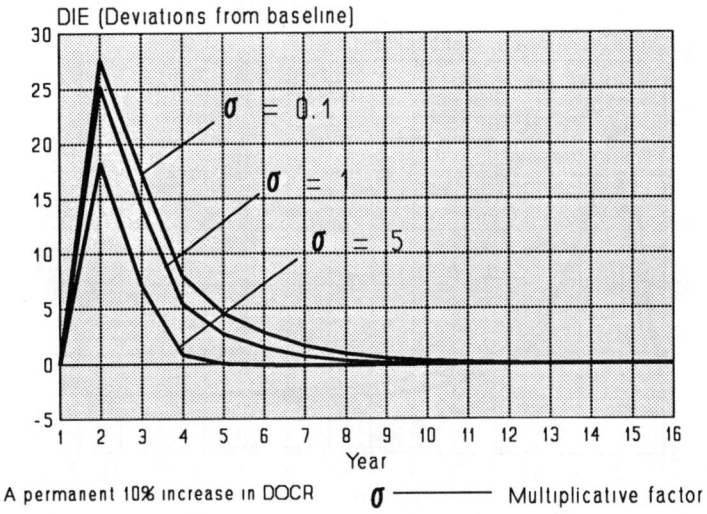

Figure 7.18 Altering the downstream investment demand-price parameter

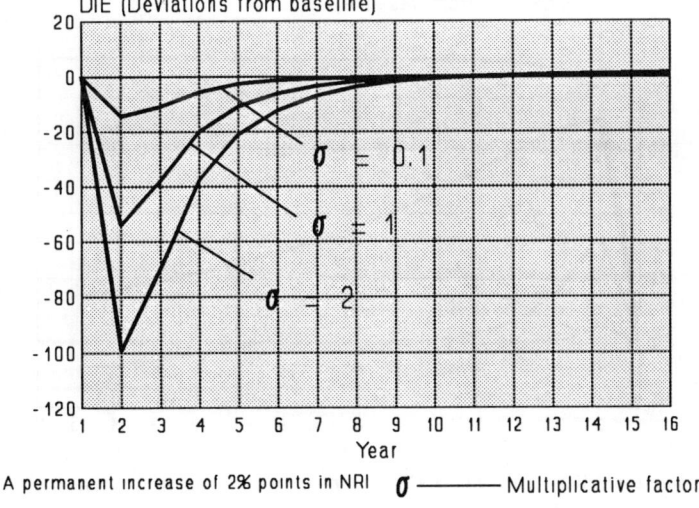

Figure 7.19 Altering the downstream investment demand-interest rate parameter

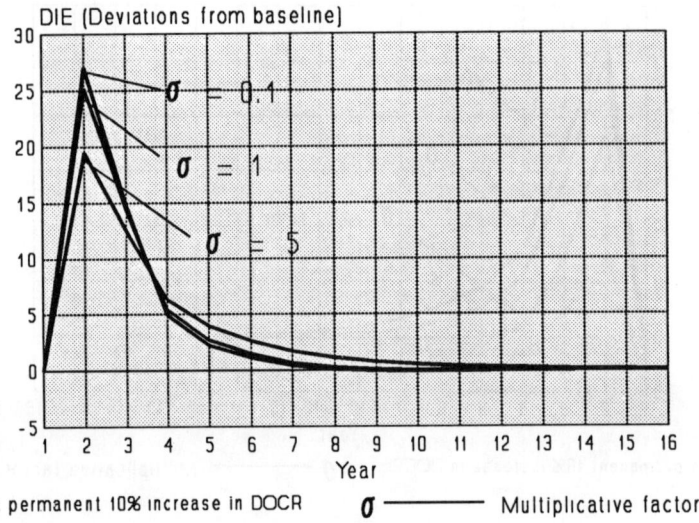

Figure 7.20 Altering the import-inflation rate parameter

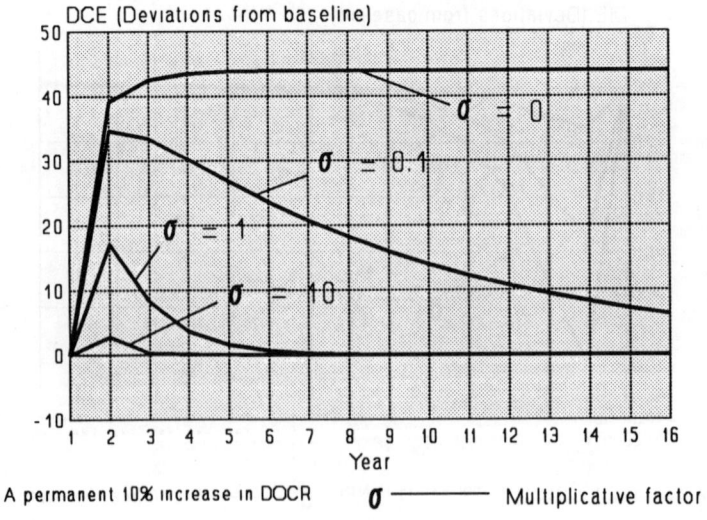

Figure 7.21 Altering the consumption price adjustment parameter

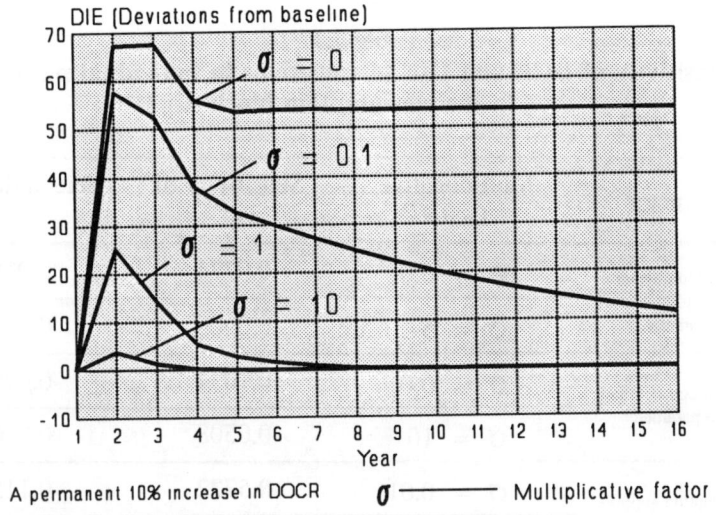

Figure 7.22 Altering the investment price adjustment parameter

Appendix 7C - Sensitivity elasticities

Table 7.1
The sensitivity of DCE and DIE to variations in individual parameters in the consumption block

Parameter	Multiplicative factor	Sensitivity of DCE	Sensitivity of DIE
Consumption demand-expected inflation rate parameter	$\sigma = 0.01$	0.0774	0.0156
	$\sigma = 5$	0.0906	0.0183
Consumption demand-price parameter	$\sigma = 0.01$	-0.1034	-0.0209
	$\sigma = 10$	-0.0508	-0.0103
Consumption supply-price parameter	$\sigma = 0.01$	-0.5722	-0.1156
	$\sigma = 10$	-0.0851	-0.0172
Current savings-disposable income parameter	$\sigma = 0.1$	0.1772*	0.0302*
	$\sigma = 5$	0.1770*	0.0302*
Current savings-interest rate parameter	$\sigma = 0.1$	0.7199*	0.0777*
	$\sigma = 5$	0.7252*	0.0784*
Current savings-its lagged stocks parameter	$\sigma = 0.1$	0.3504**	0.0450**
	$\sigma = 2$	0.3507**	0.0450**
Consumption price adjustment parameter	$\sigma = 0$	-1.2874	0.2020
	$\sigma = 0.1$	-1.1417	0.1790
	$\sigma = 5$	-0.1733	0.0270
	$\sigma = 10$	-0.0928	0.0145

Note: DCE=excess consumption demand. DIE=excess investment demand. * Using year 3's results. ** Using year 4's results. The rest using year 2's results

Table 7.2
The sensitivity of DCE and DIE to variations in individual parameters in the investment block

Parameter	Multiplicative factor	Sensitivity of DCE	Sensitivity of DIE
Upstream investment demand-inflation rate parameter	$\sigma = 0.1$	-2.5309E-5	-0.2217
	$\sigma = 5$	-1.1973E-5	-0.1062
Upstream-downstream investment demand parameter	$\sigma = -5$	-1.9079E-5	-0.1679
	$\sigma = 5$	-2.3070E-5	-0.2061
Upstream investment demand-national income parameter	$\sigma = 0.1$	4.9302E-5*	0.1652*
	$\sigma = 2$	4.7330E-5*	0.1656*
Aggregate investment supply-price parameter	$\sigma = 0.1$	7.5928E-5	-0.3550
	$\sigma = 5$	2.7743E-5	-0.1294
Downstream investment demand-price parameter	$\sigma = 0.1$	-1.1681E-5	-0.1044
	$\sigma = 5$	-7.7388E-6	-0.0690
Downstream investment demand-interest rate parameter	$\sigma = 0.1$	9.0636E-4*	0.7939*
	$\sigma = 2$	1.0833E-3*	0.8377*
Import-inflation rate parameter	$\sigma = 0.1$	1.6873E-5	-0.0789
	$\sigma = 5$	1.2265E-5	-0.0569
Investment price adjustment parameter	$\sigma = 0$	1.1214E-4	-1.6709
	$\sigma = 0.1$	9.6045E-5	-1.4338
	$\sigma = 5$	1.1973E-5	-0.1788
	$\sigma = 10$	6.3598E-6	-0.0944

Note: DCE=excess consumption demand. DIE=excess investment demand. * Using year 3's results. ** Using year 4's results. The rest using year 2's results

8 Concluding remarks

8.1 Summary and conclusions

This work is intended as a step towards the development of an experimental disequilibrium macro-model for the Chinese economy. The specification, estimation and simulation of the model has aimed to investigate the problem of macroeconomic imbalances that accompanied economic reforms being carried out in China. The results of the work support our underlying hypothesis that the problem arises from swollen demand which has its genesis in the structure of the economic system; the faults of economic policy only play a subordinate role in 'making a stormy sea stormier'. The following are the main conclusions obtained.

First, the fundamental contradiction involved in public-ownership is the root cause of macroeconomic imbalances. Indeed, due to the indefiniteness of sources of income (i.e., softness of budget constraints) and income illusion inherent in the POE, there exist various conflicts of interest between the central planner (central government) and individuals; between the central planner and sub-units (represented by local governments); and between sub-units. In the central planning system, the state-sovereignty mechanism gives no role to sub-units and individuals in the income distribution and in the determination of key economic variables, and hence these potential interest conflicts are unable to turn into actual contentions. Economic reforms to date have not yet resolved the fundamental contradictions of public ownership, but have brought these conflicts out into the open. The means has been the multi-sovereignty mechanism, under which the contentions between agents in the POE are characterized by the Nash noncooperative behaviour which gives rise to monetary competition, wage emulation and so on. The competitions of this kind defer from 'market competitions', in that costs, prices, interest rates and the underlying demand/supply relations in markets do not influence, or only to the least extent influence, the behaviour of economic agents. As result of such kind of competitions, investment demand swells and consumption demand expands, which leads to an overall augmentation of aggregate demand.

Second, in such an institutional context, demand variables are more sensitive than supply variables to policy changes. When the central government decides to speed up economic growth, even one-period expansionary policy shocks would rapidly and persistently raise demand, because this provokes a chain reaction in which economic agents compete with each other for scarce investment fund resources. Nevertheless, although there is no demand-side limitation, the supply side is restricted by limited productive capacity and more importantly by production inefficiencies, and hence always lags behind demand. On the other hand, in the case of contractionary policy shocks, we have observed a symmetrical pattern: demand declines faster than supply. The slowness of the adjustment of production to the market situation is another characteristic arising from state-owned enterprises, which are only responsible for profits but not for losses. Thus neither expansionary nor contractionary economic policy measures can move the economy towards a normal state of equilibrium, unless policy directions are changed frequently. We also have found that monetary policy is relatively more effective in controlling inflation, and fiscal policy relatively more effective in maintaining output; interest rates have a strong impact on the non-state sector's investment demand, but only a weak effect on the state sector's investment demand. The efficacy of macroeconomic policy instruments with regard to the balance between supply and demand in domestic markets depends crucially on the prevailing institutional conditions of the economy.

Thirdly, the results obtained from the theoretical and empirical studies of investment and consumption behaviour are reinforced by the reform experiments considered in chapter 7. The main contents of the policy reform package are: reducing substantially the role of the POE, so as to resolve the problem of interest conflicts in income distribution and resource allocations decisions; and shifting the economy toward more use of market mechanisms. Such further reforms would clearly enhance economic performance by suppressing the demand augmentation on the one hand, and by stimulating supply on the other. In addition, we have seen that, in such a new regime, the ability of macroeconomic policy instruments to regulate the economy be greatly enhanced. To sum up, without changing the fundamental economic relations so as to reform the public ownership and the local governments' behaviour, there will never be a genuine market economy; those indirect means of macroeconomic regulation, which have proved to be effective in a market economy, cannot be successfully employed in China; and it is very difficult for China to break such a vicious economic circle: decentralization ⇒ disorder ⇒ re-centralization ⇒ stagnancy.

Fourth, in considering household savings behaviour, a more sophisticated model was constructed to incorporate both regime shifts and repressed inflation. This is done by a distinction between forced and voluntary savings. It is interesting to discover that the higher saving rate during the 1980s was the result of both a monetary overhang (increasing shortage of consumer goods) and a behavioral change (an increase in households' propensities to save), the latter being an increasing function of real income and its upper limit 0.21. Therefore the high savings rate of the past few years may be sustained when the economy returns to 'market equilibrium' in the future.

Finally, we turn to the properties of the econometric model of the Chinese economy constructed in the present study. The earlier chapters discussed several novel properties of economic relationships in the Chinese economy. The more important ones are: income illusion; the multi-sovereignty mechanism; non-cooperative behaviour of economic agents; the indefiniteness of sources of income in the investment sector; the dynamic character of forced savings; and the time-varying parameters in the consumption sector. Since the econometric model is based on the disequilibrium indicator approach, we have assumed the existence of permanent repressed inflation, excluding 1989, when the drastic economic austerity drive began. We have tried to use carefully selected indicators to replace un-observable excess demands (supplies). The estimation results are consistent with the hypotheses proposed. The estimates of excess investment and consumption demand are as large as one might have expected. The disequilibrium indicator approach proved to be useful in identifying the forced savings, permitting an interesting explanation of the rise in household saving rates in the 1980s. The disequilibrium indicator model has thus proved to be a constructive and useful device for estimating relationships in the post-reform Chinese economy, and has yielded novel empirical implications.

8.2 Tasks for the future

It should be emphasized that the present work constitutes just the first steps in use of the disequilibrium indicator approach. Accordingly, a number of directions offer themselves for future research. Overall, the two main directions involve improvements and extensions of the theoretical model; and the widening of the data base and estimation framework. Specifically, there are some new possibilities for extending disequilibrium model-building in order to develop macromodel-building activity in China.

One of the main weaknesses of the current model lies in the incomplete specification of foreign trade processes, and in the lack of an investigation of the relationship between internal and external disequilibria. The foreign trade balance (export surplus) was positive and approximately zero in 1981-83 when disequilibrium in domestic markets was minimal; but it became negative in other years, reaching -448.9, -416.2 and -288.6 billion yuan respectively in 1985, 1986 and 1988, when there was substantial excess demand in domestic markets. This indicates that foreign trade deficits may well be driven by domestic disequilibria.

Another direction for future research would point towards incorporating labour markets. Unlike Eastern European countries, China has experienced slack in labour markets due to the huge pressure of population growth. Despite the implementation of a full-employment policy, the unemployment rate was in the range 1.8%-4.9% in the 1980s. As the reform advances, with the gradual opening of labour markets, and with more autonomy being given to enterprises to control their employment levels, we would expect a rapid rise in the unemployment rate which, in turn, may pose another challenge to the reform process.

A further point on the agenda is the in-depth theoretical study of further reforms. In this work, we have concentrated on the past reform experience, and to reveal the implied mechanisms, we have constructed a theoretical-mathematical model in strategic terms using game theory concepts. The coefficient η (see chapter 3), for example, may not only contain information about the dual systems (hence $0<\eta<1$), but also about the process of transition from the dual systems to a market system. China has taken the route of gradual reform, but what the costs, benefits and characteristics of this gradualism are, and how the transition period may be shortened without causing violent fluctuations or even chaos in the economy, requires further theoretical investigations. Our reform experiments in chapter 7 presumed an economy where the market system is basically established (hence $\eta=0$), but did not investigate the issue of transition. Therefore, we need to develop theories and models which capture the characteristics of the gradual reform process for China.

China is now in the process of drastic change. A year ago, the third plenum of the central committee of the Chinese Communist Party concluded with the announcement of a blueprint for the second phase of economic reform. It contains, *inter alia*, comprehensive measures concerning state enterprises, prices, real estate, taxes, banking, income distribution, and foreign trade. The objective of this policy package is to establish 'the socialist market economy'. This blueprint is encouraging, but new economic problems will no doubt emerge. We hope that the disequilibrium model-building technique outlined in this book will be of some assistance in solving those problems so as to smooth the path of economic reform and development in China.

Bibliography

Agenor, P. (1990), 'Stabilization Policies in Developing Countries with a Parallel Market for Foreign Exchange', *IMF Staff Papers*, Vol. 37, No. 3, pp. 560-92.

Allen, R.G.D. (1982), *Macroeconomic Theory: A Mathematical Treatment*, Macmillan, London.

Amemiya, T. (1974), 'A Note on a Fair and Jaffee Model', *Econometrica*, Vol. 42, pp. 759-62.

Barro, R.J. and Grossman, H.J. (1971),'A General Disequilibrium Model of Income and Employment', *American Economic Review*, Vol. 61, pp. 82-93.

Barro, R.J. and Grossman, H.J. (1976), *Money, Employment and Inflation*, Cambridge University Press, Cambridge and New York.

Bei, D. (1988), *Hongguan Jinrong Lun (Macro-Theory of Finance and Banking)* (the Chinese Edition), Shanghai ShanLian Bookstore, Shanhai.

Benassy, J.P. (1975), 'Neo-Keynesian Disequilibrium Theory in a Monetary Economy', *Review of Economic Studies*, Vol. 42, pp. 503-24.

Blanchard, O.J. and Fischer, S. (1989), *Lectures on Macroeconomics*, The MIT Press, Cambridge and Massachusetts.

Brandsma, A.S., Hughes Hallett, A.J. and Swank, J. (1987), 'The Robustness of Economic Policy Sections and the Incentive to Cooperate', *Journal of Economic Dynamics and Control*, 11, pp. 163-70.

Brus, W. (1972), *Shehui Zhuyi Jingji Yunxing Wenti (The Market in a Socialist Economy)* (a Chinese Translation, 1984), The China Social Science Press, Beijing.

Burkett, J. (1988), 'Slack, Shortage, and Discouraged Consumers in Eastern Europe: Estimates Based on Smoothing by Aggregation', *Review of*

Economic Studies, Vol. 55, pp. 483-506.

CESRRI (Chinese Economic System Reform Research Institute) (1988), *Gongye Zengzhang Zhongde Jiegouxing Maodun (Structural Contradictions in the Industrial Growth)* (the Chinese Edition), Sichuan People's Publishing House, Chendu.

Charemza, W. (1989), 'Disequilibrium Modelling of Consumption in the Centrally Planned Economy', in Davis, C. and Charemza, W. (eds), *Models of Disequilibrium and Shortage in Centrally Planned Economies*, Chapman and Hall, London, pp. 283-315.

Charemza, W. and Gierusz, B. (1978), 'The Estimation and Application of a Supply/Demand Quarterly Model of Retail Sales in Poland', paper presented at the Conference on Problems of Building and Estimation Large Econometric Models, Blazejewko, version in Polish published in 1980 in *Przeglad Statystyczny*.

Charemza, W. and Gronicki, M. (1988), *Plans and Disequilibria in Centrally Planned Economies (Empirical Investigation for Poland)*. Pwn-polish Scientific Publishers, North-Holland.

Chow, G. (1985), 'A Model of Chinese National Income Determination', *Journal of Political Economy*, Vol. 93, pp. 782-92.

Clower, R.W. (1965), 'The Keynesian Counterrevolution: A Theoretical Appraisal', in Brechling, F.P.R. and Hahn, F.H. (eds), *The Theory of Interest Rates*, Macmillan, London, pp. 103-25.

Cooper, Rechard N. (1984), 'Economic Interdependence and the Coordination of Economic Policies', Harvard Institute of Economic Research Discussion Paper, forthcoming in Kenen, P.B. (ed.), *Handbook of International Economics*, Amsterdam: North-Holland.

Davis, C. and Charemza, W. (1989), *Models of Disequilibrium and Shortage in Centrally Planned Economies*, Chapman and Hall, London.

Dreze, J.H. (1975), 'Existence of an Exchange Equilibrium Under Price Rigidities,' *International Economic Review*, Vol. 16, pp. 301-20.

Eichengreen, B. (1985), 'International Policy Coordination in Historical Perspective: A View from the Interwar Years', in Buiter, W. H. and Marston, R. C. (eds), *International Economic Policy Coordination*, Cambridge University Press, Cambridge, pp. 139-78.

Eichengreen, B. (1992), 'Designing a Central Bank for Europe: A Cautionary Tale from the Early Years of the Federal Reserve System', in Canzoneri, M.B., Grilli, V. and Masson, P.R. (eds), *Establishing a Central Bank: Issues in Europe and Lessons from the US*, Cambridge University Press, Frome/London, pp. 13-40.

Fair, R.C. and Jaffee, D.M. (1972), 'Methods of Estimation for Markets in Disequilibrium', *Econometrica*, Vol. 40, pp. 497-514.

Fair, R.C. and Kelejian, H.H. (1974), 'Methods of Estimation for Markets in Disequilibrium: A Further Study', *Econometrica*, Vol. 42, pp. 177-90.

Fan, G. (1989), 'Gaige, Tiaozheng, Zengzhang Yu Muocaxing Tonghuo Pengzhang' (Reform, Adjustment, Growth and the Frictional Inflation), *Jingji Yanjiu (Economic Research Journal)*, No. 1.

Fan, G. (1992), 'Lun Jingji Xiaolü, Zonggongqiu Guanxi Yu Jingji Tizhi' (On Economic Efficiencies, Aggregate Demand-supply Relationships and Economic Systems), *Jingji Yanjiu (Economic Research Journal)*, No. 3.

Fan, G., Zhang, S. and Yang, Z. (1990), *Gongyouzhi Hongguan Jingji Lilun Dagang (Macroeconomics of Public Ownership)* (the Chinese Edition), Shanghai Shanlian Bookstore, Shanghai.

Fan, G., Zhang, S. and Wang, L. (1993), 'Shuanggui Guodu Yu Shuanggui Tiaokong' (The Dual-Track Transition and the Dual-Track Regulation), *Jingji Yanjiu (Economic Research Journal)*, No. 10 and No. 11.

Feltenstein, A. and Farhadian, Z. (1987), 'Fiscal Policy, Monetary Targets, and the Price Level in a Centrally Planned Economy: An Application to the Case of China', *Journal of Money, Credit, and Banking*, Vol. 19, No. 2, pp. 137-55.

Feltenstein, A. and Ha, J. (1991), 'Measurement of Repressed Inflation in China', *Journal of Development Economics*, Vol. 36, pp. 279-94.

Feltenstein, A., Lebow, D. and van Wijnbergen, S. (1990), 'Savings, Commodity Market Rationing, and the Real Rate of Interest in China', *Journal of Money, Credit, and Banking*, Vol. 22, No. 2, pp. 234-52.

Goldfeld, S.M. and Quandt, R.E. (1975), 'Estimation in a Disequilibrium Model and the Value of Information', *Journal of Econometrics*, Vol. 3, pp. 325-48.

Grandmont, J. M. and Laroque, G. (1976), 'On Temporary Keynesian Equilibrium', *Review of Economic Studies*, Vol. 43, pp. 53-67.

Gronicki, M. and Szreder, M. (1986), 'Bayesian Analysis of Polish TV market', paper presented at the Conference on Problems of Building and Estimation of Large Econometric Models, Szczyrk.

Gronicki, M. and Szreder, M. (1981), 'Bayesian Analysis of a Simple Model of Market in Disequilibrium: Repressed Inflation Case', University of Gdansk (*mimeo*).

Grosfeld, I. (1989), 'Disequilibrium Models of Investment', in Davis, C. and Charemza, W. (eds), *Models of Disequilibrium and Shortage in Centrally Planned Economies*, Chapman and Hall, London, pp. 361-74.

Guo, S. (1990), 'Xiaofei, Touzi He Chuxu' (Consumption, Investment and Savings), *Jingji Yanjiu (Economic Research Journal)*, No. 4.

Guo, S. (1992), 'Zongxuqiu, Zonggongji-Cong Gainian Dao Xianshi'

(Aggregate Demand and Aggregate Supply-from Notions to Realities), *Jingji Yanjiu (Economic Research Journal)*, No. 3.

Hahn, F.H. (1978), 'On Non-Walrasian Equilibria', *Review of Economic Studies*, Vol. 45, pp. 1-18.

Harrison, G.W. and Kimbell, L.J. (1985), 'Economic Interdependence in the Pacific Basin: A General Equilibrium Approach', in Piggot, J. and Whalley, J. (eds), *New Developments in Applied General Equilibrium Analysis*, Cambridge University Press, New York, pp. 143-74.

Holly, S. and Hughes Hallett, A. (1989), *Optimal Control, Expectations and Uncertainty*, Cambridge University Press, Cambridge.

Hu, R. (1987), 'Duanque Guiying Lun' (On the Reasons of Shortage), *Jingji Yanjiu (Economic Research Journal)*, No. 7, 1987.

Hu, R. (1991), 'Zailun Duanque De Gongji Fangmian Yuanying' (More on the Reasons of Shortage in the Supply Respect), *Jingji Yanjiu (Economic Research Journal)*, No. 7.

Hughes Hallett, A. (1987), 'How Robust Are the Gains to Policy Coordination to Variations in the Model and Objectives?', *Ricerche Economiche*, XLI, 3-4, pp. 341-72.

Hulyak, K. (1985), 'An Econometric Disequilibrium Macromodel for Hungary', paper presented at the World Congress of the Econometric Society, Cambridge, Mass.

Hulyak, K. (1989), 'Macroeconomic Disequilibrium Model of Hungary', in Davis, C. and Charemza, W. (eds), *Models of Disequilibrium and Shortage in Centrally Planned Economies*, Chapman and Hall, London, pp. 247-60.

Ito, T. (1980), 'Methods of Estimation for Multi-market Disequilibrium Models', *Econommetrica*, Vol. 48, No. 1, pp. 97-125.

Jiang, X. (1991), '1990 Nian Zhongguo Hongguan Jingji De Shizheng Fenxi' (Positive Analysis on the Macro-economy of China in 1990), *Jingji Yanjiu (Economic Research Journal)*, No. 2.

Kemme, D.M. (1989), 'The Chronic Excess Demand Hypothesis', in Davis, C. and Charemza, W. (eds), *Models of Disequilibrium and Shortage in Centrally Planned Economies*, Chapman and Hall, London, pp. 83-100.

Keviet, J.F. (1986), 'On the Rigour of Some Misspecification Tests for Modelling Dynamic Relationships', *Review of Economic Studies*, Vol. 53, pp. 241-61.

Kornai, J. (1980), *Economics of Shortage*, Amsterdam, North-Holland.

Kornai, J. (1982), *Growth, Shortage and Efficiency*, Blackwell, Oxford.

Lee, L.F. (1986), 'The Specification of Multi-market Disequilibrium Econometric Models', *Journal of Econometrics*, Vol. 32, pp. 297-332.

Li, J. and Liu, S. (1994), 'ZhongGuo Jingji Fazhan: 1993 Nian Tedian, 1994

Nian Zoushi Ji Youguan Duice' (Development of the Chinese Economy: Its Features in 1993, tendency in 1994 and the Countermeasures Proposed), *Jingji Yanjiu (Economic Research Journal)*, No. 2.

Li, L. (1991), *Tonghuo Pengzhang Jili Yu Yuqi (The Mechanism of Inflation and Expectations* (the Chinese Edition), The People's University Press, Beijing.

Li, M and Hu, J (1990), 'Chuxu Zengzhang Zhong Jidai Yanjiu De Liangge Wenti' (Two Issues in the Savings Growth Needing to Be Considered Ungently), *Jingji Yanjiu (Economic Research Journal)*, No. 4.

Ma, G. (1993), 'Macroeconomic Disequilibrium, Structural Changes, and the Household Savings and Money Demand in China', *Journal of Development Economics*, No. 41, pp. 115-36.

Ma, Q. (1989), *Xing Duanque Jingjixue (New Economics of Shortage)*, Qiushi Publishing House, Beijing.

Maddala, G.S. and Nelson, F.D. (1974), 'Maximum Likelihood Methods for Models of Markets in Disequilibrium', *Econometrica*, Vol. 42, pp. 1013-30.

Malinvaud, E. (1977), *The Theory of Unemployment Reconsidered*, Basil Blackwell, Oxford.

Michalak, K. and Starzynska, W. (1979), 'Application of Disequilibrium Indicators in Econometric Models of Some Foodstuffs Markets', paper presented at the Conference on Models and Forecasts, Polanica.

Mishkin Frederic, S. (1979), 'Simulation Methodology in Macroeconomics: An Innovation Technique', *Journal of Political Economy*, Vol 87, pp. 816-36.

Muellbauer, J. and Portes, R. (1978), 'Macroeconomic Models with Quantity Rationing', *Economic Journal*, Vol. 88, pp. 788-821.

Neary, J.P. and Roberts, K.W.S. (1980), 'The Theory of Household Behaviour under Rationing', *European Economic Review*, Vol. 13, pp. 25-42.

Pagan, A. (1984), 'Econometric Issues in the Analysis of Regressions with Generated Regressors', *International Economic Review*, Vol. 25, No. 1, pp. 221-47.

Patinkin, D. (1956), *Money, Interest and Prices*, Harper and Row, New York.

Pesaran, H. M. (1987), *The Limits to Rational Expectations*, Basil Blackwell Ltd, UK.

Portes, R. and Santorum, A. (1987), 'Money and the Consumption Goods Market in China', *Journal of Comparative Economics*, No. 11, pp. 354-71.

Portes R. and Winter, D. (1980), 'Disequilibrium Estimates for Consumption Goods in Centrally Planned Economies', *Journal of Comparative*

Economics, No. 1, pp. 351-65.
Portes, R., Quandt, R. E., Winter, D. and Yeo, S. (1987), 'Macroeconomic Planning and Disequilibrium Estimates for Poland, 1955-1980', *Econometrica*, Vol. 55, pp. 19-42.
Portes, R. and Winter D. (1980), 'Disequilibrium Estimates for Consumption Goods Markets in Centrally Planned Economies', *Review of Economic Studies*, Vol. 47, pp. 37-59.
Qian, Y. (1988), 'Urban and Rural Household Saving in China', *International Monetary Fund Staff Papers*, Vol. 35, No. 4, pp. 592-627.
Quandt, R.E. (1989), *The Econometrics of Disequilibrium*, Basil Blackwell Inc., Oxford/New York.
Quandt, R.E. (1989), 'Disequilibrium Econometrics for CPEs', in Davis, C. and Charemza, W. (eds), *Models of Disequilibrium and Shortage in Centrally Planned Economies*, Chapman and Hall, London, pp. 147-77.
Reynolds, B.L. (1987), *Reform in China: Challenges & Choices*, M.S. Sharpe, Inc., Armonk, New York/London.
Sheffrin, Steven M. (1983), *Rational Expectations*, Cambridge University Press, Cambridge, New York, Melbourne.
Shi, J. (1989), *Shehui Zhuyi Tonhuo Pengzhang Daolun (Introduction to the Inflation in the Socialist Economy)* (the Chinese Edition), Shanghai Shanlian Bookstore, Shanghai.
Shoven, J.B. and Whalley, J. (1984), 'Applied General-Equilibrium Models of Taxation and International Trade: An Introduction and Survey', *Journal of Economic Literature*, Vol. XXII, pp. 1007-51.
Sims, C.A. (1980), 'Macroeconomics and Reality', *Econometrica*, Vol. 48, pp. 1-48.
Sun, Y. (1990), '1979-1988 Nian Wuoguo Touzi Zongliang Taishi De Shizheng Yanjiu' (Positive Studies of Aggregate Investment in China in 1979-1988), *Jingji Yanjiu (Economic Research Journal)*, No. 4.
Svensson, L.E.O. (1980), 'Effective Demand and Stochastic Rationing', *Review of Economic Studies*, Vol. 47, pp. 339-55.
Welfe, A. (1989), 'Savings and Consumption in the Centrally Planned Economy: A Disequilibrium Approach', in Davis, C. and Charemza W. (eds), *Models of Disequilibrium and Shortage in Centrally Planned Economies*, Chapman and Hall, London, pp. 317-32.
Welfe, W. (1978), 'Disequilibria in Econometric Macromodels of Centrally Planned Economies', paper presented at the Conference on Colloques sur Structures Economiques et Econometrie, Lyons.
Wickens, M.R. (1982), 'The Efficient Estimations of Econometric Models with Rational Expectations', *Review of Economic Studies*, Vol. 49, pp. 55-67.

Wigle, R. (1986), 'Summary of the Panel and Floor Discussion', in Srinivasan, T.N. and Whalley, J. (eds), *General Equilibrium Trade Policy Modelling*, The MIT Press, Cambridge, pp. 323-54.

Wijnbergen, S. (1985), 'Oil Price Shocks, Unemployment, Investment and the Current Account: An Intertemporal Disequilibrium Analysis', *Review of Economic Studies*, Vol. 52, pp. 627-45.

Wu, J. and Zhang, J. (1990), '1989 Nian Zhongguo Jingji Shikuang Fenxi' (Empirical Analysis of the Chinese Economy in 1989), *Jingji Gongzuozhe Cankao Ziliao (Reference Materials for Economists)*, Vol. 60.

Xia, X. and Li, J. (1987), 'Consumption Expansion: A Grave Challenge to Reform and Development', in Reynolds, B.L. (ed.), *Reform in China: Challenges & Choices*, M.E. Sharpe, Inc. Armonk, New York/London.

Xun, D., Ye, B. and Fang, X., 'Muqian Jingji Xingshi: Maodun Fenxi Yu Zouchu Kunjing De Xuanze' (The Present Economic Situation: Analysis of Contradictions and Choices for Extricating Ourselves from A Difficult Position), *Jingji Yanjiu (Economic Research Journal)*, No. 4.

Yang, P. (1990), 'Dangqian Jingji Xingshi Fenxi He Duice Yanjiu' (Analysis of the Present Economic Situation and Study of Countermeasures), *Jingji Yanjiu (Economic Research Journal)*, No. 7.

Younes, Y. (1975), 'On the Role of Money in the Process of Exchange and the Existence of Non-Walrasian Equilibrium', *Review of Economic Studies*, Vol. 42, pp. 489-501.

Zhang, S. (1993), 'Zongliang Guanxi Jiqi Zhidu Fenxi' (The Aggregate Relation and Its Institutional Analysis), *Jingji Yanjiu (Economic Research Journal)*, No. 1.

Zhang, J. (1991), 'Qiwu Qijian Jingji Xiaoyi De Zonghe Fenxi-Geyaosu Dui Jingji Zengzhang Gongxianlü Cesuan' (The Integrative Analysis on the Economic Effects During the Seventh Five: Estimation of the Contribution Rates of Factors to the Economic Growth), *Jingji Yanjiu (Economic Research Journal)*, No. 4.

Zhong, P. (1990), *Zhongguo Tonghuo Pengzhang Yanjiu (Study of the Inflation in China)* (the Chinese Edition), Jiangxi People's Publishing House, Nanchang.

Zhou X. (1988), *Jinrong Jingji Lun (Economic Theory of Finance)*, Economic Publishing House of China, Beijing.